D1195101

More Praise for

The Magnet Method of Investing

"Investors have long been sold diversification as the Holy Grail. Jordan Kimmel pushes investors to see a different light. He knows the big money is often made in just a few moves. Investors should embrace his big-picture wisdom."
—Michael W. Covel
Author, *Trend Following* and *The Complete TurtleTrader*

"Whether you are a novice or an experienced investor, you owe it to yourself to absorb how the MAGNET method takes a unique look into the brightest minds on Wall Street— and highlights why they ignore the call to widely diversify."
—Doug Trenary
Author, *The SuccessMind*

"If you are simply seeking average returns, do not bother with The MAGNET Method of Investing—invest in a low cost index fund. However, if you want to learn the secret to generating exceptional returns, this book is a must-read. Inside, Jordan Kimmel reveals his MAGNET method for finding the truly exceptional stocks in the stock market."
—Nicholas Maturo
CEO, Global Investor Services, Inc.

"A clear and entertaining manual on how to profit from sensible risk-taking in the market without blowing up."
—Aaron Brown
Author, *The Poker Face of Wall Street*, and
Risk Manager, AQR Capital Management
(formerly of Morgan Stanley)

The MAGNET®
Method of Investing

Founded in 1807, John Wiley & Sons is the oldest independent publishing company in the United States. With offices in North America, Europe, Australia, and Asia, Wiley is globally committed to developing and marketing print and electronic products and services for our customers' professional and personal knowledge and understanding.

The Hirsch Organization was founded by Yale Hirsch, creator of the *Stock Trader's Almanac* (providing historical information to investors since 1967). His son, Jeffrey A. Hirsch, is the current president of the Hirsch Organization and has worked with Yale for over 20 years. Jeffrey also edits the Hirsch Organization's monthly *Almanac Newsletter* and is a consulting editor on the Almanac Investor series.

The Almanac Investor series features books by the industry's brightest minds: money managers, traders, and investors who have continued to succeed in the face of the market's ever-changing environment.

For a list of available titles in the Almanac Investor series, the Wiley Trading series, or the Wiley Finance series, please visit our web site at www.WileyFinance.com.

The MAGNET®
Method of Investing

FIND, TRADE, AND PROFIT
FROM EXCEPTIONAL STOCKS

JORDAN KIMMEL

Foreword by Jeffrey A. Hirsch,
Editor-in-Chief, *Stock Trader's Almanac*

WILEY

John Wiley & Sons, Inc.

Published by John Wiley & Sons, Inc., Hoboken, New Jersey.
Published simultaneously in Canada.

The Magnet® Stock Selection Process is a registered trademark of Jordan Kimmel.

Library of Congress Cataloging-in-Publication Data:

Kimmel, Jordan
    The magnet method of investing : find, trade, and profit from exceptional stocks /
Jordan Kimmel ; foreword by Jeffrey A. Hirsch.
      p. cm. — (Almanac investor series)
    Includes bibliographical references and index.
    ISBN 978-0-470-27929-8 (cloth)
      1. Investment analysis.   2. Portfolio management.   3. Stocks.   I. Title.
  HG4529.K5633 2009
  332.63'22—dc22

                                                 2009008847

Printed in the United States of America.
10 9 8 7 6 5 4 3 2 1

To all those investors who desire above-average returns and who are willing to go the extra mile to generate them.

To my wife and boys, who have been so patient with me while I took time away from them while I worked on this book.

CONTENTS

FOREWORD

Since the early 1990s, economists Eugene F. Fama and Kenneth R. French have reported in several papers in the *Journal of Finance* that stocks with low price-to-earnings ratios, low price-to-book ratios, and low market values generate the best returns over time. The venerable *Value Line Investment Survey* has shown that since 1965 its number-one-ranked stocks have beaten "the Dow by more than 20 to 1." Why diversify your portfolio when it is well-known by Wall Street pros and leading academics that a small number of stocks account for the biggest gains? Why would you diversify and not seek out the top performers?

Overemphasis on diversification, asset allocation, and the use of modern portfolio theory have severely limited the creation of wealth in our portfolios. It is only after many years of following the failed strategies of asset allocation and systematic diversification, which have yielded unacceptably mediocre returns, that institutions and the public at large are now open to a more logical and robust methodology of seeking out, identifying, and concentrating capital in the truely superlative companies.

Future top-performing stocks are like needles in a haystack. Find them by turning your portfolio into a magnet for pulling in these hidden gems. The name of the game is isolating these future runaways, focusing your efforts on really getting to know and understand them, and then concentrating your capital on these hidden values at the right time.

Money manager Jordan L. Kimmel's Magnet® Stock Selection Process (MSSP) has been unearthing these top-performing stocks since 1997. Mr. Kimmel and his clients have reaped the gains by owning shares of these stocks before they became the darlings of Wall Street. Jordan has been asked by the financial networks to appear hundreds of times over the last ten years for a reason: He continues to unearth undervalued, overlooked stocks on the brink of the big upmoves.

Dogmatic asset allocation and overdiversification have put a drain on savings rates, wealth creation, society, and capitalism. Instead, embracing the concept of superlative stock selection increases individual savings, creates wealth, helps society, and strengthens capitalism. Mr. Kimmel's proven Magnet System zeros in on these future stock champs in their sweet spots before they take off during the companies' greatest growth phase.

The Magnet Method of Investing demystifies modern portfolio theory, efficient market theory, asset allocation, and diversification, and it details what characteristics the best stocks have in common before they produce their oversized returns for investors. In the following pages Jordan Kimmel dissects his process from conception to birth to wealth creation and capital acceleration.

Jordan Kimmel's unique mind and experiences synthesize the economics of the free market with an organic conception of the nature of all things and the power of Internet access to information that is unconstrained by time, language barriers, and space, creating a perspective of stock picking and the efficient allocation of capital that results in transformational change in investment returns.

The free market channels funds to the best ideas, solutions, and innovations. Relentless, willy-nilly asset allocation and overdiversification do the exact opposite. One's capital is spread out so broadly and evenly that large losses are mitigated over the long term, but the investment is relegated to perpetual mediocre and often inferior returns. In these pages Jordan takes aim at the asset allocation and diversification models that investors have been scared into following, proving the case that superior concentrated stock investing that benefits all investors will help alleviate many of the world's problems.

Jeffrey A. Hirsch
Editor-in-Chief, *Stock Trader's Almanac*
Nyack, New York
June 2009

PREFACE

Modern portfolio theory does not work. It has interfered with the flow of capital to superlative companies and has severely limited the creation of wealth in our nation. This is due to the misdirected importance placed on diversification.

Harry M. Markowitz introduced the concept of modern portfolio theory in 1952. At the time, the financial markets were comprised of two alternative investments: stocks and bonds. Since then, several significant trends have altered the course of investing. Now institutions, along with individuals, have the opportunity to invest in various products that were simply not available back in 1952. These products include hedge funds, commodities, real estate, and insurance products. Various investment tools have also emerged, including options, hedging strategies, and numerous leveraging devices that can control large sectors of the market with limited capital.

While Dr. Markowitz's theories shed light on the subject of diversification, the overall strategy within modern portfolio theory was still flawed. It consisted primarily of selling performing issues and reinvesting in underperforming issues. The outcome has been capital support for mediocre performers and lack of capital support for superlative performers. Clearly, reinvesting in laggards is not the most efficient use of a portfolio's capital. When looked at from this vantage point, the practice of modern portfolio theory has done more damage than good.

In addition, the implementation of modern portfolio theory's capital allocation practices and so-called reversion to the mean interfere with the growth of the free market. Diversification and asset allocation strategies have hindered the invisible hand of Adam Smith and the flow of capital to its most efficient use. They have had a direct and negative impact on investors' wealth creation capabilities and on America's role in the emerging Internet-based global economy. Mediocre companies do not—and often cannot—provide stable employment or dependable benefits for their workers, not to mention the other benefits that come with high performance.

When I wrote my first book, *Magnet Investing*, in 1999, stock market investing was starting to engulf Main Street and the Internet was still in its infancy. The mutual fund business was growing, and participation in pension and 401k accounts was bringing a greater percentage of the public into the market. It was a far cry from just 20 years earlier when most individuals did not invest in stocks. I saw a future unfolding wherein access to information about public companies would empower investors to make better decisions. This information was available to anyone who wanted it, not just to Wall Street insiders. In essence, the Internet would place the individual investor on a level playing field with Wall Street professionals by providing access to detailed information about public companies and a mechanism with which to invest in them.

My goal in writing my first book was to demystify the market and to enlighten readers on how to isolate, trade, and profit from exceptional stocks before they became the darlings of Wall Street. But tremendous losses in the aftermath of the dot.com bubble and the market crash in the technology sector left individuals with deep investment scars. The losses generated in the bear market from 2000 to 2002 created a large problem that individual and institutional investors still face. Those who suffered from overexposure to the tech bubble found salvation in increased stock diversification (modern portfolio theory). But by harboring the false sense of security of limiting risk through the ownership of a multitude of stocks and asset classes, investment returns become restricted, often not keeping pace with the market, inflation, taxes, and fees.

The mentality is even more restrictive at the federal level. The U.S. government wastes billions on pork barrel spending and endless bureaucracy while the stewards of the land struggle to figure out how to fund Social Security, Medicare, and our massive international involvement. Federal funds are invested only in low-yielding Treasuries and other U.S. government debt securities. This money is not put to work in new and growing industries here in the United States or abroad; yet other countries are deploying state-owned sovereign wealth funds to make massive equity investments in individual companies and projects all over the globe. The intent of these foreign funds is to use time to absorb the short-term volatility associated with the ownership of stocks, while reaping the long-term rewards, and they are doing it with equity positions alone and without leverage.

If invested well, these funds will enable other countries to build wealth and eventually to play a larger role in world politics. It is a shame that the United States seems to have lost its risk-taking appetite at exactly the wrong time. Only the state of Alaska has such a fund established to redistribute some of the oil revenue from the Trans-Alaska Pipeline. This is not to suggest that the U.S. Treasury should be involved in buying and selling shares of start-up tech stocks. But if Asian and Middle Eastern nations have no qualms about buying stakes in Citigroup, Merrill Lynch, or Visa International, why shouldn't the United States? Or how about following the lead of T. Boone Pickens in taking an equity stake in solar and wind power projects.

Several times over the last 20 years there have been suggestions to begin investing a portion of the country's capital into the stock market. Each time there was a backlash against the idea with suggestions that we could not afford to risk our nation's savings. Interestingly, it took the financial meltdown of 2008 for the government to change its course of action. Although it will probably turn out that the government actions were taken at a time when valuations were artificially low due to a liquidity crisis and will pay off with fair returns, the policy was to "save distressed institutions" rather than to invest in and support the healthiest companies.

We currently live in a country of immense wealth but hear that our own Social Security system is broke. How is this possible? It is true because we continue to attempt to fund our long-term financial future with short-term financial investments like U.S. Treasuries. If only a portion of the country's assets were placed in the stock market (using superior selection and portfolio management), I believe that we would develop a surplus within short order and that our country's future would be secure. This remains true for our country's foundations, institutions, and citizens alike.

America now faces a crossroad that will determine its future role in the world of global relations. It can either use its expertise—the implementation of the free market—to solidify its position as the most powerful economic engine in the world, or it can further its use of asset allocation strategies, interfering with the flow of capital to superlative companies, much to the detriment of the free market.

In this book I draw direct correlations between the outcomes of the efficient flow of capital and the future of America as a world power. The recognition that the efficient allocation of capital to superlative companies expands the collaborative methods of business management is a nearly universal and central component in the productivity of these superlative companies. Collaborative forms of management eventually lead to collaborative forms of government, a more stable society, and ultimately higher standards of living. The efficient allocation of capital within a global free market can even greatly reduce the terrible human and economic cost of terrorism, because more people would have something to lose by destroying themselves and others.

The markets today are far bigger and more global than just ten years ago when *Magnet Investing* was first published. In writing this second book, I think of one of my favorite financial authors, Gerald Loeb, who wrote a book relatively early in his career and another toward the end. Although some of the same themes were covered in both books, having lived through a few market cycles and having gained so much experience trading the market, the author was wiser in his second book. The last 25 years that *I* have spent studying and investing have been remarkable. This experience has made me a better investor, trader, and money manager, and this latest book is the culmination of this knowledge. It is intended to create profits for readers, but it also help change the destructive investing behavior we see today.

The past 30 years have seen fantastic developments in almost every field. It is time for the investment world to reap the benefits that we have seen transform and improve the rest of our world. Despite the negative slant of news in the general media, in many ways the world is a better place for most. People are living longer and eating better. We have harnessed technology to give us more leisure time. Why should you be satisfied to generate the same returns using the same tired diversification strategies that started pushing for mediocrity over 50 years ago and got us into this mess in the first place?

The adverse effects of overdiversification and asset allocation have macro- and microeconomic, political, and even social implications. Compared to failed strategies, my Magnet System of investing isolates and identifies superlative stocks during the early stages of their most powerful growth phase. By debunking the myths associated with diversification and asset allocation, I hope to guide today's investors and their capital down the path of the superlatives.

As I was writing this book in 2008 and 2009, the markets around the world experienced a vicious bear market that helped to highlight and prove many of the points I made throughout the book. The very core of the theories of diversification and asset allocation were shaken and disproved. We saw supposedly noncorrelated assets become very correlated indeed. There was nowhere to hide as stocks, bonds, and commodities alike were hit hard, both domestically and internationally. We will see, when the dust finally clears, that a liquidity crisis developed as a result of a global margin call experienced by the largest financial institutions that had drunk their own poison. Their reliance on their own models led them to overleverage themselves, attempting to generate higher returns. It was because they were so overdiversified that they felt safe and ignored other risks. It was because of the overreliance on their models that excessive leverage was used, making the use of stop-losses impossible.

If I can teach investors how to redefine risk and show them how higher returns come with fewer, well selected companies, I will rest easier, knowing that our government will not have to support a nation of citizens who cannot care for themselves. More foundations will be set up similar to the Robert Wood Johnson Foundation, which continues to accomplish great things for humanity. This foundation is in this position because their entire fortune was allowed to remain solely in Johnson & Johnson stock. Bill Gates certainly would not be doing his great charitable work had he diversified away his Microsoft stock early on.

My goal is to help secure our country's future by replacing models and strategies that continue to come up short, and to employ The Magnet Stock Selection Process, and other effective investment strategies to replace these ineffective models.

In the pages ahead, I share the results of my own research over the past 25 years and, through personal interviews, the philosophies of some of the greatest investors of all time. And so, in this book, I challenge you to discard the notion of modern portfolio theory and explore the possibility of achieving higher returns with fewer stocks.

JORDAN KIMMEL
Magnet Investment Group
Randolph, New Jersey
June 2009

ACKNOWLEDGMENTS

A special thanks to the Magnet team for all their efforts—not only on this book but in the many ways they have continued to support our great working environment over the years. Jeff Anderson and Jason Nolan—this book could not have been completed without your dedication and insights.

And, of course, thanks to the great efforts of the Wiley team and Jeff Hirsch for pulling together a loose manuscript to make this book something I am extremely proud of.

Jen MacDonald and Lynn Lustberg, your guidance and professionalism were invaluable over the course of the project.

Over the years, I have reached out to the top investors and portfolio managers of the era. Several of them have been partly responsible for my success. Among them, they manage several billion dollers in assets with their own investment style and insight. I am honored that so many of them took the time to spend with me during an extermely difficult market environment. I am grateful for their contributions.

J. K.

The MAGNET®
Method of Investing

INTRODUCTION

Throughout history investors have searched for new ways to achieve investment success. Lasting success has rarely been found by following the crowd or the latest investment fad. In fact, doing so has usually ended with disastrous consequences: the Tulip mania of 1637, the South Sea Bubble of 1720, the Internet bubble of 2000, and, most recently, the real estate bust and credit markets crash. It is reasonable to conclude that simply following the latest fad can lead to failure and has the potential for significant losses.

Investment success can be achieved only through the judicious application of a well-grounded discipline built on a solid foundation of fundamental principals and understanding of market behavior. The Magnet Stock Selection System (MSSS) is such a discipline.

Jordan Kimmel, inventor of The Magnet® Stock Selection Process, has transcended being an avid student of investment principles to a leading proponent of the art and science of investing. His knowledge and keen insight into the investment process have been gained in the trenches and on the front lines in the battle for investment survival and success.

The Magnet Stock Selection Process has evolved from those experiences. It uses conventional technical and fundamental factors within a theoretically sound framework and a clear set of practical rules to select a limited number of stocks expected to outperform broad market averages such as the Standard and Poor's(S&P) 500 and Russell 2000 indexes.

The system's underlying theory states that stocks are likely to outperform the general market if they have large and rapidly growing sales, are reasonably priced according to metrics (such as their price-to-earnings multiples and earnings growth), have above-average relative strength, and are undervalued.

The strategy underlying the model states that investors consistently underestimate the expected returns of stocks with strong fundamentals, technical patterns, and risk and growth characteristics.

Thus purchasing a basket of such stocks over time will lead to out-performance with lower risk.

We evaluated the system by performing extensive back-testing and found that it produced superior returns relative to the S&P 500 and Russell 2000 by substantial margins over a nearly 20-year history. Our study back-tested the strategy using portfolios of varied sizes—20, 25, and 30 stocks—and found that each of the Magnet portfolios produced greater returns than both the S&P 500 and Russell 2000 by substantial margins.

The results held up in the long and short term, as well as in the traditional long run only. In addition, although these Magnet portfolios have greater volatility than either index, their volatility is lower than typical 30 stock portfolios, and their risk-adjusted returns are superior to both the S&P and the Russell 2000. Moreover, the Magnet portfolios have lower maximum drawdowns from market peak to trough and shorter drawdown recovery periods.

We have back-tested many strategies over the years. On the basis of the empirical evidence, we find the Magnet strategy appears to be theoretically sound; its selection criteria and rules offer significant promise for outperforming the S&P 500 and Russell 2000. These back-tests have produced some of the highest unleveraged returns of any strategy tested to date. These results are consistent with those obtained by other researchers and reflect methodologies used by a number of "best-of-breed" money managers in major U.S. institutions.

The system's back-test results challenge a popularly held view that passively holding a diversified portfolio with a large number of securities is the best strategy. They indicate that holding a portfolio based on the Magnet system, using a small number of carefully chosen securities can produce superior risk-adjusted performance.

The Magnet investment strategy uses a disciplined two-step process for ranking approximately 8,000 stocks for which earnings estimates are available. Stock selection criteria and heuristic rules are used to rank stocks in descending order according to their potentially superior expected returns for monthly capital appreciation.

The first step in the Magnet process is to rank NYSE-, Euronext-, and NASDAQ-traded stocks by expected returns based on the fundamental, valuation, and technical criteria that research has shown are shared by stocks that have performed well historically. Among the fundamental criteria considered are those related to sales and earnings, favoring companies with superior growth over others with average or below-average growth. The valuation criteria consider a company's market value relative to its sales and earnings, favoring companies that appear to be undervalued at current prices. The technical criteria consider a company's stock price momentum relative to others, favoring those with the greatest momentum.

The second step screens out selected stocks according to a set of rules. Among these rules is one that limits sector exposure to 25 percent of the portfolio to ensure adequate industry diversification, thereby avoiding the potential for catastrophic losses in any one sector. Another rule places stop-loss limits on holdings to limit downside losses at 20 percent and partially pares back positions on stocks that have appreciated 40 percent to lock in a portion of the gain. In addition, each stock must be sufficiently liquid to have a minimum daily trading volume of 35,000 shares.

Once a portfolio is selected, it is monitored daily to ensure that each holding remains eligible. If a stock violates one of the rules, it is removed from the portfolio, and the next highest ranking stock meeting all of the criteria is chosen.

The Magnet strategy is on the forefront of portfolio selection processes that choose stocks based on valuation rather than market capitalization. Active portfolio selection processes are currently gaining acceptance among former advocates of passive or indexed investment strategies. In the last decade, many indexes on which market capitalization strategies were built have been modified. They have dropped market capitalization-weighting schemes in favor of float weighting, formally recognizing that that not all of a company's shares outstanding are available for trading.

Some of the more sophisticated index creators now use fundamental metrics to break the dubious linkage between market capitalization and intrinsic value in their search for performance. For example, Research Affiliates, a Pasadena-based firm, created a series of indexes called "Fundamental Indexes" which use factors such as sales, dividends, cash flow, and number of employees rather than market cap. In a similar vein, WisdomTree, a New York City–based firm, created a series of indexes using earnings and dividends rather than market cap. Also, First Trust AlphaDEX funds are based on enhanced indexes that employ proprietary rules based on a fundamental stock selection process.

For investors, the Magnet investment strategy is important not because of its advanced theoretical nature, but rather because of its performance. Despite holding only 20, 25, and 30 stocks, Magnet portfolios are adequately diversified by virtue of its rules limiting sector exposure. A significant gain in any one of its holdings beyond the sector limit requires that the position be trimmed to bring it back into line.

Magnet portfolios have consistently higher returns than the S&P 500 and the Russell 2000 indexes. The higher returns are occasioned by somewhat greater volatility, but the portfolios' return-to-risk trade-offs are clearly superior to the "indexes". They are also superior in what is perhaps the most relevant risk measure to investors: their maximum drawdown. The strategy's maximum drawdown from market peak to trough is less than the indexes', due in part to the use of stop-loss limits. And, more significantly, the strategy's higher returns result in shorter drawdown recovery periods.

The important lessons to be learned from the Magnet strategy could not be made available at a more opportune time. Investment survival and future investment success will rely on having a sound discipline with strong fundamental, valuation, and technical underpinnings. Such a discipline consistently applied should help investors during the impending worldwide economic slowdown and global stock market malaise.

C. MICHAEL CARTY
New Millennium
Advisors, LLC

EDWARD MATLUCK, PhD
HedgeMetrics, Inc.

1

The Road from Broadway to Wall Street

If you are ready to give up everything else—to study the whole history and background of the market and all the principal companies whose stocks are on the board as carefully as a medical student studies anatomy—if you can do all that, and, in addition, you have the cool nerves of a great gambler, the sixth sense of a clairvoyant, and the courage of a lion, you have a ghost of a chance.
—BERNARD BARUCH

Whatever method you use to pick stocks, your ultimate success or failure will depend on your ability to ignore the worries of the world long enough to allow your investments to succeed. It isn't the head but the stomach that determines the fate of the stockpicker.
—PETER LYNCH

For as long as I can remember, I have had a deep understanding of the engine of the free market. Surely it had something to do with growing up in New York City with my bedroom window overlooking Broadway. I am also sure that my interest in business operations came from having two parents who operated a retail store right below our apartment building. At the dinner table, the discussion often revolved around how the store was doing, as well as how their competitors were fairing. As the youngest of four children, I did not participate much in the conversation, but I listened intently. I saw stores opening and closing throughout the neighborhood and often thought about what made them successes or failures.

All four of my grandparents lived in New York City as well. We spent a lot of time visiting with my mother's parents, who lived in the same neighborhood as us. Those grandparents were fairly well off, enough so that my grandfather was able to retire at a fairly young age. I can remember often being in his living room as he watched his favorite financial show. He would jot down prices of his stocks throughout the day and would make note of any tidbits of information about those companies that he found interesting.

My father's grandparents, however, were not as well off. The contrast between my two sets of grandparents was very clear. Though I did not love either set of grandparents more or less, the fact that my grandfather who kept track of his stocks was the one who visited us with a trunk full of toys was not lost on me. I identified at an early age that the stock market was a vehicle that could lead to wealth generation. I was determined to understand how it worked.

HAMBURGER HELPER

The discussion of the stock market was commonplace in my childhood home. Though my parents were not very successful in the stock market when I was young, they did eventually have a major investment success that allowed them to live more comfortably in later years. One night while enjoying my family dinner—a hamburger to be exact—I asked whether Heinz was a company that you could invest in. Excited by my early interest in investing, my parents answered yes and encouraged me to dig further. Using my accumulated savings, I became an investor for the first time at age 8—the proud owner of 35 shares of Heinz. I think I enjoyed my hamburgers even more being a Heinz shareholder and followed the stock in the newspaper. A few years later, my shares of Heinz had risen substantially in price, and my opportunist older brother bought my shares from me at a discount to the current market price. I was hooked from that time forward and continued to invest in both stocks and, by high school, in stock options.

In eighth grade, I tested for and was accepted into the Bronx High School of Science. The school was considered one of the best in the country. Despite not being the most conscientious student, I used my natural affinity for math and science to bolster my grades and graduate. The hour-and-half journey each day to Bronx Science, along with working after school, may have had something to do with helping me to develop the work ethic I carry with me today. At Bronx Science, I was exposed to the scientific method as well as other method of critical thinking, which have clearly helped me throughout life.

As my time at the Bronx High School of Science was coming to a close, I knew that my choices for college were limited. First of all, I was going to be paying for college myself and the thought of a private college overwhelmed me. Second, I knew that I could not pass a college-level foreign language course and that eliminated another set of opportunities. As it turns out, the State University of New York (SUNY) system provides an excellent education at a very affordable level for in-state residents. SUNY at Stony Brook offered an accelerated five-year degree that included both a bachelor of arts and a master of science, which I completed. The program focused on using both statistical and quantitative analysis to find solutions to various problems and applications.

THE BELL TOLLS

One concept in particular that I became very in tune with during my time at SUNY was that of the bell curve, or Gaussian distribution. Karl Friedrich Gauss was a German mathematician and astronomer known for his contributions to algebra, differential geometry, probability theory, and number theory. Among other things, he was the creator of the Gaussian distribution, or the bell curve as we will refer to it going forward. By definition, the bell curve (also known as a normal distribution) plots all of its values in a symmetrical fashion where most of the results are situated around the probability's mean, with a small group of outliers at either end of the curve. In layman's terms, this means that the majority of items in any set of data will be at or near average, whereas a select few will be above average or below average. This idea can be applied to nearly anything: athletes, automobiles, air quality, or, of course, stocks.

The obviousness of the bell curve in its simplicity and its wide applications had a profound effect on me. It was very clear that, in nature, there would be some outliers on both the winning and losing side, and all else would fall basically in the middle. Through the use of the bell curve and a statistical approach adapted to identify superlative, or in other terms highest-quality, companies, I began to develop what we now know as The Magnet® Stock Selection Process (MSSP). Interestingly, years later one of the cofounders of the Urban Policy Science Department at SUNY Stony Brook would become my director of research at the Magnet Investment Group.

After college and graduate school (having earned both degrees simultaneously), I began working for Mayor Edward Koch at New York's Office of Management and Budget. Within two years, I was responsible for forecasting over $500 million in revenues from various city agencies. I was on track to becoming the youngest commissioner in New York City's history. Although I was enjoying my time in city government, I knew my true calling was in the financial markets. The Municipal Building was just a few blocks north of Wall Street, and I felt myself pulled down to The Street. I continued to invest in stocks and was a student of the market, trying to learn as much as I could.

It was not until I was 25 that I entered Wall Street and my financial career began. I started as a municipal bond salesman, but I was using my savings to continue investing in the stock market and to further develop my Magnet theories. I took the opportunity to meet as many portfolio managers, newsletter writers, and authors as I could and invited them all to lunch or dinner. I asked, "What is the number one book that you would recommend?" "What sets you apart from the rest?" What was startling to me then—and even today—is how money managers and mutual funds have pigeon-holed themselves into specific boxes: growth, value, or momentum investors. It was after years of listening to these varied approaches to investing that I realized I could develop a quantitative method to incorporate the best aspects of several different top-performing money managers and construct my own process that included the best of various styles. It was over several more years of working with more than 70 college interns from five different universities that The Magnet Stock Selection Process was developed.

Since the beginning of my investment career, I had been interested in developing a model that would try to analyze public companies to give me an advantage investing in the stock market. Several distinctly different models had been created that fell into three broad categories: value, growth, and momentum. In addition, a more passive approach was being pushed on Wall Street, and it was called the efficient market theory. As opposed to the other methodologies, the efficient market theory assumed that all relevant information about a company was already in the public domain and therefore the sum of all buyers and sellers created the correct, or "efficient," price. In analyzing price movement, however, I found it clear that the market was far from efficient. There was simply too much price movement within individual companies for the market to be truly efficient.

This observation of nonefficient price movement is supported by an idea known as chaos theory, whose proponents believe that price is the very last thing to change for a stock, bond, or other security. Though in this context the theory is adapted for analysis of the stock market, the ideas of chaos theory were originally pioneered by a meteorologist at Massachusetts Institute of Technology (MIT) named Edward Lorenz, who attempted to use computers to predict weather patterns. He kept a continuous simulation running on his computer that would output 24 hours' worth of his simulation for every minute it ran, as a line of text on a roll of paper. He intended to draw correlations between seemingly insignificant changes in weather conditions to predict likely occurrences in the future. James Gleick described it well in his book, *Chaos: Making a New Science.*

> Line by line, the winds and temperatures in Lorenz's printouts seemed to behave in a recognizable earthly way. They matched his cherished intuition about the weather, his sense that it repeated itself, displaying familiar patterns over time, pressure rising and falling, the airstream swinging north and south (Gleick, p. 15).

Applying chaos theory to the fundamentals of stock selection made perfect sense to me. I began to gather all the data I could get my hands on about public companies and set out on my quest to develop a model that would identify stocks on the brink of a massive growth spurt. Through the use of applications borrowed from chaos theory and factor analysis (as opposed to raw data mining), my theories on what makes a good company were transformed into The Magnet Stock Selection Process. At this time, I was asked to be a member of the Quantitative Work Alliance for Applied Finance, Education, and Wisdom in New York City. This is a group composed of some of the top quantitative thinkers from around the country. They hold meetings to debate cutting-edge theories and openly collaborate with one another. Shortly after my initial presentation to the group, more interest gathered in the Magnet system. Two of the largest asset managers in the world offered to do a study to see whether they would hire us to select stocks for them. Both of them offered us contracts. Our approach was closely examined by a few other institutions, and, despite its controversial and unique methodology, we received some lucrative contracts that took us to the next level.

I continued to read every investment book that was recommended to me by the professionals that I sought out and encountered. I was particularly interested in books written by those who had considerable success in the stock market. I began to embrace several aspects of the different schools of investing. Although the various proponents of growth, value, and momentum styles of investing adamantly rejected each other's approach, I saw merit in the different approaches, and it made sense to me to try to combine them somehow. I began to build a model that incorporated the best attributes of the best investors that had come before me. Within a few years, Magnet was offered contracts to select stocks for two of the biggest institutions on Wall Street: John Nuveen & Co. and Van Kampen Funds Inc.

At the time that I was under contract with John Nuveen & Co., I came across a book called *The Predictors*. The book was written by Thomas Bass and was about the use of chaos theory to analyze the stock market. In the book, two men sought patterns within the stock market in an effort to predict the movements of the stock market and traded actively using those predictions. Many at the time assumed the behavior of stocks and the stock market to be completely unpredictable. The most vocal in proclaiming the so-called random walk of stocks were the proponents of the efficient market theory.

Coupled with this assumption, others extended the notion even further. Their approach was simply to broadly diversify among many companies. This approach suggested that you could benefit from the stock market by owning a little bit of everything; with some winners offsetting some losers and therefore creating a decent return. My understanding of the market and individual companies quickly led me to reject this concept and to find a more focused and productive approach. I was not interested in a decent or average return.

The theories regarding investing were not the only areas of the world getting more complex at the time. This was a time of great acceleration in the advancement of various technologies. Personal computers had just been introduced to the world and led to the development of several new industries that did not even exist just a few years earlier. Developments in manufacturing, commerce, and seemingly all walks of life were occurring at breakneck speeds.

Many of the companies involved in these new developments had similar characteristics. They were not only growing their revenues faster than companies that had come before them, but they were also capturing the minds and attentions of the public. What was interesting was that their share prices often got bid up to unsustainable levels only to decline rapidly when competition arose. For this reason, many traditional and experienced investors had no way to analyze this rapidly changing environment.

A few quants, or investors who use quantitative analysis of companies' earnings to seek out those worth investing in, were using chaos theory to trade the market. I did something completely different. Using pattern recognition, I set out to identify the fundamental characteristics that were common among only the best companies. I found that the truly superlative companies often had several certain fundamental characteristics in common. Understanding that there can be only a few "best" companies, I was looking for a model to identify the true superlatives in the market.

COMBINATION HERO

I was convinced that a stock selection model combining the right factors of value and growth could also incorporate the new momentum of financial change occurring throughout the world.

I expanded on this theory and developed a mathematical process that I called The Magnet Stock Selection Process. I took a scientific approach that would help me include the best aspects and factors that worked for other top money managers. This system would be able to identify companies that, through their financial outperformance, would attract and pull in other investors.

It is important to take a moment to distinguish between successful data mining and what we were doing at the Magnet Investment Group. Data miners look for events or circumstances that take place and try to predict the future based on these observations. A common example of this was the observation that the stock market did well in years when the winner of the Super Bowl came from the National Conference, but was weak following years when the winner came from the American Conference. Clearly, anybody with any investment knowledge or experience would not invest based on who won the Super Bowl. What I did instead was to create a model based on my hypothesis of what made a good investment. The characteristics of a company's financials take on very clear patterns when you attempt to separate the winners from the losers. By understanding the subtleties within a balance sheet and income statement, we created a statistical approach to ranking companies within their sectors.

What was so interesting about our system was that it was proven successful in identifying the superlative companies—both in comparison to the entire stock universe and within specific industries. Wall Street is keen on having different analysts following different sectors and becoming experts in very narrow fields. Unfortunately, this specialization has in many cases led analysts to miss the forest while looking at the trees. As we have seen over the years, many analysts' overinvolvement with management has led to many a blind alley.

It is the repeating pattern of accelerating revenues and margins, the emphasis on new products, and the sum of several other important factors that lead to the identification of potential Magnets and ultimately to superior investment results. This holds true regardless of sector or market capitalization. The concept of superiority is not confined to the stock market. It is very clear that when you analyze anything in nature, there can be only a few superior anythings, whether you are looking at architects, painters, musicians—you name it. An unbiased method of finding them is the key to success.

Our work and discoveries here at Magnet have been quite exciting to me. Even more encouraging is the fact that the commonsense approach that we take to investing has been proven statistically significant by others. Through the use of our spreadsheets and ranking system, we have been able to invest in top-ranking Magnet companies that have outperformed the lower-ranked companies time after time.

But beyond finding the right characteristics by which to judge a company's success, the dilemma for me has always been the issue of how to most clearly and successfully organize our information. A professor of mine in graduate school, Dr. Stan Altman, identified this very problem. Back in the 1980s, Dr. Altman wrote an article entitled "The Dilemma of the Data Rich, Information Poor Service Organizations." In his article, he discussed the increasingly difficult task of analyzing data while there was also a steadily increasing amount of information to pore through as a result of the advancements in computer technology. Imagine, this paper was written in the early 1980s!

I began to analyze the outperformance created by investing in the 50 best-scoring Magnet companies within each sector. I found that there was still too much information and too many companies to attempt to truly understand. I then suggested that we narrow our focus to the top 40 companies in each sector in order to get a better handle on the selection system. Interestingly, the performance of the top 40 companies was significantly better than the top 50. This result led to the question, "What happens when we narrow it down to the top 30?" Again we saw stronger returns, whether investing within a single sector or across the entire stock spectrum. Through this thought process, I first recognized the dramatically negative effects of overdiversification. Ironically, at that same time Wall Street was selling the very theories that almost ensured mediocre results at best: diversification, the efficient frontier, and modern portfolio theory.

That our system was able to screen through the entire universe of stocks to select the best-performing and most promising companies was only part of the story. There was still the issue that, if we were constantly rebalancing into the top-ranked Magnet stocks, the model showed a considerable amount of turnover. Some investors have a strong predisposition against turnover in a portfolio. The other issue was that obviously some of the selected stocks would end up not working out and instead would decline in price. Over the years, I learned to use both stop losses on our declining stocks and trailing stop losses on those stocks increasing in price. Through the use of stop losses, we have been able to reduce risk and have coupled superior stock selection with superior portfolio management.

Currently the investing world is bombarded with the call for diversification. As we shall see, the original diversification studies had several flawed assumptions and cannot lead to anything beyond average results. My entire focus is on creating above-average returns.

I share my Magnet Stock Selection Process later in the book, but for now let us review some of the flawed assumptions that led to today's obsession with diversification. In preparing this book, I spent time with many of this generation's leading investors to get their opinions. In the next chapter we will hear from them as well.

CHAPTER 2

The Paradox: Diversification and Superlatives

If you can buy more of your best idea, why put [the money] into your 10th best idea or 20th best idea? . . . The more positions you have, the more average you are.

—BRUCE BERKOWITZ

The early stock market was just a place for private companies to go public and raise capital. Stock ownership was concentrated among very few wealthy individuals. Although there was great interest in the market, actual information about individual companies was scarce. The financial data was in the hands of few, and trading in stocks was done directly by investors for their own accounts. Over time, pools were created and wealthy families could have their investments handled by others with more direct access to information. As the markets continued to grow, mutual funds grew exponentially, and successful corporations began investing their pension funds in other companies' stock. Starting in the 1950s, individual participation in the stock market began to increase. But, looking back just 20 years, today's investors would be surprised at how little information was available to the public. Prior to the explosion of the Internet in the mid-1990s, all the information was in the hands of the brokerage firms.

As the markets grew, the service business of investing for others developed rapidly. The investment pools and money management industry began to replace individuals as the primary force behind the trading in the market. With the introduction of computers, the entire investment landscape changed. Although the information was still strictly controlled and was unavailable to most individuals, financial data *was* now out there. Models could now be built to quickly analyze and compare companies and to create portfolios in scientifically formulated ways. Rather than trying to isolate the best companies according to their competitive advantages, other more complex portfolio creation and management methods emerged, aimed at minimizing short-term volatility in order to maintain client comfort levels and not scare away client assets, maximizing management fees while short-changing clients with mediocre non-market-beating returns that fail to keep pace with inflation, taxes, and transaction fees.

MODERN PORTFOLIO THEORY (MPT)

As more academic attention was placed on the subject of investing, studies were conducted to determine whether there were optimal ways to construct portfolios in order to maximize returns while limiting risk. Unfortunately, two theories brought on by modern portfolio theory (MPT) have since emerged that have had a profoundly negative impact on our county's wealth creation: diversification and asset allocation. Unfortunately, both of these are failed concepts that almost eliminate the possibility of superior returns needed to achieve long-term goals. Instead, both concepts include the process of systematically rebalancing a portfolio to adjust for recent returns. Another way to put it (although nobody is willing to say it out loud) is to continuously sell your winning investments and add to your losers. Not only is this ridiculous behavior encouraged, but the studies that ushered in these practices have inherent flaws in them. In some cases, certain assumptions were made that were valid at the time but are no longer valid. The very calculations that their work depended on were not able to be generated due to a lack of computer power at the time.

Most investors are familiar with the concept of diversification, or investing in a broad group of securities or industries as a hedge against underperformance by a certain issue or sector in your portfolio. I will address the flaws and limitations of overdiversification in chapter 3 and throughout the book. I will first examine modern portfolio theory (MPT) to understand how we have become so indoctrinated with diversification and asset allocation. MPT was originally introduced back in 1952, when Harry Markowitz wrote a paper called "Portfolio Selection," which appeared in *The Journal of Finance.* At the time that he introduced his concept, the financial markets basically consisted of two alternatives: stocks and bonds. The idea behind modern portfolio theory was to have a disciplined strategy mixing the right blend of securities in your portfolio, based on a given risk profile. Theoretically, the blend would provide the optimal combination of risk and reward.

Since the initial introduction of MPT, however, significant trends have altered the entire landscape of investing. Now, institutions along with individuals have the opportunity to invest in various products that were simply not available in 1952. These products include hedge funds, commodities, real estate, and varied insurance products. Investors now also have access to other tools as well, such as the use of options and hedging strategies. In short, quite a bit has changed since the early work by Markowitz. Citing the studies originally used to develop modern portfolio theory today is like using a pencil and paper, ignoring the advent of computers.

The original MPT proposed by Markowitz tied in several other concepts that were to be used in portfolio construction and asset management. Blended together were the concepts and assumptions of the efficient frontier, the capital asset pricing model (CAPM), the alpha and beta coefficients, the capital market line, and the securities market line.

Not only were all of these overly complicated concepts included, but they all had to actually be working together at the same time. The trouble was that even these subconcepts had direct internal conflicts. CAPM assumes the ability to construct portfolios based on correlated and noncorrelated risk. However, the efficient market theory believed all investors had all the information required to eliminate all nonmarket risk.

Despite the limitations and some of the poor assumptions of MPT, the original underlying assumption was a fair and acceptable one: Given two assets that offer the same expected return, investors will prefer the less risky one. Therefore, an investor will take on increased risk only if compensated by higher returns. The problem with this assumption, however, is that volatility of the security is used as the proxy for risk, not the actual return expectation. The other flawed assumption is that the investor is actually indifferent to the size of the distribution of the potential returns. Mathematicians measure skew, which is the level of asymmetry in the distribution, and kurtosis, which is the level of nonaverage data points or the so-called fat tail. In laymen's terms, this suggests that an investor would not really care when the theory would not work or, even sillier, how badly it may miss by.

The attempt to control a portfolio's volatility using MPT is based on determining the covariance of the components within the portfolio. We will look at the complex formula and examples in a moment, but for now just think of trying to create a basket of stocks in which some zig while the others zag. The concept is to invest in companies across several uncorrelated sectors in hopes that they will act as hedges against each other, that is, offer a blended return as the economy changes. You would want to include companies in sectors that may perform best when the economy strengthens, while having other companies that remain strong when the economy contracts. By doing this, theoretically, you never have to understand what trends exist or will develop. Instead, by taking a Noah's ark approach, you have a little of everything and never worry about a single hole sinking your ship. Of course, this methodology can never provide the upside benefits that a truly insightful investor may generate. Instead, it is an approach that is expected to keep you out of trouble, but the obvious side effect is producing mediocre returns.

By looking at expected returns and expected volatility using MPT, you are attempting to build a portfolio along what is called an "efficient frontier," maximizing returns and minimizing risks based on an investor's unique risk tolerance. Quite a bit of advanced formulas and calculations are incorporated, and the expected results are very specific. With respect for all who work with MPT and the extremely bright people who introduced it, history has shown dramatic flaws with the strategy. Almost everything involved with MPT is directly aimed toward reducing variance, standard deviation, volatility, or whatever measure of risk someone determines to be relevant. Clearly, these short-term measurements of variance are important, but not nearly as important as generating superior long-term returns.

Another more important measurement is called "longevity risk," the risk that nearly everybody underemphasizes. Longevity risk, the risk of outliving one's capital, is also called terminal wealth. Rather than addressing long-term goals and achieving them, MPT takes a different approach. In fact, MPT limits progress. For instance, say an investor, whether individual or an institution, creates an original investment plan based on a risk profile. Once the initial profile is completed, a portfolio is created by blending different asset classes in an attempt to achieve an expected return without excessive volatility. Let's say you started with a 50% allocation to stocks and a 50% allocation to bonds. Over time, as your stock portfolio continues to grow, the stocks will continuously be sold off to allocate more money into the lower-returning bonds. Rather than focusing on the terminal market value of the portfolio, the emphasis with MPT is on the reducing short-term volatility.

Markowitz was offering a mathematical approach to asset selection and portfolio management. By implementing this seemingly prudent approach, institutions have not been able to generate the returns they desire because they opted for the high comfort level offered by this safe strategy. We see a business model that many asset managers have promoted: Gather assets, provide mediocre returns, and focus on damping short-term volatility so as not to lose the client.

Because of the tremendous influence that MPT has had on the world of investing, many more studies have been done over the years to evaluate the process itself. These studies address some of the flaws inherent in the original assumptions made while constructing MPT. Even at its origin, the core of this theory, mean-variance analysis (MVA), is unreliable. According to one of the developers of CAPM, Dr. William F. Sharpe, who worked closely with Markowitz:

> Under certain conditions the MVA can be shown to lead to unsatisfactory predictions of (investor) behavior. Markowitz suggests that a model based on the semi variance would be preferable; in light of the formidable computational problems, however, he bases his (MV) analysis on the mean and the standard deviation. (Sharpe, p. 428)

POSTMODERN PORTFOLIO THEORY (PMPT)

Ironically, this very analysis that uncovers the weakness of MPT simply goes on to introduce a new concept with the same inherent flaws: postmodern portfolio theory (PMPT). PMPT states that using traditional MPT for investment portfolio construction and evaluation frequently distorts investment reality. In 1987 the Pension Research Institute at San Francisco State University developed the practical mathematical algorithms of PMPT that are in use today. With just a few more added mathematics, the same weak assumptions of the original MPT remain present, maintaining the same environment and strategies that are geared to gather assets and provide mediocre investment returns.

I am now going to show the absurd math behind MPT—not to fully explain it, but to expose how many moving parts must perform as expected in order for the strategy to work. The following excerpt directly from Markowitz's paper exposes how the extraordinarily simple question of how to allocate into two securities is complicated by the calculations that Modern Portfolio Theory is based upon:

We can see this analytically: suppose there are N securities; let r_{it} be the anticipated return (however decided upon) at time t pet dollar in vested in security i; let d_{it} be the rate at which the return on the ith security at time t is discounted back to the present; let X_i be the relative amount invested in security i. We exclude short sales, thus $X_i \geq 0$ for all i. Then the discounted anticipated return of the portfolio is

$$R = \sum_{i=1}^{\infty} \sum_{i=1}^{N} d_{it} r_{it} X$$

$$= \sum_{i=1}^{N} X_i \left(\sum_{i=1}^{\infty} d_{it} r_{it} \right)$$

$R_i = \sum_{i=1}^{\infty} d_{it} r_{it}$ is the discounted return of the ith security,

therefore

$R = \Sigma X_i R_i$ where R_i is independent of X_i. Since $X_i \geq 0$ for all i and $\Sigma X_i = 1$, R is a weighted average of R_i with the X_i as non-negative weights. To maximize R, we let $X_i = 1$ for i with maximum R_i. If several Ra_a, $a = 1, \ldots, K$ are maximum then any allocation with

$$\sum_{a=1}^{K} Xa_a = 1$$

maximizes R. In no case is a diversified portfolio preferred to all non-diversified portfolios. (Markowitz 1952, p. 78)

Amazingly, in that last sentence above, even Markowitz himself clearly admits that a diversified portfolio is not preferred to non-diversified portfolios. Furthermore, look at what happened to the calculations when there were three investment alternatives factored in as opposed to just two. Seeing how the following formulas were attempting to handle an investment decision among merely three alternatives, imagine what an investment formula today must look like with the vast number of options for investment now available.

Two conditions—at least—must be satisfied before it would be practical to use efficient surfaces in the manner described above. First, the investor must desire to act according to the E-V maxim. Second, we must be able to arrive at reasonable μ_i and σ_{ij}. We will return to these matters later.

Let us consider the case of three securities. In the three security case our model reduces to

1. $E = \sum_{i=1}^{3} X_i \mu_i$

2. $V = \sum_{i=1}^{3}\sum_{j=1}^{3} X_i X_j \sigma_{ij}$

3. $\sum_{i=1}^{3} X_i = 1$

4. $X_i \geq 0$ for $i = 1, 2, 3$

From (3) we get

3'. $X_3 = 1 - X_1 - X_2$

If we substitute (3') in equation (1) and (2) we get E and V as functions of X_1 and X_2. For example we find

1'. $E = \mu_3 + X_1(\mu_1 - \mu_3) + X_2(\mu_2 - \mu_3)$

The exact formulas are not too important here (that of V is given below). We can simply write

  a. $E = E(X_1, X_2)$
  b. $V = V(X_1, X_2)$
  c. $X_1 \geq 0, X_2 \geq 0, 1 - X_1 - X_2 \geq 0$

By using relations (a), (b), (c), we can work with two dimensional geometry. (Markowitz 1952, p. 83)

Although these formulas may mean a lot to the academics, in the real world the best investors scoff at them. Warren Buffett said:

The amount of time spent at business schools—maybe it's a little less now—teaching things like option pricing and that sort of thing is *totally* nonsense. You need two courses in business school from the standpoint of investments. One is how to value a business—and the second is how to think about stock market fluctuation. Spending all of this time with formulas is very counterproductive. The problem, of course, is that the instructors *know* the formulas, and the students *don't* when they come in—so the instructors can kill time explaining them to the students. (Munger 2008, p. 20)

MPT was also expanded on by William Sharpe and Jan Mossin. By the early 1960s, the capital asset pricing model (CAPM) was being used along with MPT to account for the rate of return required to introduce new securities into a portfolio. The attempt was to delineate between systemic risk and market risk.

In the May/June 1998 issue of *Dow Jones Asset Manager*, Jonathan Burton offers us a brief history of the Capital Asset Pricing Model:

Modern Portfolio Theory was not yet adolescent in 1960 when William F. Sharpe, a 26-year-old researcher at the RAND Corporation, a think tank in Los Angeles, introduced himself to a fellow economist named Harry Markowitz. Neither of them knew it then, but that casual knock on Markowitz's office door would forever change how investors valued securities.

Sharpe, then a Ph.D. candidate at the University of California, Los Angeles, needed a doctoral dissertation topic. He had read "Portfolio Selection," Markowitz's seminal work on risk and return—first published in 1952 and updated in 1959—that presented a so-called efficient frontier of optimal investment. While advocating a diversified portfolio to reduce risk, Markowitz stopped short of developing a practical means to assess how various holdings operate together, or correlate, though the question had occurred to him.

Sharpe accepted Markowitz's suggestion that he investigate Portfolio Theory as a thesis project. By connecting a portfolio to a single risk factor, he greatly simplified Markowitz's work. Sharpe has committed himself ever since to making finance more accessible to both professionals and individuals.

From this research, Sharpe independently developed a heretical notion of investment risk and reward, a sophisticated reasoning that has become known as the Capital Asset Pricing Model, or the CAPM. The CAPM rattled investment professionals in the 1960s, and its commanding importance still reverberates today. In 1990, Sharpe's role in developing the CAPM was recognized by the Nobel Prize committee. Sharpe shared the Nobel Memorial Prize in Economic Sciences that year with Markowitz and Merton Miller, the University of Chicago economist. (p. 20)

Making matters even more complex and teetering on the boundaries of the ridiculous, according to CAPM, the expected return of a stock equals the risk-free rate plus the portfolio's beta multiplied by the expected excess return of the market portfolio. Specifically, let Z_s and Z_m be random variables for the simple returns of the stock and the market over some specified period. Let z_f be the known risk-free rate, also expressed as a simple return, and let B be the stock's beta. Then

$$E(Z_s) = z_f + \beta[E(Z_m) - z_f]$$

where E denotes an *expectation*.

Stated another way, the stock's excess expected return over the risk-free rate equals its beta times the market's expected excess return over the risk-free rate.

Unfortunately, the same assumption of normally distributed random variables was used in formulating CAPM. We know in the real world, however, that frequently the returns in equity and other markets are far from normally distributed. In fact, we often see three to six standard deviations from the mean showing up. That is, we are seeing a 100-year flood every couple of years in today's markets.

Simply put, some things prove easier to engineer than others. With experience, farmers have learned to rotate crops to improve the yield on their farmland. Operations research has helped to create efficient pickup and delivery applications. But the stock market is in a different class due to the vagaries of human nature. During periods of financial stress, all betas and volatility statistics go out the window. When a breakdown occurs in one aspect of the model, we often see an even greater discrepancy develop on the back end. Throw in the heavy use of margin and leverage that is often used due to an overreliance on a given model, and you really see how troublesome these models can become. During the 2007–2009 financial crisis, we have experienced a dose of this that will go down in history.

Mr. Markowitz's theories have indeed had a dramatic impact on the market. For many years now, investors have been following the failed strategies of asset allocation and systematic diversification, effectively trading off some volatility in favor of mediocre and frankly unacceptable returns. Institutions and the public at large are now open to a more logical and robust methodology of seeking out, identifying, and concentrating capital in the true superlative companies. If the asset allocation and diversification approaches that have been so blindly followed worked, the proliferation of the hedge fund business would never have taken place.

Today, over 50 years after the introduction of MPT and CAPM, Wall Street and academia have succeeded in selling a concept in which you should not lose all your money in one investment or experience too much uncomfortable volatility. The overemphasis on diversification within portfolios and the use of modern portfolio theory have severely limited the long-term creation of wealth within our nation. As a result, our citizens are economically suffering, earning less and less each year from their investments. In my opinion, the central problem with those early theories of investing was that the risks were not defined properly. By studying the approaches and results of the best investors over the years, my goal is to help the investment public, both individuals and institutions alike, to reevaluate their current investment strategies and ultimately improve their results.

RISK VERSUS REWARD

The concepts of modern portfolio theory and diversification were created in an attempt to provide the right balance between risk and reward. To do this correctly, however, you have to start with the correct assumptions of what risk and reward actually are. In terms of risk/reward, the goal of investing is frequently improperly defined. In one of my favorite investment books ever, *The Battle for Investment Survival*, Gerald Loeb properly defines the goal of investing (in simpler terms) as the preservation of one's purchasing power over time, after taxes, inflation, and fees.

The issue of risk is another discussion in itself. In Loeb's approach, fluctuations in prices and day-to-day account values are not the primary risk. The real risk is not achieving your goals. Ignoring this teaching, diversification strategies have attempted to minimize short-term volatility, which has led to the creation of even more issues. Today we see a country with underfunded pensions and nonprofit organizations, as well as individuals who are unable to save enough for the future. In fact, the United States overall is suffering from historically low levels of savings by individuals, not because Americans are not saving enough, but because they are not placing enough of their savings in the right investments. The reason for that is that they are not assessing risk correctly.

TRUE SUPERLATIVES

Back in Statistics 101, a professor put up a chart called "the bell curve." As simple as it was, I found the concept remarkable. According to the law of large numbers, when any group in nature is measured, 90% of its components will fall into the average level. There will be 5% below average and the other 5% above average. This applies to the height of trees, the weight of automobiles, the IQs of people, baseball players' batting averages, golfers' handicaps, and pretty much all things measurable. Although there are many

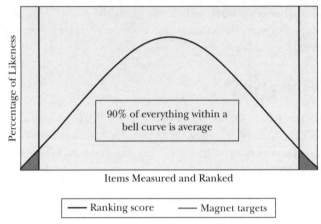

FIGURE 2.1   The bell curve's application in the stock market

Source: Magnet Investment Group, 2008.

facets to the concept of the bell curve and its statistics, this is the basic theory (see Figure 2.1).

I used to take the subway from Manhattan to the Bronx High School of Science. One of the stops along the way was Yankee Stadium. As we would pass the stadium, I would think about Babe Ruth, Lou Gehrig, and Mickey Mantle. Think about how many kids grow up and want to play in the big leagues. How many make it? How many ever bat .350 for a season or hit 40 home runs in a year? You are talking about the cream of the crop. Despite their efforts, only a few people run the 100 meters in under 10 seconds. How many ever score 40 points in an NBA game? This is the way you need to think about public companies as well.

By nature, there can be only a few superlatives of anything, publicly traded companies included. It is the natural order of things. In this way, the stock market is like the rest of the world. Having been interested in investing, I sat in my college class looking at the chart of the bell curve and asked myself a couple life-changing questions: Understanding that only 5% of companies can be truly superlative, why would anybody recommend buying the whole list? Why would anybody accept the premise of investing in all 500 companies in the S&P or all 2000 in the Russell small-cap index unless they were willing to have an "average return"?

My next thought was that, to take advantage of isolating and investing in the superlatives, there would have to be a way of measuring companies in a quantitative methodology. This became my quest over the next 20 years and remains the backbone of The Magnet® Stock Selection Process. With the advancements that have taken place in computers and technology, many investment programs now allow for variables to be tested and portfolios to be backtested. With this, I was able to test my theories and eventually come to what we believe is the best formula for strong stock selection.

Other money managers have taken various approaches. Some have studied and tried to use the suggested covariance among sectors, and others use optimization strategies, but all their approaches are based on the underlying concept of reducing volatility while owning many positions. Using our rigorous screening process, we take a different path: owning fewer but clearly superlative opportunities. Our approach is to rank many different aspects of a company's balance sheets and other fundamental and technical indicators, and then to combine them to give every company a final score. This serves to isolate outliers, companies at the absolute tip of the bell curve. While 90% of the company's stock opportunities are average, there are always the extremely poor and extremely good.

The only way investors can feel comfortable in a strategy other than that of buying the whole list is to have confidence in two things. First, they would have to believe they could isolate the best companies. Second, they would need to be able to exit the investment or strategy if it is not working. In the early and still often quoted diversification studies, it was assumed that you remained in each investment, sometimes riding a loser all the way to zero. Obviously, in the real world you have the option of using stop loss strategies or cutting your losses along the way.

Addressing modern portfolio theory directly in the book *The Warren Buffett Way* by Robert Hagstrom, the legendary investor Warren Buffett said, "modern portfolio theory tells you how to be average. But I think almost anybody can figure out how to be average in fifth grade" (p. 166). My point is that it is fine to be an average investor. After all, it is not possible for everybody to be above average. When hiring professional portfolio services, however, you should expect more than an attempt to be just average.

Buffett goes on to say, "In our opinion, the real risk that an investor must assess is whether his aggregate after-tax receipts from an investment (including those he receives on sale) will, over his prospective holding period, give him at least as much purchasing power as he had to begin with, plus a modest rate of interest on that initial stake." This is close to the definition Loeb gave decades earlier.

The entire premise of asset allocation and overdiversification—done out of a fear of loss—could be replaced with the use of a superior stock selection process resulting in a concentrated approach to portfolio construction, coupled with the use of stop losses within the portfolio to control risk.

The Bell Curve: Stock Market Superlatives

It is a funny thing about life; if you refuse to accept anything but the best, you very often get it.

—W. Somerset Maugham

There is a battle cry in today's world on Wall Street and in the money management business. More than any other recommendation is the call to be diversified. In my effort to become the best investor I could be, I have read almost every book on investing that I could find. I have met with and interviewed many of the top portfolio managers, authors, newsletter writers, and top investors of the last several decades. Interestingly, I have found a common discrepancy. The how-to books that focus on the novice investor all hold diversification out as the most important and self-evident truth of investing. The Wall Street firms and money management companies also heed the need for diversification. However, as you move up the experience ladder and talk to the most successful investors of all, you find a very different story. Invariably the top performers in the investment business all shun diversification. By taking a careful look at the theory of diversification and its related cousin, asset allocation, we can find the inherent flawed assumptions that they are based on. We can use this research to improve on the investment results we see today, hoping eventually to change the behavior of tomorrow.

Today's most common themes throughout Wall Street and portfolio management remain diversification and asset allocation.

Unfortunately, both of these are failed concepts that almost eliminate the possibility of superior returns needed to achieve long-term goals. Both concepts also go against the free markets.

DIVERSIFICATION AND ASSET ALLOCATION

The underlying concept supporting both diversification and asset allocation is that you are prevented from losing all of your money in a single bad investment. By diversifying across a broad number of stocks—or asset classes—even if some of your money or investments lose 100% of their value, at least you do not lose all of your money.

As the approach goes, you start by investing in several places; then, because the returns of each investment vary, you continue to rebalance the assets back to equilibrium, or to your initial allocation starting point. The actual result is that you continue to sell down your best investments and place the excess returns from those investments into the underperforming areas. This goes against the most important strategy of all in making real money: Let your winners run and sell your losers! In fact, diversification is a failed concept that fails to ride the economic progress of the markets.

Wall Street and academia succeeded in selling a concept in which you would not lose all your money in one thing, but, as a result, many investors now take on too little volatility. They think they are avoiding risk. They are just not correctly assessing the different types of risk. Inflation risk continues to be one of the biggest risks to all investors—individuals, institutions, foundations, and nonprofits alike. In the process of avoiding volatility, investment returns come up short and fail even to keep pace with inflation.

FLAWS IN THE ORIGINAL DIVERSIFICATION STUDIES

Many are quick to tag along and endorse the need to be diversified and often site studies to back up the concept. A couple of important flaws with the initial studies are not known by many of the current proponents of diversification. The studies were initially performed to determine a number of things.

- First, the question was asked, "What is the optimal number of holdings you need to carry to be properly diversified?"
- Next, "How much short-term volatility is removed as you incrementally added more holdings to your portfolio?"
- The last question dealt with the end result: "What was the impact on the 'terminal value' of a portfolio based on its level of diversification?"

Although these were the right questions, the problems were with two of the critical primary assumptions in the studies.

The first problem with the initial diversification studies is that they did not take stop-loss or selling strategies into account. They simply assumed that if a holding went bad, you rode it down to zero and did not try to control the downside risk. We all know that, in real life, investors have the opportunity to sell a holding at any time. Not only do investors have a chance to sell along the way, but money management is often as important as any other aspect of successful investing. We know ahead of time that even the best-looking and well thought-out prospects often fall short of our expectations. The ability to cut one's losses short and move into another opportunity is what enables the good investor to take larger, more concentrated positions in the first place.

Another major problem with the initial asset allocation studies is that they took place when the only available choices for investment were stocks or bonds. The products and opportunities we now have at our disposal in creating and managing portfolios were not yet available. In today's market, we have other tools at our disposal that can help to control risk and even enhance reward, such as options, derivatives, commodities, and futures. Studies done in a black-and-white world, where only stocks and bonds were available, should no longer dictate investors' decisions.

The other obvious problem with diversification is that, by nature, not all stocks can be equal, or winners. Only a few stocks or a few of anything can actually be superior. Peter Lynch, the acclaimed portfolio manager from Fidelity, coined the term "de-worse-ification" to describe an investment approach where people spread themselves too thin and do not concentrate on the best opportunities available.

Along the same line of thinking, it is hardly possible for any-body to think that their 160th best idea is as good as their top 10 ideas or even their 40th best idea. Whatever methodology you use to assess companies, there must be a way to rank or quantify them. By continuing to diversify into companies further down in ranking, effectively filling a portfolio of top-ranked, medium-ranked, and ultimately even poorly ranked companies, you will be significantly reducing your returns.

Another dangerous belief arose regarding diversification and modern portfolio theory that we have seen blow up in dramatic fashion. We were sold the story of non-correlated holdings and how mixing and matching them would increase returns while reduc-ing volatility. In fact, the argument was that this strategy worked so well that you could use leverage with your portfolio and enhance the returns. However, as we have seen many times in the past sev-eral years, the idea of non-correlated holdings and using them to create diversification works only some of the time. During peri-ods of extreme volatility, assumed correlations become meaning-less and predetermined models go haywire. Suddenly the models that worked so well in the laboratory did not hold up in real mar-kets with real human emotion involved. Tremendous losses have occurred as a result, in both the stock market as well as in the fixed-income markets. We saw this play out in the high-profile example of Long Term Capital in 1998 and now on an even bigger scale with the credit products than went haywire and illiquid in 2008.

Another major problem is in the handling of a so-called prop-erly diversified portfolio that most mutual funds currently hold. The average equity mutual fund currently holds 160 positions. Not even the most diligent portfolio team, let alone a single portfolio man-ager, could keep track of 160 companies. If you are following your investments as carefully as you need to be—conducting prudent, thorough, ongoing research—you simply cannot follow the ins and outs of 160 companies. By thorough research I am talking about fol-lowing their competition, their suppliers, their industry prospects, market cycles, and pitfalls, not just analyzing the quarterly earnings reports of the companies. In fact, if you researched your current portfolio holdings this carefully, you would probably find that most of them should not be held anymore. As we have seen before, in the real world there can be only a select number of truly superior performers, and that obviously includes superlative public companies.

As I have previously mentioned, I am not the only investor to find the approaches of diversification and asset allocation flawed. Over the years, several prominent investors have already begun addressing the issues and drawbacks of these two-headed monsters. Let's now take a look at the best investors of our era and see their views on asset allocation and diversification.

THE BEST INVESTORS' VIEWS

One of the early investors to comment on diversification was none other than John Maynard Keynes: "As time goes on, I get more and more convinced that the right method in investment is to put fairly large sums into enterprises which one knows something about. . . . It is a mistake to think that one limits risk by spreading too much between enterprises about which one knows little and has no reason for special confidence . . . " (Hagstrom 1997, p. 67). Despite this early warning, diversification prevailed and became a keystone among planners and portfolio managers.

William O'Neil

Also quite vocal on the subject has been William O'Neil, the founder and publisher of *Investor's Business Daily* and one of the most prominent investors of the last several decades. His exhaustive research of the stock market is clearly one of his hallmarks. In my opinion, his work and books should be read and studied by anyone serious about investing. I have learned a tremendous amount from his studies of the best-performing stocks in each market cycle. One such lesson that may come as common sense to some is that, if you are able to isolate the top performing stocks—those going up in price the most—diversifying among a broader list of companies can only dilute your return (though you may not need to be as cognizant of individual companies in your portfolio).

O'Neil's work also highlights the risk in staying in a top-performing stock past its peak, or the simple buy-and-hold strategy. In fact, according to his research, "the true market leaders—stocks that outperform all the rest by doubling or tripling or more—fall by an average 72 percent once they reach their peaks." What about being patient and waiting out corrections, you may ask? Well, if you have money in the market, a 72% drawdown does not feel like a correction; it feels more to me like a calamity. I will further address this important observation later in this book when we discuss the S-curve and its application to the stock market.

Further clarifying the risks posed by staying invested in a stock past its prime, O'Neil's studies illuminated yet another great point: "Remember this key historical fact: only one of every eight leaders in a bull market reasserts itself as a leader in the next or a future bull phase." His advice is to simply rotate among the winners of each bull market. William also addressed diversification very clearly by saying, "No one can fully know and stay on top of several dozen stocks. Over the years, I've found that it's better to put all your eggs in a few baskets and then watch the baskets very closely, knowing what's in them backward and forward" (O'Neil 2003, p. 98).

In two of his books, *24 Essential Lessons for Investment Success* and *The Successful Investor*, O'Neil asserts the shortcomings of broad diversification. Here are a few more zingers:

> Almost everyone in America today has been brainwashed into believing that wide diversification—spreading your money among many stocks rather than a few—is the secret to safe, prudent investing. But this is only partly true. Yes, the more you diversify, the less risk you have in any one stock. But you're still not protected against substantial losses, and you certainly haven't put yourself in a position to make big money when you're right. (O'Neil 2003, p. 97)
>
> If you have $5,000 or less, you should own no more than two stocks. If you have $10,000, two or three stocks is appropriate. With $25,000, perhaps three or four; with $50,000, four or five; and with $100,000 or more, you should own five or six.
>
> There's no reason to own twenty or more stocks. You simply can't know all you need to know about that many. You'll also dilute your overall results.
>
> For the individual investor, real money is made first by buying stocks of the very best companies in their fields, and then by concentrating your portfolio on a limited number and watching them carefully. I don't believe in the principle

of wide diversification, or trying to reduce risk by spreading your money across many stocks or many types of investments. (O'Neil 1999, p. 10)

Warren Buffett

The most successful and prominent investor of our era, Warren Buffett, has also commented extensively on the futility of both asset allocation and diversification strategies. The results of his investments at Berkshire Hathaway are legendary. He has achieved such results by means of a highly concentrated portfolio, which he writes about extensively in his annual reports. If you have not read his reports, you are only doing yourself a disservice; they are now widely available on the Internet (easily found on Berkshire's website) and are well worth your time.

One of the things that Buffett talks about is the need to allow for fluctuations in the stock market, which the academics confuse with volatility or risk. Buffett is very clear about this: To construct a portfolio without allowing for fluctuations will basically leave you with bonds and low returns. Addressing diversification, he is even clearer. "Diversification is a protection against ignorance. It makes very little sense for those who know what they are doing." He adds, "Wide diversification is only required when investors do not understand what they are doing." Quoting from his 1966 report:

> This year [1966], in the material which went out in November, I specifically called your attention to a new Ground Rule reading, "7. We diversify substantially less than most investment operations. We might invest up to 40% of our net worth in a single security under conditions coupling an extremely high probability that our facts and reasoning are correct with a very low probability that anything could drastically change the underlying value of the investment." (Buffett 1966, p. 10)

Buffett continues in his report:

> We are obviously following a policy regarding diversification which differs markedly from that of practically all public investment operations. Frankly, there is nothing I would like better than to have 50 different investment opportunities, all of which have a

mathematical expectation (this term reflects the range of all possible relative performances, including negative ones, adjusted for the probability of each—no yawning, please) of achieving performance surpassing the Dow by, say, fifteen percentage points per annum. If the fifty individual expectations were not inter correlated (what happens to one is associated with what happens to the other) I could put 2% of our capital into each one and sit back with a very high degree of certainty that our overall results would be very close to such a fifteen percentage point advantage. It doesn't work that way. (Buffett 1966, p. 10)

Buffett goes on to say later in the report:

There is one thing of which I can assure you. If good performance of the fund is even a minor objective, any portfolio encompassing one hundred stocks (whether the manager is handling one thousand dollars or one billion dollars) is not being operated logically. The addition of the one hundredth stock simply can't reduce the potential variance in portfolio performance sufficiently to compensate for the negative effect its inclusion has on the overall portfolio expectation. (Buffett 1966, p. 11)

Buffett concludes:

I am willing to give up quite a bit in terms of leveling of year-to-year results (remember when I talk of "results," I am talking of performance relative to the Dow) in order to achieve better overall long-term performance. Simply stated, this means I am willing to concentrate quite heavily in what I believe to be the best investment opportunities recognizing very well that this may cause an occasional very sour year—one somewhat more sour, probably, than if I had diversified more. While this means our results will bounce around more, I think it also means that our long-term margin of superiority should be greater.

Many years later, in his 1993 Letter to Shareholders, Buffett put it yet another way that I think is worth noting:

The strategy we've adopted precludes our following standard diversification dogma. Many pundits would therefore say the strategy must be riskier than that employed by more conventional investors. We disagree. We believe that a policy of portfolio concentration may well decrease risk if it raises, as it should, both the intensity with which an investor thinks about a business and the comfort-level he must feel with its economic characteristics before buying into it.

Buffett and his partner Charles Munger also share some great insight in the August 2008 edition of *Outstanding Investor Digest*. When asked about his confidence in making such concentrated investments, Buffett replied:

> Well, there have been several times where I've had 75% of my net worth invested in one situation. Over a long period of time, you will see things that if you're working with smaller sums, it would be a mistake not to have half your net worth in. Sometimes, you see things in securities that are lead-pipe cinches. (Buffett 2008, p. 12)
>
> And you're not going to see them often—and they're not going to be talking about them on television. But there will be some extraordinary things that will happen in a lifetime where you can put 75% of your net worth or something like that into a given situation. (Buffett 2008, p. 13)

When prompted about his thoughts on diversification specifically, Buffett replied:

> There's nothing wrong with the know-nothing investor practicing it—it's exactly what they should practice. But it's exactly what a good professional investor should not practice.
>
> And there's no contradiction in that. A know-nothing investor will get decent results as long as they know they're a know-nothing investor—and diversify as to the time they purchase their equities, and as to the equities they purchase. That's crazy for somebody that really knows what they're doing. And you will find opportunities where if you put only 20% of your net worth in, you will have wasted the opportunity of a lifetime by not really loading up. (Buffett 2008, p. 13)

In the same line of questioning, Buffett's business partner Charles Munger also had some great insight:

> Well, the students of America go to these elite business and law schools and learn corporate finance and investment management the way it's now taught. And some of these people write articles in the newspaper and other places and say, "Well, the whole secret of investment is diversification." That's the mantra.
>
> They've got it exactly back asswards. The whole secret of investment is to find places where it's safe and wise to non-diversify. It's just that simple. Diversification is for the know-nothing investor. It's not for the professional. (Buffett 2008, p. 13)

Charles Munger

Although almost everybody has heard of Warren Buffett, not many are as familiar with his investment partner, Charles Munger, who has greatly aided in creating the tremendous returns at Berkshire Hathaway. Like Warren, "Charlie" is a phenomenal source of wisdom in the investment world and offers a great deal of insight on the subject of diversification. Although he is famous for saying he has "nothing to add," Charles authored a wonderful compilation of his thoughts and ideas entitled *Poor Charlie's Almanack*. In the book, he speaks volumes on the subject in just a few words.

Mr. Munger says in several places in his *Almanack* that a portfolio of three companies is plenty of diversification. Accordingly, he is willing to commit uncommonly high percentages of his investment capital to individual "focused opportunities." "Find a Wall Street organization, financial advisor, or mutual fund manager to make that statement!!" he challenges. His investment style of so-called focus investing implies ten holdings—not 100 or 400—according to his *Almanack*. In his extensive discussion of diversification, Munger makes a bold claim: "The idea of excessive diversification is madness. We do not believe that widespread diversification will yield a good result. We believe almost all good investments involve relatively low diversification." He goes on to say:

> I have more than skepticism regarding the orthodox view that huge diversification is a must for those wise enough so that indexation is not the logical mode for equity investment. I think

the orthodox view is grossly mistaken. In the United States, a person or institution with almost all wealth invested long term, in just three fine domestic corporations is securely rich. . . . I go even further. I think it can be a rational choice, in some situations, for a family or a foundation to remain ninety percent concentrated in one equity. (Munger 2006, p. 331)

Munger summed up his thoughts by saying:

> We believe that almost all really good investment records will involve relatively little diversification. The basic idea that it was hard to find good investments and that you wanted to be in good investments, and therefore, you'd just find a few of them that you knew a lot about and concentrate on those seemed to me such an obviously good idea. And indeed, it's proven to be an obviously good idea. Yet 98% of the investing world doesn't follow it. That's been good for us. (Munger 2006, p. 102)

Although more studies have been done that clearly identify the problems with overdiversification, most mutual funds' portfolio managers and private asset managers alike continue to construct portfolios with between 100 and 200 holdings, the current average number of holdings being 160. Why? Mr. Munger does a great job of addressing this issue: "It is sad that today each institutional investor apparently fears most of all that its investment practices will be different from the practices of the rest of the crowd."

He goes on:

> Berkshire's whole record has been achieved without paying one ounce of attention to the efficient market theory in its hard form. And not one ounce of attention to the descendants of that idea, which came out of academic economics and went into corporate finance and morphed into such obscenities as the capital asset pricing model, which we also paid no attention to. (Munger 2006, p. 377)

It is obvious by looking at the chart of the returns generated in Berkshire Hathaway that they could not have come from mirroring the indexes. Notice that while there were periods in which significant

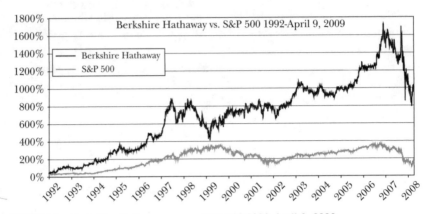

FIGURE 3.1   Berkshire Hathaway versus S&P 500 1992–April 9, 2009

Source: Hirsch Organization.

volatility occurred, because we are looking at a 15+ year period, those periods of volatility seem muted and the excess returns justified Buffet's willingness to ignore the call to diversification.

Jim Rogers

Recently I conducted an hour-long interview with one of the most successful investors of the last 30 years, Jim Rogers. As a cofounder of the Quantum Fund with George Soros, Rogers amassed great personal wealth in the markets. Our discussion was nothing short of stellar. While his investment results have been exceptional, his approach sounds like just plain old common sense.

I asked Jim to reveal the secrets of his successes, as well as the lessons learned from his failures. His two answers were nearly identical. He admitted that he was so afraid to make mistakes that he did a tremendous amount of research before he made his investments. When he finally made the decision to invest, he continued with his careful research and scrutiny of his investments with equal diligence. When I asked him about his feelings about diversification, he was at first somewhat apologetic. Thinking the interview was going to be tailored to novice investors, he said he was sorry but he did not believe in diversification. His comment was specifically, "If you do enough research and stay on top of your holdings, there is no need for diversification." He agreed that diversification is a cop-out by Wall Street managers intended not to lose clients by having periods where you significantly underperform the market. His biggest caveat is critical and important: If you are undiversified and wrong, you can lose too much money. The cure for that problem, of course, is the use of stop losses.

Gerald Loeb

Another great investor of his time, Gerald Loeb, also has interesting insight into the use of diversification. In 1935, he wrote *The Battle for Investment Survival.* It is a wonderful book and every bit as timely today as it was when it was first published. In the book, Loeb talks about the evolution of investors.

Toward the end of his career, Loeb followed up with another book titled, *The Battle for Investment Profits.* It was written with the accumulated knowledge he had gained through trading actively in the market for over three decades. Both of his books are difficult to come by, but well worth finding. Over the course of the years, having had dozens of interns work with us, I have made my library of such books open for their education. Unfortunately, somebody never returned Loeb's second book, which discussed in depth his beliefs on diversification. His feelings were that novice investors should use diversification to protect themselves while gaining experience, but that once they develop confidence and experience, they should become less diversified over time. He also reminded investors that while diversification may save them from dire calamity, it also significantly limited any success they may have achieved. Loeb went on to discuss the advantage of being a "lone wolf"—his term for an investor unshackled by the burdens of fiduciary responsibilities. Similar to Charlie Munger's belief that investors are best off in three securities or less, Loeb believed that investors can generate extraordinary returns by being concentrated in only a few securities, which is just not practical in the professional money management industry.

Charles Ellis

In *Classics: An Investor's Anthology,* Charles Ellis covers the strategies of David and Thomas Babson. When an investor takes the right approach to diversification, according to the Babsons:

> [h]e has diversified his holdings among various industries, not by following any mechanical formula but by analytical selection of those companies and fields of activity most likely to spear-head the long-range expansion of the American economy. That is, he has looked upon diversification not merely as a device for spreading risk but as a means of broadening opportunity for the progress of his investments. And he has avoided scattering his holdings among more companies than he could conscien-tiously follow. (p. 178)

This sums up what I believe to be the correct application of diversification.

In another one of Ellis's excellent books, *Investment Policy: How to Win the Loser's Game,* he addresses the diversification of man-agers and gets back to my central point regarding the nature of things.

> The problem with multiple managers is that the positive rea-sons become increasingly ephemeral as the number of man-agers increases. While it may be feasible to select one or two superior managers in a particular specialty, it's harder and harder to pick three or five or seven. There just aren't that many truly superior managers around. (p. 78)

Cabot Heritage Corp

One of my longtime favorite newsletters comes from The Cabot Heritage Corp. Their emphasis has always been on maximizing their readers' investment return by studying the market and iden-tifying the best companies to invest in. I have been a long-term subscriber to their services. I shared with them the subject of this book, and they were kind enough to have Michael Cintolo, the current editor of the *Cabot Market Letter,* write the following for our book:

Concentration versus Diversification

Do You Want to Be Average or Above Average?

We've all heard the financial jargon that the Wall Street pundits (and salespeople) spout. It seems you can't read a money magazine or turn on the TV without hearing mantras like, "Stay invested for the long term," "Buy more on the way down to lower your cost," and "It's impossible to time the market."

We're not huge fans of any of those tactics. We've successfully timed the market for years, for instance, and we've proved many times (especially during punishing bear markets) the value of cutting losses short.

But one of the biggest offenders in finance-speak is the oft repeated line: "Be sure to diversify your holdings; too much concentration leads to too much risk." We couldn't disagree more.

What the diversification-versus-concentration topic comes down to is simple: Do you want to be average? Do you want to earn average returns from stocks, bonds, or mutual funds? Do you want to be passive and hope the market continues to deliver 7 or 8 percent annual returns? In our minds, the only thing diversification guarantees is an average result.

But most investors don't want to be average. *We* certainly don't! We want to be above average. And if you do too, you must concentrate your assets in your very best ideas, and then watch those stocks closely to see whether they're acting normally (i.e., under accumulation by institutions) or abnormally (i.e., under distribution). Think about it: Would you rather have your money invested in your five best ideas? Or your next five best ideas?

With the help of sound buy and sell rules, having most of your money in just a handful of your very best ideas can produce huge returns during good times. And when bad times arrive, you'll be able to quickly raise cash; with fewer holdings, all you need to do is sell a couple of stocks and you'll be well on your way to protecting your portfolio.

Here's another way to look at it. Let's say, if fully invested, you own just 10 stocks; each stock makes up 10 percent of your portfolio. If one of those stocks doubles, your overall portfolio just rose in value by a solid 10 percent. That's meaningful! And it's from just one stock. In a strong bull market, if you own a few true leaders, you can rack up gains in a hurry.

However, let's say you own 25 stocks; each stock makes up a mere 4 percent of your portfolio. If you're able to grab hold of a true leader that doubles, your overall portfolio's value will rise just 4 percent—not bad, but not exactly thrilling. And, as mentioned, if you need to sell out and raise cash (say, during a bear market), selling a few stocks will have little impact—even if you sell five stocks in this scenario, you'd have just 20 percent in cash and 80% in stocks!

(Continued)

But, you ask, what if you're concentrated, and a stock or two falls by a large amount? That's a good question, and it demonstrates why you should always cut losses short. With growth stocks, you shouldn't take a loss of more than 20 percent from your purchase price (we often cut them smaller than that). Thus, while your risk is never more than 15 to 20 percent in any one stock, your upside potential is many times greater. Knowing that the math is in your favor, your returns will only increase by running a concentrated portfolio.

In our own *Cabot Market Letter*, we've run a model portfolio for decades that, when fully invested, contains up to 12 stocks. That provides plenty of diversification (owning names in different sectors), while also providing the upside punch every growth investor wants.

Source: Michael Cintolo, *Cabot Market Letter*.

OTHER VIEWS ON DIVERSIFICATION

In an attempt to measure the impact of diversification, it is critical that you evaluate the right things. Although most people just look at standard deviations among portfolio sizes, the most important measurement is what is called "terminal wealth dispersion" (TWD), or the range of the future value of your portfolio. The value of an account at an endpoint, or at each ten-year period, is a lot more important to an investor than the month-to-month volatility. In their study, "Stock Diversification in the U.S. Equity Market," H. Christine Hsu and H. Jeffrey Wei do an excellent job of approaching the subject. In their findings they demonstrated that the dispersion of terminal wealth is cut by more than 25 percent when the portfolio size is increased from 10 to 20 stocks and by more than 50 percent from 10 to 50 stocks in each holding period studied. The assumed benefit of risk diversification is somewhat limited when the number of stocks in the portfolio goes beyond 50.

Adding to the list of great minds exposing the flaws of diversification, in April of 2004 Mark Hulbert wrote an article in *The New York Times* entitled "Diversify! Well, Not So Fast." In the article he talks extensively about Warren Buffett's success with a lack of diversification. More importantly, he references work done by the University of Michigan finance professors Clemens Sialm and Lu Zheng. Analyzing over 1,800 mutual funds and their performance over a 15-year time span, the professors' studies produced dramatic results. Over the 15 years studied, the funds with the highest divergence in readings—those with the least diversification—produced the greatest average returns. By contrast, the most diversified funds lagged behind the market. This result persisted even when adjusting the performances of the least diversified funds for any greater risk they may have incurred. Even among smaller funds, the least diversified fared better then the most diversified. Hulbert wrote, "The study has several implications for investors. Generally, researchers say that stock picking ability does exist—that investors are not necessarily being irrational when choosing an actively managed fund over an index fund."

Another very interesting study can be found at the U.S. Securities and Exchange Commission's website, titled "Beginner's Guide to Asset Allocation, Diversification, and Rebalancing." I was surprised to see the statement that "You'll need at least a dozen carefully selected individual stocks to be truly diversified." I thought that they would claim a much higher number. Even the SEC is saying you need only a dozen stocks to be diversified, yet we continue to see money managers, in an attempt to act in a fiduciary manner, holding in excess of 100 stocks in their portfolios.

Peter Krass edited a wonderful book, detailing some of the greatest insight from our era's most successful investors. *The Book of Investing Wisdom* compiles the most influential ideas from the greatest stock pickers and investing legends around. In Part I of the book, Paul F. Miller Jr. does an excellent job of addressing modern portfolio theory (MPT). He says two things of particular interest:

> Portfolios that fluctuate more violently should be expected to provide higher returns than more stable portfolios.
>
> Non-market risk can be diversified away, and probably should be. (p. 52)

I found it fascinating that, of all the individuals profiled in the book, not one of them recommended diversification within portfolios. The list included Warren Buffett, Philip Fisher, Jim Rogers, Peter Lynch, Sir John Templeton, Mario Gabelli, Gerald Loeb, Bernard Baruch, Michael Steinhardt, George Soros, Donald Trump, and many more. Not one of them mentions anything about diversification. So, although diversification is the central theme of Wall Street's advice, we see the opposite approach taken by the greatest investors over time.

Derrick Niederman tackles the issue of diversification in his book, *The Inner Game of Investing*.

> Diversify your portfolio, by all means, but do it purposefully, not just because you heard it was the right thing to do. In particular, you don't have to own oil stocks, airline stocks, or forest products stocks just because there's a spot open for them. If you don't understand an industry well, you're better off staying away from it entirely, rather than investing in it just to round out your portfolio. (p. 185)

He continues:

> As corollary, you might find that as you fill your portfolio one stock at a time, certain areas become disproportionately represented. Don't panic, at least not yet. It could be that your overweighting is entirely appropriate because the over weighted area of the market, whether it be technology or interest-sensitive stocks, might well represent unusual value. If that's the case, your portfolio will surely outperform those who artificially restrict their holdings of any one market sector. (p. 185)

One of the most respected mutual fund managers over the last 15 years is Bill Miller, the portfolio manager of the multibillion-dollar Legg Mason Value Trust. What he is most known for is having the longest streak ever of S&P 500 outperformance in his large mutual fund. Although many mangers fail to beat this index, Miller's streak ran for 15 consecutive years, ending in 2005. Of course, he was not able to do this with a widely diversified portfolio, but instead managed the fund with 35 holdings.

It is interesting to see the reaction to his methodology, now that he has in fact underperformed the indexes for a couple of years. His thoughts were profiled in a May 11, 2008 *New York Times* article by Geraldine Fabrikant entitled "Humbler, after a Streak of Magic." Despite his long-term outperformance, it amazes me how quickly confidence can fade. In one part of the interview, Miller clearly says that broader diversification still does not appeal to him:

> I have never found it as a useful policy because what it guarantees is that you will be in the worst sectors of the market as a matter of policy. That is why so many managers are justly criticized as closet indexers because they don't get too far away from the index because they are afraid to be wrong. My view is that being wrong is part of the business. You need to focus on making the best investments you can, instead of trying to smooth things out. (p. 2)

But after a short period of underperformance, already Miller is questioning himself: "The question we are asking ourselves is: Should we think more broadly now about probability, about high-impact events and protecting against them by having broader exposure to the market?" Personally, I hope he sticks to his original philosophy and remembers that being wrong some of the time will occur. That is the hard part of managing money, not just being a closet indexer.

We can now see, by studying strategies of the most successful investors, that asset allocation and overdiversification are done simply out of the fear of loss (or the fear of loss of clients) and that they could and should be abandoned and replaced. Using a more selective and concentrated approach to portfolio construction, in tandem with the proper application of portfolio management and adherence to a stop-loss strategy to control risk (or some sort of sell strategy), higher returns are available. (An important note, though, is that selecting a money manager based on the fact that he invests in fewer companies is just not enough.)

Following many exhaustive studies, much has been written addressing the question, "Does an investor benefit with less diversification?" One such study that sheds light on the industry's view on this subject was conducted by Travis Sapp (Iowa State University) and Xuemin Yan (University of Missouri–Columbia). The 2008 study—"Security Concentration and Active Fund Management: Do Focused Funds Offer Superior Performance?"—sought the answer to that recurring question. They referenced a database covering the period from 1984 through 2002, containing information on 2,278 funds, totaling 16,399 fund years' worth of data. The study excluded funds with fewer than 12 holdings as well as those with less than $1 million in assets.

The interpretation of the results of the study interested me more than the results themselves. As far as I was concerned, the authors of the study were unfair. They examined gross returns based on the number of securities held and concluded that there was no evidence that focused funds outperform diversified funds. They further claimed that, after deducting expenses, focus funds actually significantly underperform. There was no discussion of the actual distribution of the results going back to my discussion of the bell curve, no understanding that there can only be a few superlatives, and no recognition that this fact obviously applies to money managers. A portfolio that utilizes a superior selection system and makes better money management decisions in handling the portfolio will have better returns than its peers. If the results showed that nobody had outperformed the market, you could make the statement that passively managed diversified portfolios are preferable to a concentrated approach. If all other things were held constant—the same selection process and the same portfolio management techniques— then you could make a better determination. In the study, a few managers did outperform significantly, but, as I would expect, only a few. It was interesting to me how the authors of the study did not even address the superior returns that did appear in the study and recognize them.

DORSEY, WRIGHT MONEY MANAGEMENT

One group continues to utilize a focused approach with considerable success: Dorsey, Wright Money Management, run by Harold Parker and Michael Moody. Using relative strength and point-and-figure charts, they keep their minds clear and their portfolios concentrated in about 25 holdings. Their experience, clarity, and exceptional returns offer yet another view on diversification. In Moody's words, "Concentration is not in itself a panacea. If you do not have a process, concentration can be a recipe for disaster. Your process has to have an edge. A portfolio manager that holds

160 stocks probably does not believe he really has an edge. As long as you have a back tested strategy with an edge—your focus needs to be on sticking to your edge." He also reiterated the fact that some portfolio managers simply use diversification to reduce what he called "career risk," or the fear of being fired for underperforming an index.

Although I understand that many investors do not have the expertise and knowledge to manage concentrated portfolios, professionals are in a different position. Using a professional money manager who acts as a closet indexer, holding over 100 stocks, and who produces average returns that match the market at best is unnecessary. You would be better off in a low-cost index fund. In Chapter 11, I will empower you to go beyond average and seek higher returns, if you are willing to put in the effort. It may not be easy or always achievable for everyone, but higher returns are available. One thing should be clear at this point—anybody looking for higher-than-index returns needs to avoid the very thing that keeps investors mired in mediocrity: overdiversification.

CHAPTER 4

The Inefficient Market: Reallocate into Superlatives

The generally accepted view is that markets are always right—that is, market prices tend to discount future developments accurately even when it is unclear what those developments are. I start with the opposite point of view. I believe that market prices are always wrong in the sense that they present a biased view of the future.

— GEORGE SOROS

I'd be a bum on the street with a tin cup, if the markets were always efficient.

— WARREN BUFFETT

There is a fundamental decision that all asset management firms need to make. Do they grow their firm by focusing on gathering as many assets as possible and earning a modest fee mirroring index returns? Or do they focus on outperforming the markets substantially and attracting assets with their exceptional returns? Having been in the industry for over 20 years, I have been exposed to a great many firms and have seen all kinds of business models. There are many ways to operate in today's tremendously large asset management market. In my opinion, as long as a firm is not taking advantage of the clients—and the client actually makes a reasonable return—I have no problem with any of the approaches they take. Be aware however, that at most asset management firms, the goal is simply to obtain the most assets under management as possible. Very basically, the more assets a firm manages, the more money they can make in management fees.

INDEX FUNDS

Several financial firms have been created based primarily on the efficient market theory. The huge industry of index funds dominates the financial industry. They believe that no manager or system can beat the market over time. Operating under that assumption, trying to beat the market is not the most lucrative avenue to travel. Instead, those companies go about providing market, or index, returns and compete for business by being the lowest-cost provider. In fact, the largest mutual fund in the world is an index fund. Although this may sound like an easy approach, it is not. Even this relatively simple approach requires a fair amount of effort. The good news is that it may not be all that difficult, because these firms exist and have made many millions of dollars for their employees, shareholders, and investors. Trillions of dollars are currently invested passively around the world in the various stock markets in index funds. The returns over the years have far exceeded other, presumably less risky alternatives like cash and bonds to date.

The easiest choice for investment is simply to index, and, frankly, for many investors it is an adequate choice. Quite a few asset managers have grown their assets under management tremendously over the last decades simply by delivering index returns. They make no bones about it: They offer market returns, no more or less. They like to point to studies showing that, in fact, most active portfolio managers routinely underperform the indexes. Furthermore, when you factor in the taxes on short-term gains, it reduces the net returns of active managers even further.

Aside from the tax benefits and lower volatility, there is even another reason that indexing is a good idea for many investors. Industry studies have shown that many investors find a way to lose money in top-performing mutual funds. How is this possible? Investors are often attracted to funds that have just run up and delivered strong returns over a period of time. What they often do not consider is the fact that stocks and indexes need room to "breathe" and may often pull back after long runs to the upside. Many so-called return chasers invest in a hot manager, only to sell the fund at a loss during an ordinary and acceptable drawdown of which all funds and managers encounter. For these investors, indexing may be a more prudent choice. Once you accept the fact that you are simply indexing, you can stop losing money chasing hot managers and looking for the next hot thing. Although simply mirroring the indexes surely has outperformed bonds and cash over the last 80 years, many investors will justifiably seek higher returns.

Understanding that the financial markets are expanding, most asset management companies do not want to blow their opportunity and encounter career risk. When you simply invest in the biggest and most widely known companies, nobody faults you when you lose money. It is only when you lose money in less known companies that you are called to task, and investors are quick to find another money manager. This is why most money managers would rather hear, "What's wrong with IBM?" instead of "What's wrong with *you*?" Even so, it is obvious that if you want to attempt to generate above-market returns, you cannot simply invest in the whole market.

ALTERNATIVES TO INDEXING

Realizing this, the next step some asset managers started to take was to optimize to get slightly better returns. I know many incredibly smart mathematicians involved in this practice. They have figured out how to hold 350 out of the 500 companies in the S&P 500, while getting the approximate return of the index itself. The incrementally lower cost of holding fewer stocks can help squeeze out slightly higher-than-index returns, without significantly increasing the volatility of the smaller portfolio. Although the added value seems trivial, it is surprising how many assets this approach has attracted.

The next rung up the latter in volatility and return is enhanced indexing. Here the approach is to adhere to the sector weightings within an index. However, rather than buying the full list, you eliminate as many companies as you feel comfortable with. Many variables of this strategy have emerged over the years, each based on the same concept. Although this style of investing cannot offer dramatically greater returns than the index itself, it was another step in the direction of seeking higher returns. In most instances, the determination not to look too different from the benchmarked index was the overriding mandate. What I found interesting is that even the creative funds benchmarked themselves against the major indexes. Not only did they decide to benchmark against an index, but they picked the index that contains only the largest companies and in many cases companies that are already too big to show continued upside outperformance. I address this subject more extensively in Chapter 5, which is dedicated to the S-curve and its place in the stock market.

Another interesting approach that is being used to cut down on diversification to enhance returns is to try to eliminate the worst companies and invest in the rest. Rapid Ratings International, Inc., for example, uses their own "junk detector." They are simply benchmarking against the Russell 3000, identifying the 400 worst companies according to their process, and investing in the other 2,600! Although this seems like a relatively small step, they are beating the index by several percentage points and at the same time have a lower volatility than the full index. It amazes me how many different approaches there are to beat the indexes.

RELATIVE VERSUS ABSOLUTE RETURNS

The next discussion in the investment timeline became one of relative return versus an index, not one of absolute returns. In strong bull markets it is okay if you slightly underperform. Investors will be forgiving, at least for a short while, if you miss the hot sectors or stocks, as long as they see the overall values increasing. But in weak and declining markets, losing less than the index becomes unacceptable over time. Outperforming "relative to the market" but still losing money is just not going to retain certain clients and assets. To create absolute returns, you can no longer mimic, mirror, or even enhance an index; you need to do something different. In this approach, sector over- and underweighting come into play, as do individual stock selection strategies. Managers may also use alternative asset classes like hard assets and commodities and even short selling the market to generate their returns.

In a relative performance approach, an investment manager tries to favorably compare investment returns to a stated index or benchmark. The investment process attempts to mirror the index, while the manager figures out a way to slightly outperform. A manager accomplishes this by trying to over- or underweight sectors or individual companies in an index. Unfortunately, this approach leads to mediocre returns and often even underperformance against the benchmark.

In an absolute return strategy, the investment manager takes an approach independent of indexing. Within an absolute return approach, the manager is free from many of the constraints and the Wall Street mentality that impede superior returns. Instead, the emphasis is on identifying superior opportunities, whether that is accomplished through stock selection, sector emphasis, or adjusting appropriate cash levels according to market conditions. This is a much more hands-on, customizable approach than the always fully invested and fully diversified gibberish that is traditionally recommended and too often followed.

Often asset management companies will establish artificial barriers that prevent their own portfolio managers from investing in timely opportunities. Arbitrary rules are often set up, all with the aim of protecting the client—or not losing clients. For example, an asset management company may set up rules allowing managers to invest in businesses that have been in operation for a minimum of ten years or companies that trade on a certain stock exchange. Any one of these obstacles only interferes with the free flow of capital and ultimately impairs investment returns. It seems as though the least used but most effective alternative is the use of the free market, that is, simply identifying the best companies and letting money flow to those superlatives—without any constraints. This is what we do at the Magnet Investment Group.

Insisting on diversification assures mediocrity. Remember, whenever the subject of diversification comes up, it is used in reference to protecting your assets, not about making money or generating high returns. Investors, individual and institutional alike, that have successfully identified the best strategies are now in a different position than the many underfunded pension plans and nonprofit organizations. Today, we are seeing some of the most successful institutions achieve superior returns by effectively allocating capital to alpha strategies that do not practice overdiversification but that instead concentrate their portfolios in a small number of select holdings. The endowments at Harvard, Yale, and The World Bank have been managed by forward thinking administrators who are often cited as having used alternatives to simply indexing. Excess return strategies are available not just to the superlarge investors. The same method of deploying capital to the superlatives is available to anybody who is willing to take the same road.

As we get ready to go to print, some new data has become available that further sheds light on the perils of diversification and unfortunately casts the financial industry in a poor light. In his book, *The Investor's Dilemma*, Louis Lowenstein compares the results of mutual funds to the results of the companies that manage the funds. With the vast increase in assets under management in recent years, the investment companies have earned tremendous fees. With this I have no problems. The book reveals, however, that too many management companies have simply taken an approach aimed at maximizing their assets under management, rather than enhancing investment returns for their shareholders. The fund managers have been encouraged to mirror the returns of the indexes, not to provide the value-added research, the stock selection, or the risk taking required to truly outperform the average return of a passive index.

Furthermore, the managers were compensated according to the assets they kept under management, not according to the returns they generated. Lowenstein cites an industry report in which an analyst describes the indexing approach as the type "you would feel good about your granny investing in." He counters, "Maybe your grandma, but not mine." In other words, although indexing may serve to limit downside risk, it is hazardous not to be aggressive. You run the great risk of not achieving a high enough return to fund your future. Allow me also to clarify. By aggressive I mean aggressively doing the extra research needed and isolating those investments that will most likely outperform their peers, rather than simply conforming to the indexes. Risk taking is part of investing, dying from starvation because you are afraid to cross the street to get food just does not work.

Compare the paltry returns generated by the average fund manager to the list that *Forbes Magazine* put out in June 2008 about the fund managers who made the most money in 2007, while making the most for their investors as well. Although the names of the managers often change, the approach taken does not. This year's list again consisted primarily of managers who isolated the right sectors and made large concentrated investments in those areas. One of the new names on the list was John Burbank, who has closely studied and followed the methodologies of the great investors Warren Buffett and Sir John Templeton (Kitchens, 2008). He sums up his strategy simply by saying, "diversification is for those who don't know what they are doing." Although that statement might be a little brash, it echoes the mantra of the greatest investors of our time.

Despite the latest academic studies and the advice of the top investors of all time, most money managers still prefer to take a widely overdiversified approach. Several quality firms effectively deliver market returns at low cost. For many investors, or for at least a portion of their holdings, the widely diversified portfolio is a great idea. For other investors, or for a portion of one's portfolio, seeking a higher return using a more selective strategy is the way to go.

Truly superlative companies do not come and go daily. They need not be day-traded according to moving averages, volume, and whether they close at the high or low end of the daily trading range. Those strategies are promoted by the trading software companies, the data sellers, and the media that have brainwashed investors into thinking that they need to pay attention to each price tick and economic data release. Most trading strategies lead to confusion, over-trading, and short-term small gains that are eaten up by short-term capital gains taxes.

Great stocks to own are shares of companies with a certain exceptional combination of characteristics. Early in my career I understood this and set out on an exhaustive study to identify the best stocks for investment. My first book included a disk with an introductory offer for a computer program called Telescan. It was a program way ahead of its time. At the head of the company was David Brown, who along with Kassandra Bentley, wrote *Cyber Investing*. In the second edition of their book they address diversification. They cite some experts recommending investing in only five stocks to maintain a well-balanced portfolio, with others recommending 20 or more. Notice that they never spoke of carrying 160 holdings, the current average number of stocks held in mutual funds today. Brown opted in favor of the larger number of holdings, 20, because his computer program enabled users to properly manage and keep track of that many. His excellent advice to others was, "We suggest you spread your risk over as many stocks as you can comfortably follow."

RICHARD DRIEHAUS

Another fund manager who helped to dispel the myth of the random walk theory is Richard Driehaus. I like the way he describes his philosophy. The great book *Classics: An Investor's Anthology* by Charles Ellis is full of useful knowledge shared by Driehaus. As opposed to "buy and hold a big diversified portfolio," he says in the book: "High turnover reduces risk when it's the result of taking a series of small losses in order to avoid larger losses. I don't hold on to stocks with deteriorating fundamentals or price patterns. For me, this kind of turnover makes sense. It reduces risk; it doesn't increase it." When he describes what he needs to buy a position, you can see how selective he is. "It had everything I look for in a growth stock: accelerating revenues and earnings and proprietary products in a rapidly expanding market." Then he talks about the need to take an even narrower approach that requires a company to have both good fundamentals *and* momentum, he says, "I won't buy a stock when it's dropping even if I like the fundamentals. I like to see the stock's relative strength in the top 10 percent of the market, or at least the top 20 percent." This is a manager willing to pay more taxes with his active narrow selectivity, in exchange for significantly higher net gains. You too would be happy to pay those taxes if you had made his kind of returns!

Driehaus spoke of taking a less traveled path: "Absolutely! There's a definite market inefficiency there. Typically, the more the street covers a stock, the less opportunity there is."

Rather than looking for value in the new low list, Driehaus said, "I would much rather invest in a stock that's increasing in price and take the risk that it may begin to decline than invest in a stock that's already in a decline and try to guess when it will turn around." Again, ahead of his time, Driehaus took on the issues of risk and volatility head-on:

> [Investors] tend to confuse short-term volatility with long-term risk. The longer the time period, the lower the risk of holding equities. People focus too much on the short term—week-to-week and month-to-month price changes—and don't pay

enough attention to the long-term potential. They look at all movement as negative, whereas I look at movement as a constructive element. For many investors, the lack of sufficient exposure to high-returning, more volatile assets is their greatest risk. In my opinion, investment vehicles that provide the least short-term volatility often embody the greatest long-term risk. Without significant price movement, you can't achieve superior gains. (p. 223)

Given today's emphasis on asset allocation, the unfortunate result has been the selling of winning stocks and expanding the positions in the losers. In this approach, sadly, the winners are deprived of the very capital that may enable them to make a major impact on society. By adding capital to the superlatives, we are aiding the free market rather than working against it.

Many investors are complaining about the lower returns they have been generating lately in the stock market. Since the mid-1990s, powerful investment returns have been hard to come by in the stock market. We have seen sectors rotating in and out of favor, while various bubbles quickly inflate only to take back multiyear gains quickly. It was refreshing to see Harvard University announce continued strong returns over the last several years on their nearly $30 billion endowment. Along with several other institutions like Yale University and The World Bank, Harvard has earned its returns by breaking away from the barriers that continue to hold back most institutions along with individual investors. Although diversification remains the battle cry of Wall Street, the top investors have ventured beyond the mediocrity created by overdiversification and have accepted the reality that, as in all of life, there can be only a few superlatives. Taking an absolute return strategy, as opposed to simply comparing relative returns, has given rise to a new asset class that has steadily grown in viability and credibility over the last decade: hedge funds. Through these funds, excess returns have in fact been available over the last several years, but only to those who accept this approach with its often increased volatility.

LET WINNERS RUN AND CUT LOSSES

If the asset allocation and diversification approaches that have been so blindly followed actually worked, hedge funds would never have proliferated. Investors, individual and institutional alike, that successfully identified the best stock selection strategies are now in a quite different position than the many underfunded pension plans and nonprofit organizations that did not.

For many years the concept of an efficient market has dominated Wall Street. That is, with accurate information available to all investors, any past or future information regarding the markets is already factored into current prices. Long discussed by the indexers were the inabilities of most to outperform the broader indexes. Over time and throughout every decade, select individuals have shown a consistent ability to outperform the market. By studying the successes of these individuals—Gerald Loeb from years past, the superb mutual fund manager Peter Lynch, and Warren Buffett, to name just a few—one cannot dispute that some individuals and methodologies can and do deliver superior excess returns. And the investors who achieved them did not take an overdiversified approach.

The majority of our country's institutions, nonprofit organizations, and foundations, along with most individual investors, currently find themselves underfunded as a result of failed investment practices. Their focus on diversification, MPT, and asset allocation practices has forced them to continue to cut gains by selling their winners, while placing more money into their underperforming holdings. I believe that it is time to break away from the reversion-to-the-mean strategies and provide a permanent endowment for America through superior investment returns.

The economic and market conditions of 2007 and beyond represent an ideal time for the tremendous amount of capital currently sitting in short-term low-yielding financial instruments to come into the market. The world is in reality experiencing a dramatic global expansion, despite the often sensationalist problems that the media continue to focus on. We are seeing the free market adopted on each continent and capitalism spread abroad, regardless of which political institution is running the government. Harvard University, for instance, cites their success in the international markets as fuel for their superior returns. By allowing capital to flow to the few existing superlatives, Harvard has clearly enhanced its investment returns significantly.

As explained in Chapters 2 and 3, and according to the theory of large numbers, the bell curve does wonders to bring order into what otherwise appears to be a chaotic distribution. Under this theory, 90 percent of anything closely examined falls into an average range. The other 10 percent is distributed among winners and losers, 5 percent on either end. Taking this into consideration, we have developed and utilize a highly quantitative methodology that we call The Magnet® Stock Selection Process. Using our business model of what we believe makes a great company—top-line revenue growth, profit margin acceleration, low price to sales, and price momentum, among other things—we screen and analyze stocks by sector and by market capitalization to find the true superlatives in each niche of the market.

Why anyone would choose instead to broadly diversify and force a reversion to the mean just does not make sense to me. One of the greatest investors of all time, Gerald Loeb, theorized that as a well-informed investor you could be successful placing all of your eggs in one basket and watch that basket very carefully. Although this approach could not work for fiduciary organizations (trust companies that hold and manage assets for the benefit of other entities) because of their lower tolerance for exposure to downside risk, my belief is that a small basket of top-ranked Magnets in the top-performing market sectors would generate the excess returns that investors require. I cannot stress enough that, once a portfolio is constructed, the disciplined use of stop-losses can be your strongest tool in effectively controlling risk and providing downside protection. The initial studies trumpeting diversification as the appropriate methodology never included the use of stop-losses. This little known fact is one of the reasons that diversification has continued to engulf Wall Street dogma so completely.

The common theme that runs through every successful investment philosophy is to let your winners run and cut your losses. Unspoken, but inherent to diversification and asset allocation theories, is to cut your winners and reallocate your profit to your lesser performing assets. My goal is to share our unemotional, unbiased system for identifying superlatives to help those who do not have access to the top-performing, unreachable money managers.

CHAPTER 5

Nature's S-Curve: Buying Stock Sweet Spots

Our philosophy here is identifying change, anticipating change. Change is what drives earnings growth, and if you identify the underlying change, you recognize the growth before the market, and the deceleration of that growth.
— PETER VERMILYE

I never buy at the bottom and I always sell too soon.
— BARON NATHAN ROTHCHILD'S SUCCESS FORMULA

Like other investors, I also utilize technical tools that show over-bought and oversold levels. I look at the short-term signals but try not to pay attention to them. I keep an eye on them only to stay abreast of the trading climate, not to make buy and sell decisions. If you follow the short-term buy and sell signals, you do not allow yourself the opportunity to compound your assets and often end up paying too much in taxes. Transaction fees, once cited as a major drawback to short-term trading, have all but disappeared. The unfortunate consequence has been the reduction of too many investors' time horizons. Once powerful trends are established, it is best not to play the wiggles, but instead, like the great Jesse Livermore said many years ago, "Be right and sit tight." Earlier in my career I was also enamored with the old quote attributed to Bernard Baruch, "I made my money by selling too soon." My personal experience has been that often when I find undiscovered companies that nobody is talking about by using The Magnet® Stock Selection Process, they can appreciate far beyond my own expectations. There does come a point, however—and it may happen for a variety of reasons—that the best time to invest in an individual company has already passed. One of Wall Street's dirty little secrets is that, although the market indexes go higher in the long term, long-term investing in individual companies can be disappointing and even hazardous. This leads us to another natural phenomenon that appears in many facets of life, called the S-curve, and its place in the stock market cannot be ignored.

THE S-CURVE

As in nature, companies should also be allowed to grow old and obsolete. Well-known within the science of biology is the S-curve. Organisms grow slowly at first. A stage of development occurs when rapid growth is seen, followed by a period of maturity, stability, and slower growth. Ultimately, a time comes when an organism is simply too big or too old to continue to grow, and then it enters a period of decay. This same growth and decay pattern is clearly seen in the stock market with individual companies. Often the best companies to invest in are the ones entering into their rapid growth period; these are companies that are still unfamiliar to the public and still under the radar of professional managers at the large firms.

Why the Indexes Keep Going Up in the Long Term

Interestingly, the indexes continue to go higher over time precisely because they continue to change the components of the index. So, although long-term investing in indexes has proven profitable, investing in the individual components has not worked out as well. Many former index components such as Pan Am and Bethlehem Steel have gone bankrupt. The index creators simply replaced these names with new companies that help the indexes go higher. Fewer than 50 companies in the S&P 500 today were in the index 30 years ago, and less than a handful of these have actually outperformed the index itself. Although several of the names that have been removed from the index were involved in mergers or acquisitions, the majority of the names were removed due to underperformance. New industries continue to emerge, and new market leaders show up unannounced. It is up to individual investors to find their own way to identify these industries and companies. Also, it is important to remember that it is widely known that the leaders of prior bull markets are often not the leaders of the next.

It amuses me when I hear so-called experts citing the lack of growth in the United States and highlighting the problems of General Motors as their proof. Back in the 1800s, there was a filibuster in Congress with a proposal to close the U.S. Patent Office. The argument was, "Now that everything has already been invented, why are we wasting taxpayers' money?" On the contrary, with the advancement of communication and computational powers, new discoveries are actually accelerating. Interestingly, these breakthroughs usually do not come from the larger companies, which are too set in their ways. Investors looking for true growth need to be involved with the innovative companies making these breakthroughs. Initially, small, niche companies create the new, enabling industries: Microsoft in 1987–2000, AOL in 1992–2000, or Google in 2000–2008. In the beginning of the twentieth century, Ford and RCA were the Magnets of their day, but they eventually lost their leadership role in the stock market.

Maybe Charlie Munger said it best in August 2008's *Outstanding Investor Digest*:

> You've got to remember that it's in the nature of things that most small businesses will never be big businesses. It's also in the nature of things that most big businesses eventually fall into mediocrity or worse. So it's a tough game out there. In addition, the players of the game all have to die. Those are the rules of the game—and you have to get used to it. (p.19)

Stan Weinstein

The first time I saw the S-curve discussed in conjunction with the stock market was while attending a presentation given by Stan Weinstein. His approach was radically unique, unlike any other methodology I had ever seen. His focus was strictly on price movement and had absolutely nothing to do with a company's actual fundamentals. I reached out to him while writing this book, and it is good to see that he is still successfully using the same approach and that he maintains his focus with the same discipline. When you think of the great market-leading companies that dominated their industry, and the swiftness in which they came and went, it is hard for anyone to believe in the buy-and-hold approach in the stock market. To stick with a company that clearly has lost momentum and has deteriorating fundamentals is hazardous to your wealth. Weinstein's opinion is that the current state of the market requires an even sharper focus on stock selection because the market indexes may not yield significant results for years.

Companies, Like Sports Stars, Do Not Dominate Forever

It is helpful to think about the entertainment business when you invest. In sports we are used to seeing young athletes come into their prominence early on in their careers. Later on we see them lose a step, then get too slow, and eventually be forced into retirement only to fade into obscurity. That is the S-curve played out within a sports scenario.

The same patterns are found while investing in individual companies. It is the same in each sport, and it is the same in each industry. International Rubber, Pan AM, Lucent, Bethlehem Steel—the industries that these great former companies once dominated are now larger than ever. However, these companies, along with countless other brilliant success stories along the way, are no longer in business. You would have lost all of your investment in them had you bought and held them. The key to avoiding the same fate is in realizing that there are always future market-leading companies just beginning their ascent. For a brief period of time, growth takes place rapidly in these companies. These are the Magnet stocks. They throw off free earnings and are firing on all cylinders as they hit their sweet spot of exponential S-curve growth. In the latter chapters of this book I will show you how we uncover and trade these under-the-radar stock gems.

Do Not Be Afraid to Get in before the Crowd

It is also critical to remember that you do not need to run with the largest crowd to be profitable. In fact, most mutual funds, due to their massive size, all buy the same largest publicly traded companies. For this reason, I believe the individual investor has a significant advantage over the institutions today. The individual investor who invests in the best small companies and operates with a three- to five-year time horizon will have the opportunity to reap the most superior investment results of all. Once such an underfollowed and undervalued company is identified, you must have a certain patience to let the investment find its way into the news and collective consciousness of investors. It may take time, but big healthy trees do not grow overnight. Once companies show continued revenue and margin growth, it is only a matter of time until the institutions begin to come on board and you are able to achieve superior returns by riding the upside momentum spurred by heavy accumulation.

By operating with The Magnet Stock Selection Process, we can easily and clearly monitor the financial progress, or deterioration, of our top-ranked stocks through unbiased fundamental measurements, not by management's updates about "how the story is going." This disciplined system of identifying future Magnets and staying patient, while monitoring the progress of each company in your portfolio for continued growth, enables you to generate true wealth over time.

Once you are free of simply trying to match or exceed benchmarks and indexes, you can go about seeking higher returns. The key is then to identify and invest in the few individual companies that are true superlatives in their industry, the statistical outliers on the bell curve. All of the greatest investment results, whether in large mutual funds or in the hands of individuals, have occurred as a result of superior stock selection while investing in fewer companies.

Jack Dreyfus

Jack Dreyfus, the founder of Dreyfus, posted remarkable returns while managing his namesake mutual fund, The Dreyfus Fund, from 1953 through 1964. During this period the fund returned 604 percent, besting the next highest return by over 100 percentage points. Over the same period of time, the Dow Jones Industrial Index returned 346 percent. Outperforming the market by nearly two to one over a ten-year period can be accomplished only by someone with true insight. William O'Neil, the founder of *Investor's Business Daily*, studied Dreyfus's funds to gain a better understanding of how his returns were generated. He noticed that the only time Dreyfus would start to buy a stock was just as the company traded at an all-time high. Dreyfus was one of the early successful users of momentum investing.

MAGNET LEARNING CURVE

The Magnet System is detailed in Chapter 11. For now, I will share the method I used earlier in my career. Before I developed the patience to hold stocks until they either dropped in the Magnet ranking model or got stopped out when the price dropped, I was more interested in identifying the best swing trades. I would look for oversold stocks that ranked highly on my Magnet System, but I was only willing to hold them for a trade. Over time I realized many of the companies I was identifying ended up becoming the biggest winners of all and that I was leaving too much money on the table. I developed more patience as my career went on, but early on I was following the advice that "you never go broke taking a profit."

Here are a couple of nice trades from my old records that resulted from technical analysis applied to the Magnet rankings.

Equity Marketing (EMAK)

This trade highlights the use of the stochastic technical indicators. I have always maintained a watch list of the companies I liked and that had all the characteristics of a Magnet stock. This original note (Figure 5.1) was sent to my clients when I worked at Dean Witter. Notice the disclaimer on the bottom; it was highly unusual for a

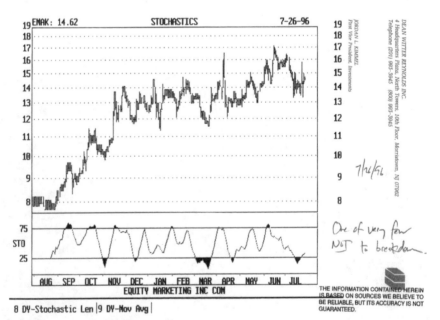

FIGURE 5.1   The EMAK note to clients

Source: Telescan.

broker at Dean Witter to be allowed to send out this kind of chart, but my branch manager trusted me. We both knew I would not work at a place where I was forced to sell the house mutual funds. The stock was rising slowly in a difficult market. Its move out of the oversold range was the buy signal. In a weak market, the stocks that are bucking the downtrend can be explosive.

Two and a half months after the buy, the trade produced over a 50 percent return. In a second note (Figure 5.2), I congratulated my clients on a great trade. In this chart I was showing them the MACD buy signal. At this point the chart was clearly extended, and I am sure we just took the proceeds and looked for another Magnet stock in an oversold position. I never got into day-trading, but this kind of swing trading was exactly what I did for years. Over the years some of the stocks I traded went on to become such outrageous winners that I was ultimately disappointed I did not hold them for a longer term. Although it is true that "you never go broke taking profits," maintaining a rising trailing stop loss can keep you in a stock and often is a better strategy.

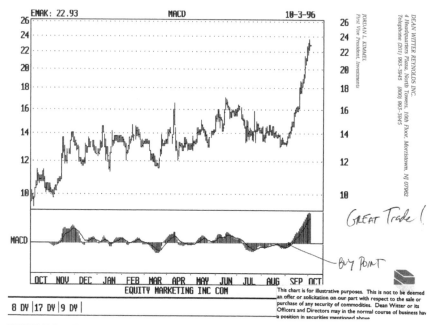

FIGURE 5.2   The congratulatory notes to clients

Source: Telescan.

DEAN WITTER REYNOLDS INC.
4 Headquarters Plaza, North Towers, 10th Floor, Morristown, NJ 07962
Telephone (800) 993-3945
(201) 993-3945

JORDAN L. KIMMEL
First Vice President, Investments

THE INFORMATION CONTAINED HEREIN
IS BASED ON SOURCES WE BELIEVE TO
BE RELIABLE, BUT ITS ACCURACY IS NOT
GUARANTEED.

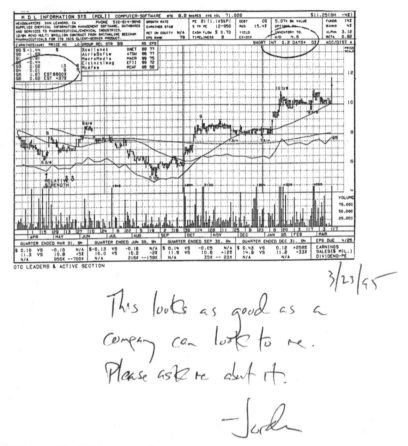

This looks as good as a company can look to me. Please ask me about it.

3/23/95

—Jordan

FIGURE 5.3   The MDLI note to clients

Source: DailyGraphs, Inc.

MDL Information Systems (MDLI)

In my files I found the original note I sent to clients back in 1995 when I came across MDLI (Figure 5.3). I would circle certain things right on the charts for clients to zero in from the *Investor's Business Daily* graphs. Notice the huge jump in earnings and revenues, zero debt, relative strength breaking out to new annual highs, and an outrageously high up/down ratio. This microcap stock was under clear accumulation.

A little over six months later, MDLI had already risen over 70 percent and my followup note was right on target (Figure 5.4). I never wanted to have more than ten positions in any account. Although all trades certainly did not go as well as this one, this was exactly the way I invested. I would go back at the end of each year to every one of these trades to try and understand what went right and what went wrong. There is no substitute for experience in the market itself.

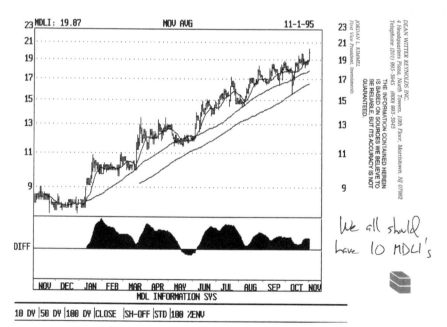

FIGURE 5.4   The follow-up note to clients on MDLI

Source: Telescan.

FREE CASH FLOW MAKES THE WORLD A BETTER PLACE

As cash flow for a company grows, the focus of that company turns from simply staying in business to growing their client base, their personnel, and giving back to their community. We have seen many companies, both domestically and internationally, become the backbone of their community. Starbucks, Microsoft, Heineken, Toyota, Nokia, and Johnson & Johnson come to mind. Over time and around the world, there have been several examples of the most successful companies working hand in hand with their respective communities for the betterment of society. These companies have been able to give back to the local people and enrich their communities because they were able to grow beyond the level of simply making payroll and paying bills, primarily through investments in the stock market. By allowing the free market to operate, we offer companies the opportunity to grow without restrictions and to receive the new capital they need to fund continued success and development. In times when the market is disrupted, they often get this capital from the likes of private equity funds or Berkshire Hathaway. Thankfully we have seen this happen recently. Comanager Charlie Munger says in August 2008's *Outstanding Investor Digest*, "I think there's one metric we use that others should use more. We tend to prefer the business that makes so much money, that it drowns in cash. One of the main reasons for owning it is you have all of this cash coming in" (p. 17).

It is through market interference, whether through governmental concerns of competition or because institutions insist on diversifying away—selling the winners to add to the losers—that society itself is made to suffer. It is only during their period of generating great free earnings that the truly superlative companies are in the position to do great things for society.

Most companies with the excess capital to do so spend enormous amounts of money conducting research to stay on top of their business and expand their market share within their industries. This research ultimately provides breakthroughs and advancements that benefit not just the company, but the public at large. These are the companies for which the most aspiring and driven people want to work. These employers provide the best benefits, environment, and tools with which to become successful. Other successful companies are then free to benefit by adopting and integrating the advancements brought forth by these leading companies. Without enough capital and the freedom for it to flow where it is best utilized, these advancements simply would not take place.

One of the most important activities that larger successful companies engage in is research. Although research is often conducted for the purpose of furthering profits and market share, the end result often benefits the public and society in general as well. Think about the advances in safety that General Motors was able to develop using the cash flow coming into the company years ago. Think about the money spent on the crash testing to enhance seat belts and braking systems. Think about Toyota, who has made tremendous strides in manufacturing that then benefited other companies further downstream. Even the old AT&T, which was interfered with because the government was concerned about monopoly, has helped to make the communication breakthroughs we see still taking place today. No doubt, Microsoft too will continue to provide future advancements that will benefit the entire world. Over the years, Microsoft was fighting the government as much as they were competing with other companies. We now see Bill Gates, their founder, as one of the leading philanthropic individuals in the world.

There is no question that we do not want evil public monopolies working against the general public's interest. Much effort is spent on behalf of the government to regulate business to prevent monopolies from coming into being. Internationally we see companies allowed to grow large enough to benefit society. Think about Heineken in Holland and Nokia in Sweden. These highly profitably run companies think as much about their employees, their communities, and their environment as they do about quarterly earnings releases. We can learn a lot about patience from them.

CHAPTER 6

Reevaluating Risk: Volatility Is Not Risk

During the first period of a man's life the greatest danger is not to take the risk.

—Soren Kierkegaard

It is not how right or how wrong you are that matters, but how much money you make when right and how much you do not lose when wrong.

—George Soros

It is impossible to win the great prizes of life without running risks.

—Theodore Roosevelt

The biggest obstacle I see that precludes most investment philosophies from achieving adequate returns is that they start with the wrong definition of investment risk. Depending on how you define risk, you either place yourself in a position to create significant returns or you can restrict yourself sufficiently in the beginning to assure yourself mediocre returns in the end. To obtain truly significant returns you must allow for volatility in the day-to-day pricing of your portfolio. Those who equate volatility with risk will end up with significantly lower returns. Volatility is the daily, weekly, monthly, and annual fluctuations in stock prices. A more important risk is not getting a high enough return on your capital to outpace trans-action fees, taxes, and inflation over a multiyear time horizon.

YOU CAN EAT *AND* SLEEP WELL

Often we hear the question, "Do you want to eat well or sleep well?" This question assumes that the answers are mutually exclusive. The truth is that you can do both, if you have the proper investment timeframe. In today's world, many investors—institutional and individual alike—look at very short-term timeframes to measure volatility and, as a result, are using the wrong measurements and definitions of risk. There are many types of risks in the investment world, and the understanding of the different risks should not be minimized. When an overemphasis on short-term volatility becomes the main factor in assessing risk, real long-term problems occur.

Over my career in the financial markets I have encountered investors of all sizes and types. Almost without exception, all of them told me they were long-term investors. Unfortunately, saying it and acting accordingly are often two very different things. Most investors simply cannot handle the fast paced and changing market environments without becoming overly absorbed with short-term results. Though the amount of information to help you create a plan and monitor it is available to everybody, it tends to become overwhelming. Many people lose their head or lose their way; they just cannot stick with an investment plan once volatility kicks in.

A long-term approach that can absorb the volatility is needed to generate higher investment returns. Institutions, endowments, and pension plans with clearly written investment policies are better able to stick with a plan. The unfortunate thing for many of these institutions is that they usually equate risk with volatility and end up creating forced allocation polices that invest in the assets that generate the lowest returns. They think they are avoiding risk, but they are in actuality just not correctly assessing the different types of risk. Inflation risk is one of the biggest risks to institutions, foundations, and nonprofits. Whereas individual investors may not have the ability to absorb the volatility financially, the institution does. Even so, the administrators do not have the fortitude to ignore the volatility, even though the institute has the time and money to ride out the short-term volatility.

DEFINING RISK

In his various writings and speeches, Warren Buffett makes it clear that he has thought about the subject of risk quite a bit. In his own words:

> In stating this opinion, we define risk, using dictionary terms, as "the possibility of loss or injury. Academics, however, like to define investment "risk" differently, offering that it is the relative volatility of a stock or portfolio of stocks"—that is, their volatility as compared to that of a large universe of stocks. In their hunger for a single statistic to measure risk, however, they forget a fundamental principle: It is better to be approximately right than precisely wrong. (1993 Letter to Shareholders, www.berkshirehathaway.com)

The risk to Buffett would be that he would be investing in a bad business or an average company with poor management. The question was not, "How would the relative short-term volatility of these companies react with each other and affect the value of my portfolio this week?" Instead, it was a focus on identifying the few exceptional companies run by excellent managers and buying them at reasonable prices. Over time, this approach offers superior returns; it just cannot be done with both eyes focused on day-to-day volatility.

In his book, *Value Investing: From Graham to Buffett and Beyond*, Bruce Greenwald looks at volatility from Buffett's view, a view that was originally discussed by Ben Graham. In the *Intelligent Investor*, Graham introduced Mr. Market, or the day-to-day gyrations offered up daily in the stock market. Once you identify a given company that you may want to invest in, market volatility often comes in and knocks down the stock during periods of pessimism. In fact, the true investor welcomes volatility, according to Graham. Learning to accept volatility rather than shunning it has helped the best investors over time.

Stanley Druckenmiller was another investment superstar that George Soros had on his team during his days running the Quantum Fund. He earned his reputation and a lot of financial rewards by understanding risk and return. Whatever he has written is worth your time to read. I remember reading an interview in which he discussed volatility, risks, and returns. In the discussion he refers to a study that conclusively demonstrated that asset classes and securities that have the lowest short-term volatility also generate the lowest long-term returns. Therefore he argues that if you genuinely have a long-term time horizon and you seek higher returns, you should invest in higher-volatility asset classes.

Types of Risks

Portfolio risk is composed of systematic risk, also known as undiversifiable risk, and unsystematic risk, which is also known as idiosyncratic risk or diversifiable risk. Systematic risk refers to the risk common to all securities, that is, market risk. Unsystematic risk is the risk associated with individual assets. Unsystematic risk can be diversified away to smaller levels by including a greater number of holdings in the portfolio. The same is not possible for systematic risk within one market. Depending on the investor's ability to accept volatility, a certain number of securities will give them the proper diversification. The question for each investor is, "How many?"

I had the pleasure of interviewing Joel Greenblatt on my radio show that I have hosted for several years now. He has produced strong long-term results managing money over many years and has written a couple of excellent books as well. On the subject of diversification, he took the time to address different kinds of risks and diversification:

> While simply buying more stocks can't help you avoid market risk, it can help you avoid another kind of risk—"nonmarket risk." Nonmarket risk is the portion of a stock's risk that is not related to the stock market's overall movements. Statistics say that owning just two stocks eliminates 46 percent of the nonmarket risk of owning just one stock. This type of risk is supposedly reduced by 72 percent with a four-stock portfolio, by 81 percent with eight stocks, 93 percent with 16 stocks, 96 percent with 32 stocks, and 99 percent with 500 stocks. (Greenblatt, 20)

If you can diversify away 93 percent of risk away with 16 stocks then why do we fund managers often carry 160?

You can do a good job of mitigating many kinds of risks. Look at the following list provided by one of the first investment houses I worked at, a bond firm. Although bonds were considered safer than stocks, it is interesting to see that many of the risks surrounding bonds are less prevalent within the stock market. Over time, the most devastating risk is inflation risk, when your assets lose value as their rates of return are about the same as or lower than the rate of inflation. Due to the focus on market risk, investors with too short a timeframe will sacrifice returns in attempts to minimize short-term volatility. Reeducating investors about the real risks to their portfolios and capital enable them to maximize their long-term returns. Institutions and individuals alike need to reevaluate and redefine risk before it is too late.

Investment Risks

- *Market risk.* Market risk is simply the uncertainty of the market valuation of an investment asset at a particular time.
- *Inflation risk.* The risk that inflation will erode the value of investment assets, unless those assets provide a rate of return that is greater than inflation.
- *Interest rate risk.* Fixed-income securities and some equities are subject to interest rate risk, because rising interest rates will generally cause market values to decline.
- *Credit risk.* This consists of the possibility that the company or organization that issued a fixed-income security will default.
- *Liquidity risk.* The risk that an asset cannot be converted to cash when needed.
- *Tax risk.* The risk that a change in the tax law will reduce the market value of a particular investment.
- *Reinvestment risk.* The risk that maturing investments will be reinvested at lower rates of return.

Two of the largest areas of individual and corporate spending, health care and insurance costs, are increasing significantly. Everybody is fighting this stealth inflation that has a profoundly negative impact on future purchasing power. For years we have been told by the government that inflation is running between 1 and 3 percent. Anybody that is running a family, company, or a nonprofit organization knows better. If you are saving for retirement, college education, or trying to grow an organization, you need to be aware of the true challenges the increase in the costs of living create.

The point is that inflation risk is one of the biggest threats to investors of all kinds. Being willing to remain in an overdiversified portfolio to beat the reported inflation numbers will leave you with a purchasing power deficit in the future. Over the last several years the public has accepted the reported inflation numbers in the 2 to 4 percent range. One of the excellent services I frequently use is Shadow Government Statistics, run by John Williams. In his revealing chart (Figure 6.1), you can see that real inflation is more than double the reported number. This requires you to redefine risk as outpacing inflation, taxes, and fees, not avoiding short-term volatility.

We often hear about America losing its dominance in the global financial world. All over the world, young entrepreneurs are taking the same risks that our nation has been known for and built on. They are becoming millionaires and billionaires and helping to reinforce

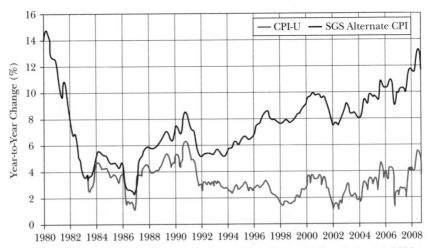

FIGURE 6.1   Annual consumer inflation: CPI versus SGS Alternate through October 2008

Source: ShadowStats.com.

and help spread the free market society. Foreign governments are using sovereign funds to buy into the equity market of the global stock markets. These funds, which are invested with 50-year time horizons, will reap tremendous rewards to their investors. It is difficult for me to see this great nation losing its economic strength. We are seeing enormous wealth being generated outside our country as others are willing to take on risks that our citizens took on previously. My goal is simply to remind everybody that the free market and calculated risk taking are what made this county great and powerful.

In an ironic twist of the financial market meltdown of 2008, the U.S. government may end up making significant returns on the strategic investments made within the financial institutions during the liquidity crisis. Only a few years prior, a suggestion that the Social Security fund invest a small portion of their assets in the stock market was soundly defeated because of a concern of "blowing up the fund"—or seeing it fluctuate too much.

During the height of the financial crisis in 2008, we saw billions of dollars invested by the Saudis and other foreign sovereign funds directly into U.S. institutions. Over decades to come, they will reap great rewards from these investments. Maybe our government and others can relearn the definition of risk and benefit as well.

CHAPTER 7

The Search for Superlatives

The worst mistake investors make is taking their profits too soon, and their losses too long.

—MICHAEL PRICE

Knowledge born from actual experience is the answer to why one profits; lack of it is the reason one loses.

—GERALD M. LOEB

Buy a stock the way you would buy a house. Understand and like it such that you'd be content to own it in the absence of any market.

—WARREN BUFFETT

If I were able to tell you with exact certainty where the market would be in five or ten years, you may think that is important information. Interestingly, however, your rate of return may not be as great as you may think. That is because most individual investors' returns are dependent on their own individual basket of holdings, not on the index itself. If you were to invest in an index fund, your rate of return reflects the gain on that index. But if you were to invest in the superlatives of the index, it is more likely that the rate of return would outperform the index fund by a significant amount.

Although there have been dozens of recessions over the last 70 years, the S&P 500 continues to climb over time because of a dirty little secret of Wall Street. Long-term investing works with indexes, but it does not work with individual stocks. The reason is that over time industries are created and new market leaders are born. All of the major indexes are actively seeking the new leaders and replacing the companies that are in dying industries. Owning the best buggy whip manufacturer turned out to be a poor investment once cars came around, unless you had a great management team that was adaptive.

If Roger Federer played a club professional, Federer would beat him the same way Tiger Woods would beat a club professional in 99 out of 100 head-to-head golf matches. After you have isolated your true superlatives, why would you want to diversify and hedge your bet because of that 1 percent chance that your superstar or your superlative may not go well?

Think about putting together a Davis Cup tennis team or a Ryder's Cup golf team to compete internationally. One choice would be to select 500 team members and rotate them among the matches. Another approach would be to select 20 team players more carefully and focus your efforts and capital on them—really get to know and understand them. Which approach would you think would yield the better results?

This same mentality can be carried over into the stock selection system. Once an individual or portfolio manager isolates the superlative securities in the marketplace, the capital concentration should remain focused on those superlatives. The need to diversify and hedge against a bet on those superlatives diminishes because all diversification would serve to do is limit your upside potential.

Once you are confident in your process and have identified the superlatives, you need to keep the same analogy in mind. Imagine firing Tiger Woods after a poor performance at a golf tournament. How about not allowing Steven Spielberg another opportunity to make a movie if, by chance, his last movie was not a blockbuster at the box office. This is exactly the way certain momentum investors react to a single poor quarterly earnings report. It is always easier to buy than it is to sell. There is a fine line between being too patient and being too hasty. Over time even the leaders cannot continue to outshine their contemporaries, and then it is the time to move on; success takes a combination of patience and confidence. If you are investing at good valuation levels to begin with, you can give smaller, more volatile stocks a chance to become big winners.

By monitoring the proper fundamental metrics, you can think long term while staying abreast of short-term developments. By long term I do not mean buy and hold. The forces of nature apply to corporations as well as to individuals. There is often a period of years during which a corporation dominates its industry. The S-curve that exists in all living organisms works with corporations as well. This is such an important point that I have given this subject its own chapter. There is often a period of time after a company completes its initial development phase when it grows rapidly and represents an exceptional investment opportunity. Ironically, it is usually following this expansion phase that most investors become aware of the company, and it is also the time when the business matures and already is entering a phase of decline.

The corollary to modern portfolio theory (MPT) is outperforming the major indexes through superior stock selection. This is the way that legendary outperformance returns are usually generated. Once I accepted the general theory of Magnet—that by the natural order of things there can only be a few superlatives of anything—my quest was to find a way to identify the real outliers, and that is where I would concentrate my capital.

MY 25-YEAR RESEARCH PROJECT

For the past 25 years I have devoted my time to studying the fascinating question, "What makes a great investment?" Throughout this complicated journey of answering this quintessential question, I made it my objective and ultimately had the privilege to meet many of the top money managers and investors of this era. My own media work has put me in a position to meet the top management at major companies, as well top authors, fund managers, newsletter writers, traders, and many of the most successful individual investors. Speaking at major investment conferences enabled me to meet almost anybody I tried to reach out to. I found out early that if you call up a truly successful individual and offer to buy lunch, you would be surprised how many great people you can meet. I want to thank everybody along the way who has made time for me when I came asking.

Seth Glickenhaus

Although taking a more concentrated approach to the stock market to generate higher returns feels new to some, some money managers have rewarded their clients for years with this approach and generated impressive returns. It was nice to see Seth Glickenhaus profiled in a *Barron's* interview in early July 2008, entitled "War, Peace, and Dividends." Since 1963, Glickenhaus has run private funds for clients. That is over 45 years, folks! His Glickenhaus & Co. maintains this investment philosophy: "We believe our first obligation is the preservation of the future purchasing power of our client's capital." In addition, their philosophy also states that "[t]his approach demands that we continually evaluate the potential for loss against the perceived opportunity for gain in markets and individual securities." Their investment philosophy leaves them with the ability to initiate moves into any security, in any market, at any time.

I would like to share the discussion I had at Seth Glickenhaus's office. Visiting with Glickenhaus was quite a treat; it became obvious quickly that his stellar returns have been generated as a result of being willing to do intensive research on individual companies. His conviction in what he uncovered allowed him to invest in no more than 30 to 40 of the best opportunities he could find. The idea that he would look different from other managers did not concern him. I asked him how he felt about narrow diversification as opposed to broad diversification. His comment was, "Diversification is the worst possible thing you can do. I do not even like your term 'narrow diversification'—selectivity is the right approach. When you have 160 stocks it is inevitable you will be average. Look at each company and ask 'What is the downside risk? What is the upside potential over time?'"

Glickenhaus's results speak for themselves, and they say he is a practitioner when he speaks of selectivity, and his investors are glad they did not settle for average.

Louis Navellier

Louis Navellier is, in my opinion, one of the most important money managers of our time. Early in my career I would use every opportunity to sit and listen to his presentations. In March 2005, BNet released an article about *Louis Navellier's Emerging Growth* newsletter, which confirmed his excellent returns. *"Louis Navellier's Emerging Growth* newsletter has been named the best-performing newsletter of the past 20 years by The Hulbert Financial Digest. According to Hulbert, the recommendations in Emerging Growth have returned over 4,064 percent from the beginning of 1985 through 2004."

As excellent as his stock picking has been, even more impressive is his ability to effectively blend superior stock selection together with MPT. It is one thing to pick the right companies, but to manage high-return portfolios that institutions can hold over long periods of time is another thing. The intuitional view of risk, with a focus on short-term volatility, requires more than choosing stocks that go up over time. Navellier has successfully blended stock selection with sector analysis, along with his own version of MPT, to achieve his superior returns.

While writing this book, I asked Navellier for his input on the big question, "How diversified should you be?" With his extensive math background and his unique adaptation of MPT, this issue is right up his power alley. For years, his staff of PhDs has pushed MPT to the limit, attempting to evaluate covariances among each stock to reduce unsystematic risk. For him, in a large-cap portfolio, 40 stocks are enough. In a small-cap portfolio, he is willing to increase the number of holdings to 70. He mentioned that benchmarking against certain indexes only ends up increasing the volatility and also tends to reduce the return of the portfolio. I then posed the interesting question: "If you used the same methodology on the same universe, what would the returns and the standard risk measurements look like?" The answers to these questions bring you to the heart of the matter: the proper level of diversification.

Navellier's operation is too sophisticated to buttonhole himself into always using a fixed number of securities in a portfolio. Depending on the health and breadth of the market, he adjusts his portfolio concentration levels. There are clearly times to hold fewer positions and times to expand the portfolio, and Louis knows this. For the benefit of our readers, Navellier had his staff perform a special analysis for this book. Using his proprietary portfolio construction methodology, he had his team do a back-test running separate large-, small-, and midcap portfolios with various levels of concentration. The charts in Figures 7.1, 7.2, and 7.3 show the results when 40, 80, and 160 positions were run in the back-test within each market capitalization. He also had his team calculate the various "consultant statistics"

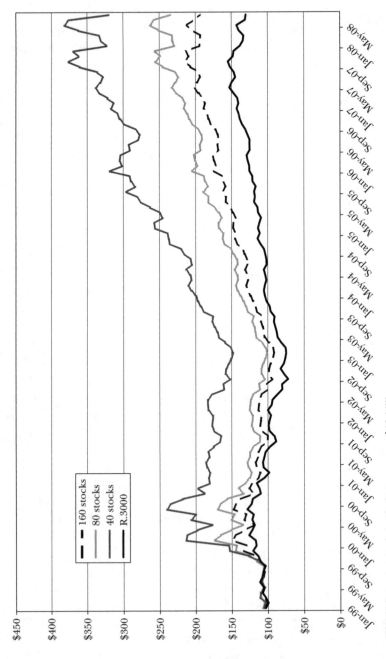

FIGURE 7.1   Large-Cap: Market cap over $10 billion

Source: Navellier & Associates, Inc.

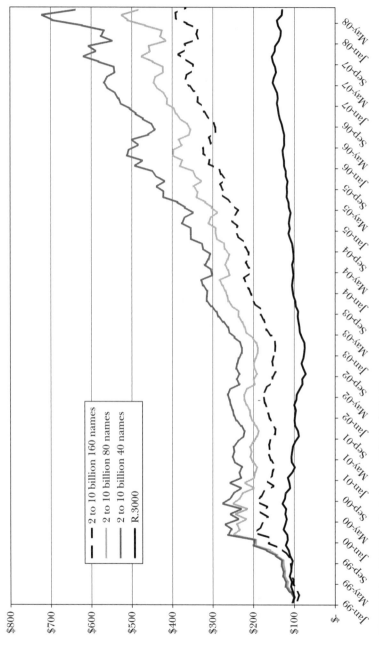

FIGURE 7.2 Mid-Cap: Market cap of $2 to $10 billion

Source: Navellier & Associates, Inc.

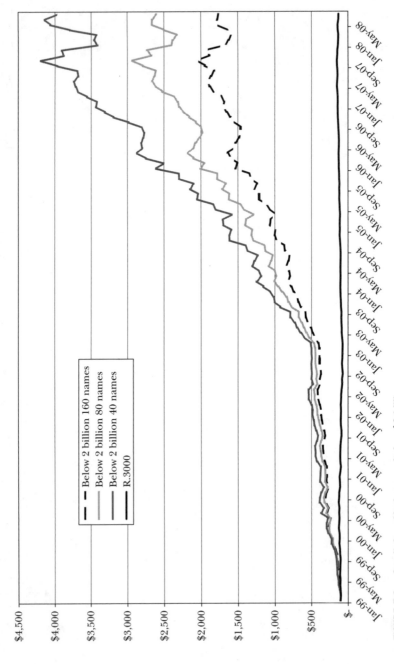

FIGURE 7.3 Small-Cap: Market cap below $2 billion

Source: Navellier & Associates, Inc.

(alpha, beta, standard deviations, etc.) to evaluate the results. The results powerfully confirmed my basic assumptions and what we see with The Magnet® Stock Selection Process. If you have a superior investment methodology, holding fewer positions will yield higher returns. The so-called risk, or volatility, will be reduced with your holding period. If you really allow yourself to stick to the plan and not base your strategy on short-term volatility statistics, your returns will dramatically outperform a presumably safe diversified approach.

Nassim Nicholas Taleb

Nassim Nicholas Taleb wrote an excellent book with an interesting title, *The Black Swan*, following his influential book, *Fooled by Randomness*. Both books address the uses of the bell curve and the handling of outliers. His focus is on the unexpected and unaccounted-for obstacles to success. His name for these highly improbable occurrences is Black Swans. He brings out the point that, while it is true the 90 percent of the time things are average, 10 percent of the time things are not so average and often *very* not average. Speculators, comforted by statistics and models, who think in terms of two standard deviations from the norm use rational MPT, and these asset allocation models often get thrown for a loop. Although it is statistically true that 90 percent of expected occurrences falls within a normal range of expectations, in the times that the actual occurrences fall outside the expected range, real problems can develop; that is, even if the event occurs slightly outside your expectations you can still be OK. It is the few times when the results are far from the expectations that disaster strikes. Unexpected external events show up more than models anticipate, and, when they do, havoc often breaks out. One of the most important realities that Taleb reminds us of is that these complicated strategies are extra vulnerable because they often seem so safe and they are therefore usually heavily margined—compounding the disaster when it does occur.

The most important concept that Taleb develops is separating process from return. By this he means that luck, whether good or bad, is often the underlying cause of an outcome. In his book, *Evidence Based Technical Analysis*, David Aronson proves through empirical scientific testing methods that the success of most trading and investing strategies is the result of luck, not superior methodology. While most investment professionals and the consultants paid to evaluate investment strategies have a hard time with this idea, you see it play out in the real world over and over again. Money came flowing into Bill Miller's fund as he gained wide recognition while setting a record of 14 consecutive years outperforming the S&P 500. Although I have tremendous respect for his accomplishments, it turns out much of his success resulted from an overweighting in the financial sector that rewarded him and his investors for years. Within just two years (2007–2008), suddenly his fund ranks toward the bottom over one-, three-, and five-year returns. I would think Miller is just as smart today as he was 15 years ago and quite a bit more experienced, but currently he is evaluated quite differently.

Barron's latest list of top-ranked mutual fund managers from their August 11, 2008 edition ranks Jan-Wim Derks as the number one manager. His ING Russia Fund had achieved an outstanding average annual return of 37.7 percent over the prior five years and an even more impressive 49.5 percent throughout the prior three years, for the period ending June 30, 2008. These performance numbers are tremendous and the managers should be thrilled. However, that particular period was a great time to be investing in Russia. The problem is that even before the *Barron's* rankings had been printed, the landscape had already changed dramatically. The global economy began to slow substantially in the summer of 2008. The driving force of recent Russian economic prowess, oil, fell about 75 percent from its high. After peaking just prior to making the *Barron's* list, the ING Russia Fund declined by over 77 percent within just five months. Again, it is a case of not confusing brains with a bull market. This is what Taleb means when he says how much luck sometimes comes into play with investment returns.

> *Financial genius is a rising stock market.*
> —JOHN KENNETH GALBRAITH

In *The Black Swan,* Taleb challenged his readers often. He said someone will read his book and soon introduce the White Swan. Not to disappoint him, I would like to introduce the Rainbow Swan. It is rainbow-colored because I use multiple factors to rank companies, like the many colors contained in the spectrum. When I run

The Magnet Stock Selection Process on the entire list of companies in the market, I will identify very few candidates for investment. By applying an extraordinary number of financial hurdles for a company to achieve and setting those hurdles high, very few companies are even isolated to look into. The top few often look beyond belief in terms of how much better they look when compared to the average company. Usually the Rainbow Swan Company has a superior idea and the superior management needed to execute the idea properly. Sales and margins are expanding, the company gets noticed by Wall Street and by big institutions, and the stock experiences a rapid price advance.

Although the company may have been around for awhile, you need to separate the company from the stock. It is at this time the company's stock is firing on all cylinders; it is in phase two of Stan Weinstein's model, it is being discussed in *Investor's Business Daily* (*IBD*), it is a number 5 on Dorsey Wright's system, and it is being added to the momentum-following newsletters. Stan's model looks at technical indicators, such as chart positions, breakouts/breakdowns, and patterns. *IBD* measures individual securities in comparison to their market competition, showing how their earnings per share (EPS), relative strength (RS), and accumulation distribution (A/D) rank out as percentages. Dorsey Wright's system is based solely on relative strength and the patterns that the relative strength develops. You get the message; once everyone picks up on these Rainbow Swans, that's when they really start to move.

Vic Sperandeo

I have highlighted Vic Sperandeo as one of the influences in the "T for Timing" section of Magnet. I met Vic years ago, and his wonderful book *Trader Vic* is a must-read for active traders. I caught up with him recently to have a discussion about his feelings on diversification. Although he has primarily moved on to indexes, it did not surprise me that his gut feelings on the issue follow quantitative studies almost exactly. His suggestion was that the minimum amount of companies in a portfolio that you need to be truly diversified would be 20. He went on to say that if you are a real stock picker and not just trying to mirror the index, the maximum that you would ever carry would be 40.

Rapid and powerful price movements can last for years and provide extraordinary gains, or they can peter out in just a single quarter. You can know only by staying on top of your holdings and not believing you can foretell the future. Tremendous gains are available to investors who can identify Magnet stocks, or Rainbow Swans, as long as they can identify them early and do not forget to sell when they lose their luster, or in our case, their Magnet ranking.

There is no question that, in each year and every market environment, some companies are clear winners, but these companies are in no way assured of continued success. The challenge is to identify them, to invest in them, and to rotate out of them before they succumb to the forces of competition, a change in the investment landscape, or often even their own hubris resulting from their early success.

John Boik

In his three great books, *Lessons from the Greatest Stock Traders of All Time*, *How Legendary Traders Made Millions*, and *Monster Stocks*, John Boik studied and documented the successes of the top stock market investors over the last 100 years. One of the first things to notice about the investors, Boik highlights, is that they were not managing fiduciary accounts. They were managing not mutual funds, but instead their own money and had the leeway to invest without the shackles of the industry's constraints.

What set these investors apart in Boik's words was their distinct pattern of patience to wait for the right setup—the right market coupled with the right set of stocks. They would sit and watch the market when it was not advancing, as opposed to being fully invested and riding out the tough periods the market often encounters. When the market turned bullish, the best investors would get fully invested in just a few names, maybe ten at the most, the pure market leaders. They also had the discipline to jump right out of any stock that did not look right. The absolute focus on very few companies is what set them apart and enabled them to generate such outstanding results. The other thing that these investors had in common was their use of stop-losses. Each one of them believed in cutting losses short, regardless of their longer-term view of any stock they bought. In fact, it is the use of stop-losses that allowed them to take such bold concentrated positions in the first place. Understanding that they would not allow themselves to take too much of a loss on any one investment created a mind-set that let them ignore the diversification strategies that would make their outsized returns impossible.

IT'S OK TO COPY

Copying on tests in school may not be OK, but copying the habits and strategies of the most successful individuals in a given field is often an excellent idea. Being the youngest of four children helped me become comfortable learning from others. As a child I was able to see what worked for my brothers and sister, as well as what got them into trouble. Even so, sometimes in life you need to make your own mistakes. It is the same way with investing. Although I read about the problems with taking gains too quickly and letting losses run too large, it is only by "having skin in the game" can you learn to control your emotions.

When it comes to developing a strategy for generating strong returns in the stock market, my advice is to learn and copy the habits of the best investors over time. As I have tried to make clear throughout this book and chapter, not a single top investor I have ever spoke to or read about ever talked about or encouraged diversification or asset allocation. Instead they all discussed the need to stay nimble, stay concentrated in your number of holdings, and cut your losses short when they occur. Think about that next time you hear about the need to be diversified.

CHAPTER 8

The InterBoomer Generation

With globalization, the big [countries] don't eat the small, the fast eat the slow.

—THOMAS L. FRIEDMAN

There has never been a commercial technology like this (Internet) in the history of the world, whereby the minute you adopt it, it forces you to think and act globally.

—ROBERT HORMATS

A lot has already been said about the international global build-out taking place. For years we have heard from the self-indulgent Baby Boomers and marketers alike about how big this group was and how they changed the supply-and-demand equations entirely. Because of the advances in communication and the Internet, the free market is spreading globally like a wildfire. The administration in Washington wants to talk about the spreading of democracy, and that is the political side. From the business side, it comes down to one thing: free markets. The communist from China goes onto the Internet the same way the socialist does from Sweden. The result of this is what I call, the InterBoomer Generation. Everyone from everywhere desires a higher standard of living that is being enjoyed around the world. The growth in the size of the capital markets over the next several decades is being ignored by today's investors, who continue to think short term.

More than any period in history, you now need to think globally, not just locally or domestically. The current global build-out is far larger and more extensive than most people realize. America's number one export is actually the free market itself. As a result of the Internet and the proliferation of mass communication, change is taking place ever faster. The development of the world population into consumers is taking place worldwide, and I am talking about economics, not politics. While our politicians are talking about democracy, the real issue is simply the opening of the free market. As a result, we are seeing increased demand internationally from the "InterBoomers," this will translate into a boom in financial assets over time. The global markets will grow significantly over time. We are building fences to keep people from coming into our country, but these barriers do not exist in the financial industry.

Only 50 years ago, the New York Stock Exchange celebrated its first time surpassing over 1 million shares traded in a single day. Now we routinely see 2.5 billion shares per day on both the NYSE and the NASDAQ. The time will come within a decade where we will see 10-billion-share days; imagine the profits of the financial service firms at that time. Over the next decades, innovative new industries will emerge. Whether it is underwater or outer space development, biotechnology or medical equipment, everything will get funded, built, and collateralized. Financial firms will underwrite these new issues and collect fees. The earnings from those new companies—companies that do not even exist yet—will help drive the economy of the future.

INTERNET-DRIVEN GROWTH

As we go to print, we are experiencing an economic slowdown occurring around the world. The financial liquidity crisis that developed in the United States. resulting from the housing slowdown, has created short-term shocks to the global markets. There is a warning that too much global growth is already built into investors' expectations. My belief is that, although business cycles are inevitable and will continue to occur, very few investors grasp the magnitude of the growing demand coming from the InterBoomer Generation over the next 100 years.

Over the last 20 years we have already seen a dramatic shift in world consumption. The accelerating growth underway on every continent has already begun to dramatically increase demand for both raw materials and finished goods. The public awareness has been focused on the BRICs (Brazil, Russia, India, and China), but those clearly are not the only areas where demand-driven growth is accelerating.

One clear example of Internet-driven growth is occurring in the Middle East. Once citizens in oppressed societies see a vision of a better life, their awareness generates desires. Regimes that were able to suppress their citizens find it more difficult once the people see the simple pleasures that others are enjoying in other parts of the world. With the resources available, indoor ski facilities are being built, and shopping malls and better schools are springing up to satisfy the population. In some countries in this part of the world, women are being formally educated for the first time. Although some governments continue to use censorship to keep their citizens in the dark, clearly the free market forces of the Internet will continue to spread consumerism.

There is a new fear-mongering campaign calling for the "great bust ahead." The claim being made is that the bust will result from the end of the cycle of U.S. Baby Boomers' peak spending consumption. The analysis may be accurate domestically, but let us not forget the percentage of the world population that is American is under 5 percent. While the United States is the single largest consumer nation in the world, a look at the worldwide consumer breakdown over the last 20 years offers a much different perspective of the future. Some view the shifts as a threat to America's dominance; I simply see a larger consumer base. If it seems America's going from four meals per day down to three while the less developed nation's citizens can enjoy a second meal per day, all the better. Americans may benefit from becoming a bit leaner, and the rest of the world's population can increase their standard of living and consumption. Many are citing the current state of affairs in the United States as troublesome, but do not forget the big picture. Given the chance to live the American dream, takers would line up to "get on board" and the line would wrap around the world.

AGE WAVE THEORY

Jason Nolan at the Magnet Investment Group has extensively studied the much talked-about Age Wave Theory and provided an excellent analysis in a research report he prepared for me. He and

I share the belief that the global economy will continue to expand and that the impact of any decrease in the America's Baby-Boomer spending patterns will be muted by international growth.

Jason detailed in his report that there has been more discussion recently about the Age Wave Theory than ever before. The retiring Baby Boomers are supposedly going to be the death of equities as we know it. But we're not convinced.

First, we have to understand the Age Wave Theory, which was popularized by economist and writer Harry Dent, who concludes that the United States and other European markets will peak between 2008 and 2012. Harry Dent's finding is that a human's consumer spending habits peak by age 50; therefore, as the Baby Boomer generation reaches this age, the economy may be approaching a peak in consumer spending and in the markets. It also states that when Baby Boomers begin to retire, which the first Baby Boomer did in 2008, it could cause spikes in unemployment, a severe decline in the markets due to selling, and a decrease in the housing market.

Let's begin by taking a look at what exactly a Baby Boomer is. At the end of World War II, birthrates spiked around the world. It's estimated that 77 million babies were born in the United States alone. A Baby Boomer is a person who was born between 1946 and 1964. The Baby Boomer generation currently represents about 20 percent of the American public and has a significant impact on the economy due to their spending. This large increase in population caused a substantial rise in consumer goods, which stimulated the postwar economy. Now you can see why most believe that when Baby Boomers retire and slow their spending, they could cause a precipitous drop in the stock market and economy.

MINOR BABY BOOMER IMPACT

Although all of this seems almost logical and expected, some commonly overlooked factors help us dispute this theory and the effects it will have on the market. We believe that the retirement of Baby Boomers is unlikely to cause any significant impact or decline in the stock market or the market's potential returns. The main issues are consumer spending habits in retirement, distribution of wealth among the Baby Boomers, an analysis of how current retirees spend down their assets. The globalization of the markets, and how what is happening overseas right now, will dwarf the Baby Boomer generation.

A study conducted by the Government Accountability Office (GAO, 2008) examined financial information from the Survey of Consumer Finances to determine what assets are held by Baby Boomers and how much they have, as well as how current retirees spend down their assets.

It is currently estimated that the Baby Boomers control roughly $7.6 trillion in assets invested in stocks, bonds, mutual funds, IRAs, and other retirement accounts. While examining the data available (Figure 8.1), we discovered that about two-thirds of all the financial assets are held by 10 percent of the Baby Boomer generation. In addition, about 33 percent of the boomers do not own any assets in stocks, bonds, or mutual funds.

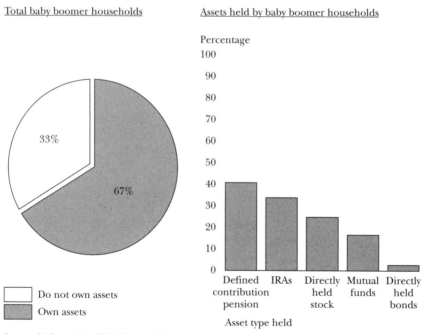

Source: GAO analysis of 2004 Survey of Consumer Finances.

FIGURE 8.1   Percentage of Baby Boomers who own financial assets and their of use different investment accounts

Source: The Magnet Investment Group with data from GAO.

It should also be noted that the distribution of wealth among the Baby Boomers is severely slanted toward the top the 25 percent (Figure 8.2), who control almost 90 percent of the retirement assets. The top 5 percent control over half of the assets. The retirees who are most likely to spend down assets to maintain their standard of living control such a small portion of the total assets of the Baby Boomers, that their liquidating of positions and accounts will have an unnoticeable effect on the markets. The bottom 50 percent of Baby Boomers, the group most likely to spend down their assets, control a mere 3 percent of the $7.6 trillion in assets held by the Baby Boomers, or $228 billion. All the recent Federal Reserve injections into money markets and bailouts total well over $4 trillion. The effect of a mass liquidation of holdings by these 3 percent would be inconsequential. Also, a mass liquidation is unlikely. Retiree habits show that assets, if spent down, are done ever so gradually over retirement. Even at a constant spending-down rate of 5 percent a year ($11.9 billion), the effects on the market would be unnoticed.

The wealthiest boomers are the ones driving the economies. The individuals with little to no investable assets will not influence the economy as the wealthy can. A large purchase such as a yacht, a second house, or a private jet can easily do more for the economy than the sum of all the purchases by an individual without any savings.

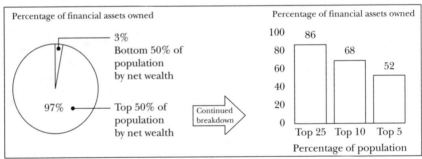

Source: GAO analysis of 2004 Survey of Consumer Finances.

FIGURE 8.2   Distribution of Baby Boomer financial assets by wealth percentiles

Source: The Magnet Investment Group with data from GAO.

A large concentration of Baby Boomer assets is held by the wealthiest 50 percent who, based on the study of current retiree behavior, will not need to spend down their assets to maintain their lifestyle and who often end up accumulating more assets over their retirement, rather than using them up. Another important thing to note is that a large number of the Boomers who do own financial assets are more likely to bequeath them to their heirs than spend them down. Also, many boomers will hold stock long into retirement as an inflation hedge and to counter their fears of outliving their savings.

In addition to the wealthiest 10 percent of the Baby Boomers controlling a large majority of the assets, it is believed that their behavior will mimic previous generations' retirement habits. In previous generations, a majority of the retirees continued to accumulate financial assets during their retirement, with only gradual liquidations occurring. In addition to the gradual liquidations that occur, there is a 19-year period over which Baby Boomers will enter retirement. This should further reduce the likelihood that Baby Boomer retirement will precipitate a sharp decline in the markets.

ASSET ACCUMULATION CONTINUES IN RETIREMENT

As explained, many Baby Boomers will continue to accumulate assets into retirement. It was also found that a majority of Baby Boomers do not plan to retire at the standard age. Over half the Baby Boomers surveyed by the Consumer Finance Committee said they plan to leave full-time employment around age 65. More than 60 percent also expressed an interest in getting a part-time job during retirement, which helps to reduce or delay the amount of investment assets they need to sell to maintain their lifestyle.

This same study found that less than 16 percent of the wealthiest retirees (the top 10 percent) spent money from their savings in investments. A large majority of them lived off the income generated from their investments. Over 65 percent of the same group reported that they accumulated more assets due to their investment income exceeding their spending.

In a study conducted by James Poterba in 2004, entitled "The Impact of Population Aging on Financial Markets," which was published by the National Bureau of Economic Research, he found that

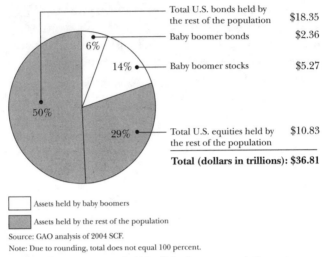

FIGURE 8.3   Total financial assets held by Baby Boomers and the rest of the U.S. population

Source: The Magnet Investment Group with data from GAO.

"holdings of elderly households suggests there is a limited decline in financial assets as households age."

In relation to the size of the U.S. economy, Baby Boomers represent a small part, only 20 percent. They hold 14 percent of all stocks, and 6 percent of all bonds. Let's keep in mind that of all Baby Boomers, roughly 5 to 10 percent will have to liquidate positions to maintain their lifestyle. At an average retirement of over 20 years, a gradual selloff should be expected, which will not impact the financial markets significantly (Figure 8.3).

A common argument for the mass liquidation of their equity positions is that, upon entering retirement, Baby Boomers will have a much lower risk tolerance for market volatility then before. In the Survey of Consumer Finances findings, it found that, of the total wealth of households with people over 70 years of age, more of their savings is still invested in stocks than bonds.

GLOBALIZATION OFFSETS BOOMER RETIREMENT

The globalization of the markets and increasing demand from developing countries will also offset the Baby Boomer retirement issues.

In a statistical analysis conducted by the Government Accountability Office, it showed that in the time period from 1948 to 2004, macro-economic and financial factors, such as industrial production and dividends from stock, have been responsible for more of the variation in stock returns than any demographics or shifts in the population's age structure ever have.

More importantly than the minimal effect that the Baby Boomer generation will have on the markets, we have to look at the bigger picture. No longer can we think just domestically about the markets. The economy is now global, and it must be looked at as so. Seventy-seven million Baby Boomers become insignificant in the big picture. Total U.S. population accounts for approximately only 5 percent of the world population. Baby Boomers' power is lost on the world stage. Economic clout is building in the new Internet generation influencing the global economies.

With the standard of living rising around the world and with developing nations building infrastructure, something much bigger than the Baby Boomer phenomenon is happening: the InterBoomers. Around the world right now, billions of people are having their second meal for the first time, and billions of people are tasting their first Egg McMuffin. When your standard of living begins to increase like this, you cannot go back to the old ways. You find a way to continue that path of improvement, regardless of what it takes. The result? *Growth.* The amount of worldwide growth taking place is more than enough to offset any effect that retiring Baby Boomers could have on the domestic or global economy. We are no longer just domestic investors. The world is our market, and new power-houses are coming up.

Figure 8.4 tells a great story of how the rest of the world is developing. Since 1980 the United State's GDP as a percentage of the world's GDP has increased by 30 percent, and developing countries such as China have increased over 1,000 percent. China has gone from having 1 percent of the world's GDP to over 10 percent. India and Russia have more than doubled as well. These developing countries are housing billions of people who are just starting to taste what Americans have become accustomed to. Their growth is continuing while U.S. GDP as a percentage of global GDP has actually dropped 13 percent since 2000. It would not be surprising to see an individual country surpass the United States in terms of GDP in the near future.

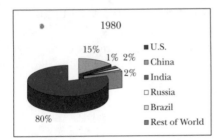

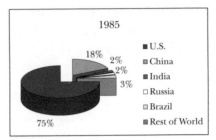

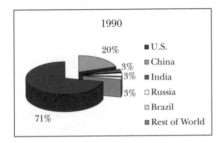

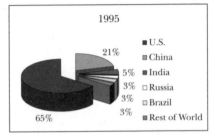

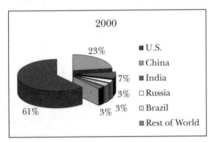

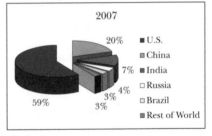

FIGURE 8.4   How the rest of the world is developing

Source: The Magnet Investment Group with data from GAO.

These European and Asian nations have also had much more time to compound their money and grow their assets. The United States has been around only a few hundred years, while Europe and China have been around thousands. This has allowed for old money to continue to grow for centuries.

The InterBoomer generation is larger than anything we have seen before. Consisting of not millions, but billions of people, this will be the driving force of the market and economies in the future. The effect that the Baby Boomers had on the economy and will have in the retirement will be minimal compared to the global effect the InterBoomers are having right now.

Coinciding with the development of these countries is the development of the people living there as well. Never have more people been educated as they are today. Innovations in every field are being made every day by InterBoomers who want to continue to better their lives. The InterBoomer Generation is being opened up to entirely new paths for their lives to develop and grow. This in turn will result in higher employment, increased GDP across the board, and wealthier people as well. The increase in consumption will be dramatic and noticeable around the world as more people line up to live what for the time being is the American Dream.

There are thousands of future billionaires around the world that no one has heard of yet. Whether they make their money by curing cancer or inventing a more effective solar cell, new people will rise to the top, and new money will be acquired. GDPs will continue to increase long term as countries throughout the planet become more and more developed, and the citizens continue to educate and improve their lives and lives of every citizen of earth as well.

9

Implications of Market Interference

If you destroy a free market you create a black market. If you have ten thousand regulations you destroy all respect for the law.
—WINSTON CHURCHILL

All the features and achievements of modern civilization are, directly or indirectly, the products of the capitalist process.
—JOSEPH A. SCHUMPETER

The majority of the nonprofit organizations that support the philanthropic infrastructure of our society are operating under great duress. This comes as a result of underfunded endowments, infrastructure costs, and the projected growth of those costs to support the increasing need for their services. America's economic role in the world is threatened by trade deficits that demonstrate our inability to export America's inherent free market expertise.

Despite the benefits offered by some of the actively managed hedge funds, they have also had some severe negative impacts in the markets. The hypercompetitiveness and short-term orientation of most hedge funds have led to extra volatility and even faster rotation from stock to stock and from sector to sector. This added volatility, coupled with a dramatic reduction in trading costs, has resulted in drastically shortened holding periods. With shorter holding periods shifting the focus toward short-term gains, the net result is that companies are often unable to make prudent, long-term strategic decisions. Instead, they are focused on showing as strong a quarterly earnings number as possible, as opposed to growing more slowly and steadily in a more sustainable way. Unfortunately, this approach usually curtails progress and disappoints almost everyone over time.

There is no question of a quest for higher returns across the investment world. We are seeing more funds taking less diversified approaches. We are also seeing the most successfully funded institutions using hedge funds and seeking alternatives to straight indexing. It is hard for others to sit back and watch successful investors generate these excess returns while they remain in diversified strategies receiving mediocre returns. All over the world, investors are reevaluating risk and achieving higher returns with fewer holdings. I look for these trends to continue to expand.

DOMESTIC IMPLICATIONS OF MARKET INTERFERENCE

The practice of asset allocation and broad diversification has multiple drawbacks. Not only do these strategies create mediocre investment results, they also have other negative repercussions. As new money comes available for investment to the indexers, the portfolio managers buy more shares of all the companies in the index. Depending on the index and the approach, usually not all companies are added to equally. Some indexes are cap weighted, in which case the larger companies are added to more extensively. Other indexes are price weighted, and—believe it or not—the highest-priced stocks are added to the most and the lower-priced companies get added to less. In this case, like the Dow Jones Industrial 30, when a company splits its shares, it actually takes on a smaller weight in the index.

To have an impact on their industry and community, companies need capital to grow. As a company begins to make strides, it gains investors' attention and raising capital becomes easier. As a company continues to gain market share and grow its revenues, a virtuous cycle is in effect. New talented employees are attracted by the buzz and the opportunity for wealth through stock options. This is a very exciting time for the company.

Unfortunately for society as a whole, shares of companies that are past their prime and currently deteriorating continue to be invested in by indexers, simply because they have made it in to the index previously. When new money comes into an indexer's hands, even more shares of these current losers are purchased. Such an inefficient use of capital only prolongs the decline of the former market leader, as well as making new capital unavailable for the purchase of more shares in emerging market leaders.

The world markets are now fully global and accessible to investors across many nations. Capital is flowing to where it is treated best and where there is full transparency. If a new market leader appears in the United Kingdom, then capital will find a way to get there. If market leaders are in Hong Kong indexes, then capital will find its way there as well.

Any interference by the market to slow the growth of an emerging market leader, or to maintain a former market leader after its growth stage had passed, only hinders the natural competition. This ultimately is unhealthy for society because it fuels the fire of a company that is undeserving of the designation as a market leader.

GLOBAL IMPLICATIONS OF MARKET INTERFERENCE

Over the last several quarters, since the third quarter of 2008 and even earlier, despite the seemingly relentless moves in most commodity prices, we have seen several violent shakeouts. In fact, we are experiencing another one at the time of writing. But despite the slowdown in the activity of the domestic consumer, the spreading of the free market is generating an almost insatiable demand for almost every commodity you can think of. In the early 1990s, Sir John Templeton gave a tremendous presentation in which he discussed the impact of the fall of the Berlin Wall. He said it would have the single biggest impact on investments of any event that has occurred in his lifetime. Consumers exposed to the free market would expand from the current 250 million living in the United States to another 250 million living in Eastern Europe. And how right he was! But that event is now dwarfed by the explosion in the growth taking place around the world today. Although the focus is on China, growth is clearly taking place on every continent. Whereas China itself currently accounts for 50 percent or more of the worldwide demand for copper, aluminum, zinc, lead, and steel, you cannot underestimate the demand that is building in every corner of the planet.

As development continues to spread around the globe, an ever greater number of people are in a position to improve their diets. The same yield improvements within the farming industry that took place in the United States are just taking place now overseas. It is back to basics in many ways. With the increase in the overall population and the ever increasing standard of living just becoming available in some places, do you really believe that the demand for the large machinery that enables people to eat better is going to fall out of favor?

It is in the interest of everybody to allow the same forces of nature to operate within the public securities marketplace. That is, superlative companies should be allowed to grow and attract capital from anywhere in the world.

THE FREE MARKET

The leading export of the United States is its free market system; each country represents a potential trading partner and buyer of our products. As our nation is the primary consumer of many products, we are also happy to contribute to the growth of the global economy by purchasing foreign products. The understanding and exportation of the free market are the very source of human capital; that is the U.S. strength. More and more countries are expanding their international trade relationships and adopting free market policies. It will be because of this international trade expansion that in the upcoming decades we will see a global build-out that will bring the international trade to unseen levels.

All over the world, young entrepreneurs are creating new businesses, taking the same risks our nation has been known for in the past. They are becoming millionaires and billionaires, thereby helping not only to reinforce and spread the free market society, but also to promote and increase trade expansion.

This leads us into a discussion of Microsoft. Founded in 1986, Microsoft rode the wave of the free market. Anybody lucky enough to have identified this company at its early growth stage was advised to continually sell stock to protect their gains. There are a few notable exceptions to those who took this poor advice, namely the founders and early employees. In an interesting conclusion, these few individuals who rode the wave of the free market put themselves in a situation to make a difference in this world. They are the stewards of the largest personal endowment funds and have chosen as the target beneficiaries of their wealth to be the international community. The Gates Foundation, along with others, is spreading the benefits and the realities of the free market in a way strikingly different from the U.S. military. The practitioners of our free market society simply expose the advantages of capitalizing on the opportunities that the markets gave to them; in doing so, they allow the mind-set of the free market to spread worldwide. As this mentality gets spread worldwide, we will see other Microsoft-type success stories appear in the international market, and those new leaders will follow the footsteps of their free market predecessors.

It is difficult for me to see this great nation losing its economic strength. We are seeing enormous wealth being generated outside our country because others overseas are willing to take on risks that our citizens took on previously. My goal is simply to remind everybody that the free market and calculated risk taking are what make this county great and powerful. Although the demise of our nation's international power frightens some, I know that there will always be a promising future for the country that exposed the great number of benefits made attainable by a free market society.

ALLOCATION OF ASSETS

Once you decide to invest your money, you can put your assets to work in only two areas: equity (the ownership market) or bonds (the lending market). The lending market is by far the larger asset class, this includes opportunities such as bonds, government treasuries, certificates of deposit (CDs), and money market funds. The other investment vehicle is the ownership class. This includes property and the equities market. When my parent's generation was buying homes for $15,000, prices were at a different level. As inflation continued to take hold, those who took the path of ownership, rather than lending, were able to outpace inflation. Time has shown that the larger the percentage of assets allocated to the ownership asset class (the equity market), rather than the lending market (the bond market), the greater the potential will be for a higher return on your investment.

In trying to capture the greatest gains on your investments, you constantly fight stealth inflation. We are told inflation is running at 1 to 2 percent. Anybody who is running a company or a non-profit organization knows better. The largest areas of spending, our health care and insurance costs, are increasing significantly. This means that not only do we have to realize gains to fight inflation, but we have also to outpace the health care and insurance expenditures. In an earlier chapter I touched on the power of compounding. This method of investing needs to be exposed to gain the greatest returns, and it is going to be through this power that individuals will be able to outpace the expenses that individuals typically face. The power of compounding goes beyond putting $1,000 dollars into a mutual fund, keeping it for 30 years, and hoping it gains 7 percent a year so that you obtain your financial freedom. What individuals have to think about is dollar cost averaging, narrow diversification, and not being fearful of the market but being confident in the capitalist system developed by our forefathers.

After many years of following the failed strategies of asset allocation and systematic diversification that have yielded unacceptable mediocre returns, institutions and the public at large are now open to a more logical and robust methodology of seeking out, identifying, and concentrating capital in the truly superlative companies. This change of strategy has been caused by numerous factors that have unfolded over the last several years. The high-profile corporate scandals of WorldCom and Enron did severe damage to the public's confidence in the stock market. The government's misreporting of tame inflation also led to the undercommitment to the higher returns offered by the ownership of rapidly growing companies. Many investors—individual and institutional—perceived that earning the low returns from bonds was enough to offset the effects of taxes and inflation. What we see as a result are several long-term problems that need immediate attention.

Remember, it is a well-known fact that hospital wings are donated by individuals who have made their fortune through concentrated ownership of the right companies, not by making their money through lending instruments.

SMALLER COMPANIES HAVE DIFFICULTY GETTING WALL STREET RESEARCH

Even with all of the things that we have already covered that inhibit the progress of smaller companies, yet another factor impedes small but profitable companies from attracting the capital they require to grow. Many years ago I spoke out about the bias inherent in the research coming out of Wall Street. I came to realize this bias quite clearly in the early 1980s, when I identified a few small companies that were clear leaders in their market niches. I could not understand why no research reports were coming out on them. Over time I got to know the management at one of the companies well and was kept informed of the company's progress. I was excited to hear of an upcoming visit by a major Wall Street firm, believing the company was about to be written up and "discovered" by others. The attention would certainly allow the company to attract capital and ultimately expand their operations. After ten minutes in a meeting with management, the research analyst determined that the company had no interest in issuing more common stock, bonds, or convertible securities. This meant no investment banking fees from the firm. The "research" meeting ended abruptly.

At this point I became aware of the complete breakdown of the Chinese Wall, as it is called on Wall Street. Though the investment banking and research departments at brokerage firms are supposed to be separate and unbiased, the truth is, as it was exposed a decade later, that many companies were "buying" research. They would offer lucrative investment banking deals by issuing public securities through brokerage houses, only to see glowing buy recommendations written 30 days after the brokers received large underwriting fees.

Free Earnings: A New Metric

Never overpay for a stock. More money is lost than in any other way by projecting above-average growth and paying an extra multiple for it.
—CHARLES NEUHAUSER

Over long periods of time, a company's stock price should correlate closely with its earnings. Each quarter, every public company is required to provide an accounting of its business. In a perfect world you would be able to properly evaluate a company's prospects by looking at its current valuation and judging whether the market is factoring the company's growth prospects into its share price fairly. Unfortunately, we do not live in a perfect world. Companies are acutely aware that their quarterly earnings releases are being scrutinized to the penny and as a result have become fond of engineering those earnings to appear more favorable to analysts. Back in the late 1990s I went on television to highlight this issue—long before it was popular to discuss. Even now, as companies are held to a higher standard, there are still many legal ways for quarterly earnings to be dressed up and manipulated. In my quest to mathematically differentiate one company from another, I developed a new metric to rank companies: I call it Free Earnings.

CALCULATING FREE EARNINGS

The PEG Approach

More money is lost by investors in the stock market through overpaying for stocks than for any other reason. While you may be looking for a company with strong growth characteristics, you also want to be careful not to overpay for your shares. In an effort to measure a company's earnings growth rate relative to its valuation, Standard & Poor's developed the PEG ratio 25 years ago. Since then, it has been widely popularized by Peter Lynch, who explains the details of the ratio in his book, *One Up on Wall Street*.

The PEG ratio is defined as:

$$PEG\,Ratio = \frac{Price/Earnings}{Annual\,Earnings\,Per\,Share\,Growth}$$

Interpreted simply, the lower the PEG ratio is, the better the valuation is.

GARP Approach

Others following the same thought process have adopted the GARP style of investing, or Growth at a Reasonable Price, also popularized by legendary Fidelity Money Manager Peter Lynch. GARP investing combines elements of both growth and value strategies by seeking companies that are growing faster than their valuations, while avoiding companies with high valuations. Followers of GARP believe that when buying a growth stock you may need to pay a higher P/E ratio than "old timers" are used to. By seeking out companies with a PEG ratio of one or less, GARP investors can invest in stocks that are growing at a solid pace, yet are still selling at a discount to their growth rate. While it is a value approach, its proponents justify paying a higher earnings multiple because it looks reasonable compared to the company's earnings growth rate.

EVALUATING QUALITY OF EARNINGS

Because of the inconsistencies between the definitions of earnings used in the PEG and GARP approaches, I prefer to analyze the cash flow generated by a company. There are a lot of ways to evaluate the quality of earnings, and this is where the hard work comes in. Too many investors, and even some professionals, do not spend enough time on this task. Making life easier, several services now can help you quickly travel though a company's balance sheet to evaluate what is really going on. They even allow you to cross-verify items within a company's balance sheet and can sometimes help you isolate inconsistencies.

One such service is Market Grader, a terrific service available to the individual investor that would have been unimaginable several years ago. Using over a dozen metrics, the program delves deep into a company's income statement not only to provide a relative valuation level, but also to address the quality of the specific company's earnings.

Another excellent service, Stock Diagnostics, uses its own proprietary fundamental analysis. Realizing the shortcomings associated with reported earnings, the developers have sought solutions to this plight. Established in 2002, the service developed a new metric for financial analysis called OPS, or Operational Cash Flow per Share. Not nearly as easily manipulated by companies as earnings per share (EPS), OPS is calculated by dividing a company's cash flow from operations by the total number of shares outstanding. Stock Diagnostics created OPS to focus stockholders on the real values of a company as opposed to the artificial values that can be produced by creative accounting under EPS, cash flow per share (CFPS), or earnings before interest, taxes, depreciation, and amortization (EBITDA). There are so many ways to engineer earnings that the more sources you can use to check on the quality of earnings, the better off you are.

Investor's Business Daily (*IBD*) also provides its own EPS ranking, their proprietary tool that ranks each company by IBD's own internal methodology.

Having supplementary tools like these allows you to obtain a great insight into a company and has, while helping to reshape Wall Street, minimized and replaced analysts' often skewed or influenced reports.

It is one thing to understand a company's cash flow and act accordingly, and another thing to overreact to each quarterly earnings release. For instance, some earnings momentum players jump into and out of stocks based on each quarter's numbers. Some analysts encourage companies to fully report sales at least monthly. We even have a movement taking place in the United States, lobbying for big companies to report more frequently. We now see monthly updates on the number of automobile sales, retailers' sharing of monthly same-store sales figures, and even weekly sale numbers from Wal-Mart. Although everyone is entitled to operate in the market in his or her own style, short-term traders have done little more than create increased volatility.

Justifiably so, there is much criticism on Wall Street of the focus on bottom-line reported quarterly earnings. Without long-term investors, corporate management has no incentive to think and act long term. Instead they are forced to make decisions based on keeping Wall Street analysts happy. A bad quarterly earnings number will often result in a massive decline in the stock price, only leading to further selling by the more active momentum crowd.

OTHER CRITERIA

If your primary focus is still on reported earnings when evaluating a company's growth potential, it is time to look into other criteria. One of the excellent technical research services I use, Dorsey Wright, explains why earnings do not drive their process:

> An important role of the SEC is to require public companies to disclose meaningful financial information, such as earnings. With this in mind, it is interesting to consider the comments of former SEC Chairman, William Donaldson, when he spoke at an event sponsored by the CFA Centre for Financial Market Integrity and the Business Roundtable Institute for Corporate Ethics in July 2006. "Imperfections in the accounting system make quarterly earnings numbers meaningless." (Associated Press, July 25, 2006.) It would be one thing for a technician to make such a statement, but it is entirely different coming from the establishment! He said that thanks to assumptions allowed under accounting standards, quarterly earnings numbers are, "so vague." Among the most important information used by a fundamental analyst for stock valuation are quarterly earnings. In fact, the theory underpinning fundamental analysis is that to truly make money in the long run, an investor must focus on the company itself rather than merely on the movement of its stock price. Earnings multiples are commonly used to determine a company's "intrinsic value." As they say, garbage in, garbage out. (Moody, 3)

Numerous studies have shown that the relative strength of a stock, or the measurement of a price trend that indicates how a stock is performing relative to other stocks within its industry, is one of the best tools for isolating improving companies. So much so that many prominent investors no longer even rely on reported earnings. These so-called momentum investors aim to capitalize on the continuance of existing price trends, as opposed to analyzing fundamentals. Momentum investors believe that, once a trend is established, it is more likely to move in the direction of the trend than to move against it. For those who trade on charts, valuation is not really important. They are simply following chart patterns and have no use for valuation measures. In fact, they may not even care what the company does. However, in my opinion, paying attention to valuation and knowing as much about a company as you can are critical requirements for investing your money.

One of the other troubling problems with using the age-old price-to-earnings (P/E) ratio as your guide is the cyclical earnings phenomena. When a cyclical company is running on all cylinders during the peak of a business cycle, its P/E is often quite low. To someone who invests in low-P/E companies, the stock looks cheap. This low P/E goads the buyer into accumulating a position near the cycle's high.

The problem occurs when a cycle turns downward. As companies begin to "take charges," as it is said, during periods of earnings regression, the P/E suddenly becomes very high due to artificially lower earnings. Following the theory that a high P/E represents too high of a valuation, investors often end up selling at exactly the wrong time when the stock is beaten down. As the share price drives lower, the P/E consequently goes higher. Rinse, repeat. My experience with the market itself is that each sector and industry seems to be cyclical, and no segment of the market is excluded.

When you can buy strong cash flow acceleration in a company trading at a discount to the current market valuation, you are effectively buying Free Earnings. This occurs when a company is delivering earnings and providing free cash flow, not just promising to be profitable sometime in the future. At this time, the company is growing even faster than the market is currently valuing the company's ability to do so. During this period the company will have a low PEG and GARP ratio and begin to show up on value investors' screens. Aside from the benefits delivered to shareholders, by generating free earnings a company puts itself in a position to do great things for their employees and communities as well. This is a wonderful time for the company and the right time to participate in its stock. It is this brief period in a company's life cycle that makes it a Magnet stock.

11

The Magnet System: Putting It All Together

No profession requires more hard work, intelligence, patience, and mental discipline than successful speculation.

—ROBERT RHEA

Even being right 3 or 4 times out of 10 should yield a person a fortune if he has the sense to cut his losses quickly on the ventures where he has been wrong.

—BERNARD BARUCH

To significantly outperform the market, you cannot be a closet indexer. You have to have a superior stock selection process. You also need to be willing to own a small number of holdings in your portfolio and then handle that portfolio with discipline. The passion that originally pulled me into this business revolved around my curiosity to find the best companies to invest in. The more than 20-year study of what makes a great company and what makes a great company to invest in has lead to the development of The Magnet® Stock Selection Process (MSSP). Although I obviously cannot share the math behind the actual ranking process, I can share the basic concept of our model. The MSSP has been developed over many years and has been enhanced though the generosity of the many great investors who have taken the time to confer with me. This long-term collaboration with many of the top investors of our time has had a profound influence on me. The least I can do is continue to give back to others. That is one of the major purposes of this book.

MSSP STRATEGIES

For a company's stock to appreciate rapidly, it must attract buyers. Ideally the company would be attractive to a wide spectrum of money managers because significant accumulation by "big money" is what drives stocks higher. Over the years of studying the most successful money managers of all time, I uncovered which factors interest the top value, growth, and momentum investors, and I became familiar with the screening process managers use to choose their holdings. By incorporating the best aspects of what these successful managers look for, I was able to create the MSSP. Not only did I combine the most robust factors contained in growth, value, and momentum investing, but I merged fundamental metrics with technical analysis (Figure 11.1).

The Magnet Stock Selection Process is a unique and proprietary process that blends growth, value, and momentum investing to achieve superior long-term risk-adjusted returns.

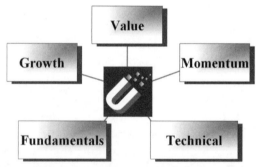

FIGURE 11.1   The Magnet Stock Selection Process incorporates several strategies
Source: Magnet Investment Group.

"Magnet" is also an acronym that represents the pillars of my stock picking philosophy.

Management must be outstanding, and the stock must have Momentum.

Acceleration of earnings, revenues, and margins is essential.

Growth rate must exceed current valuation.

New product or management may be the driver.

Emerging industries or products create great opportunities.

Timing needs to be technically opportune for price appreciation.

Management and Momentum

Nothing is more fundamentally important to a company than the capabilities of its management. Management must foster excellence, attract talented personnel, encourage employees to develop new products, deploy assets, market the company's product, and provide leadership. Management ownership of a substantial percentage of its stock is also very important. It would be foolish for those executives with large stock holdings to act in a manner detrimental to the best interests of the company. Competitive salaries that include generous management bonuses tied to enhancing shareholder value must be structured correctly. With so many recent high-profile abuses, this is obviously more critical than ever. A discussion of management can be found in each company's 10-K, 10-Q, quarterly, and annual reports to shareholders. Call the company's investor relations department to obtain these documents. They are also readily available on the Internet.

The momentum of a stock is the relationship of its share price to the overall market. This characteristic is commonly referred to as relative strength, although many market technicians have created their own methods of computing and describing momentum. The easiest way to follow and track the momentum or relative strength of a company, without using your computer, is by reading the *Investor's Business Daily* (IBD) and its weekly supplement, *Daily Graphs*. The relative strength line should be in an uptrend for at least a few months. It is best to find a stock whose relative strength line is hitting an annual high. In addition to price momentum, just as importantly, we measure financial momentum, also known as the acceleration of earnings, revenues, and margin growth.

Acceleration of Earnings, Revenues, and Margins

The acceleration of earnings, revenues, and margins is the central characteristic of a momentum growth company. There should be a minimum increase of 15 percent in quarterly revenues and earnings. This standard will eliminate most companies from consideration in

The Magnet Stock Selection Process. In fact, many companies in which I have invested will be growing at a rate of 30 percent or better. The modest 15 percent is used in this model to avoid eliminating larger companies that may dominate their industries but that are simply too big to maintain the same rapid growth rate as a smaller company.

Gross profit margins are also an important consideration. While the profit margins need not be continually rising, they should not show a decline from prior reporting periods. If the profit margins begin to slip, something is amiss at the company. It is common in today's stock market for a company to report great earnings, only to see the stock's price decline dramatically. Often when profit margins are declining, the most aggressive and astute momentum investors are selling. They are anticipating a future earnings slowdown, telegraphing a loss in momentum.

Management will often use acquisitions as a way to grow a company's revenue. It is important to watch profit margins to see whether the acquisition was a good fit for the company.

Growth at a Discount

Although individuals should own stocks in companies that maintain high growth rates, it is critical not to overpay for the stock based on its growth prospects. Ideally, when the stock is purchased, the current market valuation of a company, based on its P/E (price-to-earnings ratio) should be one-half its growth rate. Therefore, if the company can reasonably grow at a projected 20 percent rate over the next several years, an investment in this stock should be made when the market temporarily assigns it a P/E of 10. This valuation normally occurs either before the company becomes popular with investors or when the stock is temporarily out of favor.

It is not often you find large-cap companies growing at a very rapid clip. Sometimes it is fine to invest in a company growing their earnings at only 15 percent, as long as you are still buying at a discount to the growth rate.

New Product or Management

When a stock enters into an increasing price momentum phase, something new is usually occurring at the company. It may be new management that creates a change in direction or a new product that is creating a renewed awareness of the company. Companies usually exhibit rapid growth in both revenues and profit margins only when it introduces a new product.

New industries are spurred by new technologies, and these new companies are often growing the fastest. In today's momentum driven market, a stock hitting new highs will also gather new investors. A company's stock price tends to run up whenever something new catches the attention of investors.

Emerging Industry or Product

Companies in emerging industries represent some of the best investments. The dramatic advancements currently taking place in such fields as technology and medical science can result in extraordinary investment profits. Large gains can be made by experienced investors who possess a clear understanding of the future direction of technology and/or the medical fields. Learn as much as you can about emerging industries.

Since my first book came out ten years ago, new industries have emerged and are on the verge of blossoming. Fuel cell, nanotechnology, alternative energy, Internet security, and solar power companies were not even around ten years ago and have created tremendous profit opportunities for the astute investor.

Timing

Timing is critical to ensuring success in the stock market, as discussed in earlier chapters. Every investor must develop a method to answer the question, "When should I buy?" Once a stock has met the fundamental requirements of the Magnet model, I incorporate several technical indicators that enhance timing. These include moving averages, stochastics, MACD (moving averages converging diverging), relative strength, volume analysis, insider ownership, and point and figure charting.

One of the most disappointing results comes from buying stock in a great company at the wrong time—and not holding on. The result is the same as having made an investment in a subpar company: The investor loses money.

These six signposts of a Magnet evolved through my exposure and study of the greatest investors that came before me. Table 11.1

TABLE 11.1 Magnet Origins

Magnet Signpost	Primary Influence	Current Influences/Users
Management	Buffett, Fisher	Buffett
Acceleration of earnings, revenues and margins	Magnet, O'Shaughnessy	Louis Navellier, Jim Collins
Growth must exceed current valuation	Graham and Dodd, Buffett	GARP, PEG
New product or management may be the driver	O'Neil, Loeb	
Emerging industry or product creates great opportunity	O'Neil, Loeb, Lynch	
Timing needs to be right	Livermore, Darvis, Loeb, Dreyfus	Sperandeo, Stan Weinstein TCNet,

Source: The Magnet Investment Group.

gives you an idea of the influences and operators utilizing each of these main Magnet selection criteria.

BASICS OF THE MAGNET STOCK SELECTION PROCESS (MSSP)

The Magnet Stock Selection Process has been developed to isolate and find the best companies to invest in. Many years were spent developing a quantitative model to utilize proprietary ratios to rank companies. We use a quantitative model that screens for the best value, growth, and momentum criteria according to those unique investing styles. Top-line revenue growth leads our model, followed by profit margin acceleration. Companies that rank highly for us must be generating cash flow, while also trading at an acceptable valuation. These companies must have already started to appear on some radar screen, thereby creating positive price momentum. Ideally, we also want to find these Magnets early, when management is still receiving modest salaries, and owns a considerable percentage of the outstanding shares. This is the time in a company's growth phase that management is most focused on doing what is best for the company. This is the sweet spot of growth in the S-curve discussed in Chapter 5.

The Magnet System has been shown to work through independent studies on almost all of the market sectors and, just as importantly, across the full spectrum of the market, including large cap, mid cap, and small cap. Our model is able to identify those companies who are growing their financials rapidly, trading at a discount to their growth rate, and undergoing accumulation, thus showing superior potential price performance. However, the really high performance of our portfolios comes from several of the individual holdings producing outlier-level returns, not from all of our holdings. The Magnet Investment Group is therefore currently engaged in the implementation process of The Magnet Stock Selection Process through our managed accounts and funds. Given the observation that there can be only a few superlative companies, we have conducted a 25-year research project to determine exactly what makes a company more attractive than all others. By quantitatively searching for companies that are experiencing pricing power, accelerating top-line revenue growth, margin acceleration, and accelerating free cash flow—and not becoming preoccupied with "how the market looks"—we are able to focus on identifying the best companies. If the market continues to take these companies higher, and they continue to score out properly on our model, we will own them until their rank drops or until they fail to prove themselves as market leaders. Pessimistic conditions, like those we face at the time of this writing, provide the best buying opportunities.

The Magnet system targets the fastest growing companies that are still trading at a discount to their intrinsic value. Companies in this category are likely to enjoy dynamic earnings growth. We call these companies "Magnets." They tend to stimulate investor response and create powerful returns. The approach is designed to isolate the strongly performing stocks in the equity market. It involves a rigorous bottom-up stock screening and ranking process that evaluates each company, industry, and market sector based on numerous fundamental criteria. Companies that rank highly on our process tend to have some common characteristics:

- They have high top-line revenue growth.
- They are leaders within a market niche.

- They are internally financed by their growth.
- They have conservative accounting.

The most important factor driving all these characteristics is a sound management team. We have even devised a quantitative methodology of assessing management to make this important factor unbiased.

I believe that excess market returns can be achieved through the construction and management of a fundamentally sound portfolio of companies whose revenue growth and profit margins are accelerating above market expectations. We construct our own proprietary measures for company fundamentals, some of which are proxies for what would be earnings performance from corporate financial data. As a result, our Magnet analysis is not misled by reported earnings and responds much more directly to strong sales, low price-to-sales ratios, and other value measures taken from corporate balance sheets.

When I first introduced The Magnet Stock Selection Process several years ago, I suggested that the screening approach would gain in popularity. Now most stock market software packages include this feature. Utilizing our screening processes, the universe of companies can be quickly brought down to a manageable list to further investigate. Investors must understand a company's balance sheet enough to create individual simple screens that feel right for them. They can then establish a set of criteria that feels comfortable to them. You can select a combination of criteria, such as a minimal level of revenue growth, a maximum debt-to-equity level, or even a number of consecutive annual dividend increases. The individual investor now has a significant advantage over the big institutions. They can identify companies with strong fundamentals that are still too small to be picked up by the bigger institutional funds. Once the institutions find them and drive them higher, the real profits materialize. By just placing a few of these companies in your portfolio and then being patient, you can achieve outstanding results. Individuals willing to continue to do their homework to find these companies will be rewarded. The results are not only financially satisfying, but equally personally gratifying.

It is important to look at companies individually by both sector and market capitalization. For example, large caps trade differently than small caps, and most sectors are unique in their own right. Biotechnology companies cannot be compared directly to utilities. To keep our screened lists organized, we use a software package that is readily available to the public. As I manage our various funds according to our proprietary scoring system, it is critical to see companies organized in separate discrete lists. For this purpose I use a program called TCNet, which has won Software of the Year for 12 straight years in its category. Many of the charts I use as examples come directly from their charting system, preset with my own indicators. In the back of the book is a trial offer for you.

One of the ways we try to control volatility and continue to generate high returns is by adjusting the level of securities in our portfolios and the level of concentration of companies within a given sector. This can be illustrated by demonstrating the use of The Magnet Stock Selection Process within the S&P 500. First, we would rank all 500 companies through our process and put them in scored order. From there, we can take one of several approaches.

- A conservative approach would be for us to invest in the 60 top-ranked companies. If we wanted to reduce volatility, we could add the constraint that no single sector could represent more than 30 percent of the portfolio.
- A slightly more aggressive approach would be to invest in only the 35 to 40 top-ranked companies. Our expected return would significantly increase, but our volatility would increase as well.
- An even more aggressive approach would be to invest in just 20 of the top-ranked companies in the S&P 500.

Clearly, as we reduce the number of holdings in a given portfolio, the approach continues to move further away from the direction of relative performance and closer to providing a more absolute return. Holding fewer securities in this case clearly moves us further up the volatility scale, but the added returns justify the move. This is an approach of portfolio concentration through stock selection as opposed to simple broad diversification. A formal backtest using the MSSP to invest exclusively in the top-ranked S&P 500 companies is included in the Appendix.

The Magnet Stock Selection Process is a quantitative approach that assesses a company's ability to execute its business plan from a balance sheet perspective. As a result, the process works across all sectors and all market capitalizations. The strength of our process is that, through the use of the same system, we can manage assets in all segments of the market, from the biggest large caps down to the smallest tradable companies. We do not specialize in any one sector. Our system, because it is so thorough, is very discriminating. After all, only a few companies can simultaneously rank highly on our measures of growth, value, and momentum. I recognize that our more concentrated portfolios will be more volatile than widely diversified portfolios—both on the upside and downside for periods at a time. Because some view the intramonth volatility as risk, they may not feel comfortable being undiversified. Those unwilling to incur higher levels of volatility are forced to accept investment returns that may ultimately leave them short of their goals and financial needs.

Summary

The Magnet Stock Selection Process is a proprietary approach that blends the best of the traditional investment characteristics of growth, value, and momentum strategies to identify the best companies to invest in. To maintain strong cash flow for its future growth, a company must demonstrate growth of sales, margins, and cash flow. Companies that demonstrate this strong top-line growth and still trade with good value will rank highly in our system. We also need to see price appreciation or relative strength in the companies we invest in. This blend of growth, valuation, and momentum is expressed in our proprietary performance measures and then put through our unique ranking process to create an ordered list of stocks for the construction of our portfolios. Top-ranked Magnet companies are expected to perform well, and those with poor rankings are expected to underperform.

The MSSP is scientific by nature and practical in application. It started with the theory, was thoroughly back-tested, and is now in full implementation. Although we pride ourselves on being unique, we use several outside financial information services to confirm and, as importantly, challenge our findings. In the examples of current Magnet stocks that I share with you at the end of this chapter, I have included the charts, tables, and data I use from

Dorsey-Wright, Navellier, Market Grader, Stock Diagnostics, and Daily Graphs for additional support.

THE IMPORTANCE OF A MULTIFACTOR APPROACH

A very interesting article, titled "A Quantitative View of the Stock Market," appeared in the October 2008 issue of *Equities Magazine*. The article, by Richard Tortoriello from Standard & Poor's, discusses his extremely informative and well researched book, titled *Quantitative Strategies for Achieving Alpha*. In his article, Tortoriello discusses at length the importance of having a multifactor approach. To me, his article reads almost like a validation of our Magnet Stock Selection Process. In Tortoriello's words, "From a quantitative point of view, valuation and cash-flow generation are our two strongest basics—valuation and cash-flow factors should be included in almost all quantitative models or screens" (Tortoriello, 2008a, p. 15). He goes on to say:

> One major conclusion of our work is that fundamentals matter, valuations matter, and technicals matter. The investor looking to achieve strong stock market returns over a six-month to one and one-half year investment horizon would do well to consider all three of these factors.

Richard concludes:

> The seven basics presented above and covered in detail in my book provide investors with strategies that work in all three of these important areas. Another important conclusion is that quantitative analysis, qualitative analysis, and technical analysis, far from being unrelated subject areas, form mutually complementary disciplines—investors who learn the lessons taught by each are apt to increase their ability to make money consistently in stocks.

I thought Richard's article was so insightful that I contacted him to find out his opinion on diversification. It was very obvious from our conversation that he has done a tremendous amount of research on quantitative strategies, and his thoughts proved very interesting. Based on his work, Richard would hold no more than 20 to 30 companies at a time. He made a great additional point that quantitative screens can include one-time anomalies. You could see a one-time charge or benefit to earnings that is unsustainable and misleading. If he was blending a purely quantitative approach along with a qualitative second look to understand the companies even better, he would bring the portfolio down even further to only 15 companies.

LESSONS OF THE PAST

One of the things that separate the best investors from the rest is their ability to look back and learn from their own trading history. I was reminded early in my career to learn not only from my mistakes, but also from my successes. Al Frank, a legendary value investor, reminded me many years ago: "Learn as much from your winners as you do from your losers." To this day I continue to be a student of the market. As you know by now, I do not believe in buy and hold, but neither do I try to short-term trade the market. My ideal holding period would be forever, but unfortunately investments just do not turn out that way. Once an investment is made, we continue to monitor the company extensively. For a company to remain in our portfolio, it has to continue to rank highly on Magnet and also needs to continue to exhibit strong relative strength. Often, the market moves ahead of fundamentals. A company will break down in price on increasing volume, sending off warning signals, despite its apparently strong fundamentals. Following are a few Magnet experiences that were especially enlightening for me. Although I believe that investors need to learn from their own experiences, learning a few lessons from others may help too.

As each stock was purchased, I would open a due diligence file that would also provide me with an opportunity to look back upon and analyze the position of the company at the time of purchase. While reviewing these files to look for examples, I came across many ideas that I would like to share in this section. Basically, the essence of what I do requires that I follow the Magnet System without ego. Through the use of stop-loss strategies, I can make a purchase without hesitation because I am not risking the full investment. Over the years I have bought and sold shares in several hundred companies. The following actual trades come from my old files and include some of the original notes I sent to active clients at the time. Please remember that many ideas did not work so well.

CyberOptics (CYBE)

Early in my career, in 1995, CYBE showed up on top of the Magnet ranks. This tiny company had accelerating earnings, margins, and revenues, but it had not been found yet by many others. Notice the 1 percent ownership by funds and the tiny number of shares outstanding. Relative strength was breaking out to new highs, and I loved the product the company had (Figure 11.2).

As I was adding to the position, you can see on my letterhead I was asking my firm to begin making a market in the stock. Volume, still quite small, was increasing, as were the revenues and earnings. A few quarters later, the stock ranked out as the number one in IBD's Week in Review (Figure 11.3).

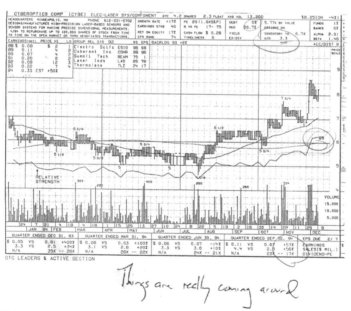

FIGURE 11.2   The CyberOptics recommendation

Source: DailyGraphs, Inc.

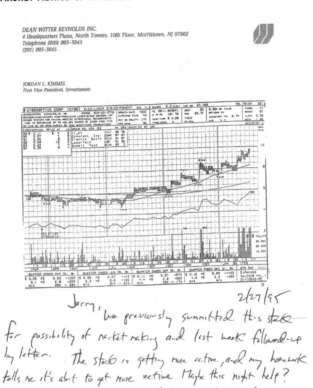

DEAN WITTER REYNOLDS INC.
4 Headquarters Plaza, North Towers, 10th Floor, Morristown, NJ 07962
Telephone (800) 993-3045
(201) 993-3045

JORDAN L. KIMMEL
First Vice President, Investments

2/27/95

Jerry,

I've previously summitted this stock for possibility of market making and last week followed-up by letter. The stock is getting more active, and my homework tells me it's about to get more active. Maybe this might help?

thank you, Jordan Kimmel
(800) 993-3045

cc. Art Roseberry, BRANCH MGER - 615.

FIGURE 11.3   The CyberOptics follow-up

Source: DailyGraphs, Inc.

CyberOptics was one of my first *big* winners. In addition to having all the right financials at the time, it also had a wonderful story. Miniaturization was a powerful, new commercial application and they were a leader. So many of my clients continued to call and ask when we were going to take our profits, that I ultimately took profits too soon. Because of our success in the stock, we went back to the well a few times and traded this stock very successfully. I still keep an eye out for another move (Figure 11.4).

If you had bought and held this stock from when we first found it until today, you would not have made a dime. For me to stay invested in a company, I need to see the combination of fundamentals and technicals.

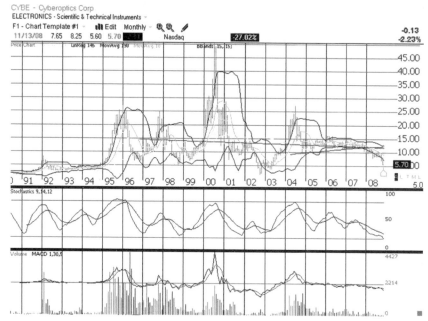

FIGURE 11.4   CyberOptics lately

Source: TCNet Telechart

Gaming Partners International Corp. (GPIC)

GPIC offered my clients tremendous profits from our entry point. I became involved with this stock more deeply than any other stock previously. Because I became frustrated with leaving too much on the table and because this company totally dominated their niche industry, I was prepared to hold this until it became discovered. Figure 11.5 shows the original chart that I had in my folder of a Dorsey Wright point and figure chart showing the first sell signal in a bullish trend, following a long consolidation. First sell signals almost invariably lead to a new high, and this was taking place right as Paulson Gaming became a top-ranked Magnet stock. The name of the company was later changed to Gaming Partners International Corp. From this buy point of around $4.00, the stock went on to a six-fold move.

Paul-Son Gaming Corporation (PSON)
Updated Through- 02/20/2004 (3.95 Down 0.05)
Gaming Favored (Status: **Bull Confirmed 84% Os**)
Wkly Mom: **Neg (3 Wks)**
Mkt RS = Sell, 12/22/2003; col=Os Peer RS = Sell, 02/03/2004; col=Os
Trend Chart Broke a Double Bottom on 02/03/2004
Tech Attrib: 1

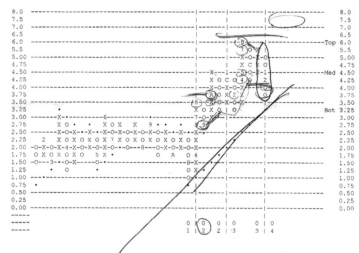

FIGURE 11.5   The buy signal for Gaming Partners International Corp

Source: Dorsey, Wright & Associates, Inc.

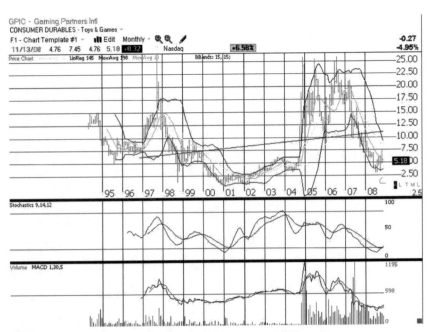

FIGURE 11.6   Gaming Partners International Corp. in the long term

Source: TCNet Telechart.

Despite my conclusion that this was a buy-and-hold, I learned a difficult lesson about staying with a company after it no longer ranks highly through the Magnet system (Figure 11.6).

Central European Distributors (CEDC)

Right near the bottom of the bear market of 2002, CEDC showed up on the top of Magnet's list. Notice the huge revenue and earnings growth. The margins were accelerating, something IBD did not show in these graphs. A more expensive supplemental service of IBD does reflect this. Notice also the very small institutional holdings of the company at the time. The relative strength was climbing all year and was now breaking out to new highs and the float was tiny at that time (Figure 11.7).

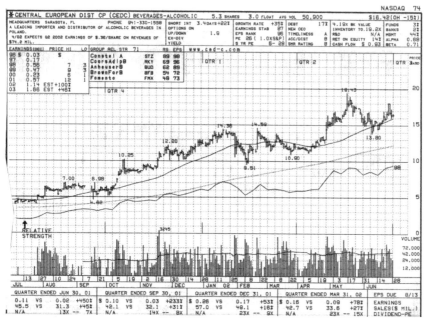

FIGURE 11.7   The CEDC buy signal

Source: DailyGraphs, Inc.

CEDC went on to be a truly fabulous stock for years. When you see stocks produce gains like CEDC did, you can see the benefits of using trailing stop-losses and the wonders of compounding. Just a few of these winners can be the difference between generating average returns and never needing to worry about money again (Figure 11.8).

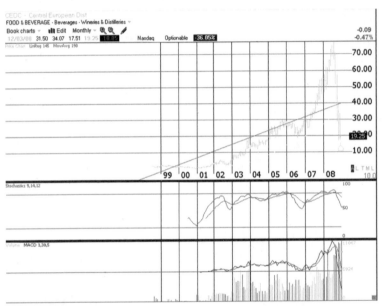

FIGURE 11.8   CEDC's long run up

Source: TCNet Telechart.

Allis-Chalmers Energy (ALY)

Revenues, margins, and earnings were all accelerating at this time for this small-cap oil service company. You see the relative strength breaking out to new annual highs, a small number of shares in the float, an AAA IBD ranking, and a modest P/E relative to the growth of the company. The stock was also generating a moving-average buy signal with the 50-day moving average crossing through the 200-day moving average—something that attracts technical buyers (Figure 11.9).

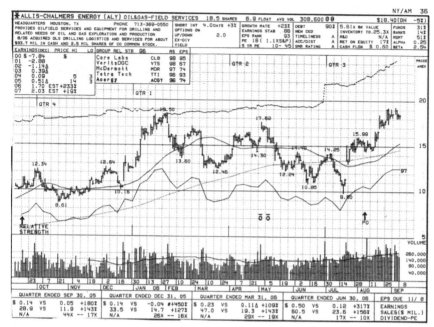

FIGURE 11.9   The Allis-Chalmers Energy buy signal

Source: DailyGraphs, Inc.

It is a little hard to see on the monthly chart shown in Figure 11.10, but ALY was getting more volatile. I saw a high-volume reversal and the Magnet ranking had dropped. That is all I needed to make the decision to sell. At this point of my career, I have learned not to fall in love with *any* company. The news at the time of the sell was incredibly bullish for this sector. A reminder: Stocks break down well ahead of bad news regarding the company or its industry. At the time of writing, oil is diving back to $40. per barrel after flirting with $150 per barrel just a few months ago (Figure 11.10).

Home Depot (HD)

Looking at long-term charts can be very revealing. While HD was by now a household name, it had gone sideways for years while it was consolidating from a huge run from the mid-1980s to 1992. As the stock emerged from its base, it was now poised for another big run—and indeed it did run again (Figure 11.11).

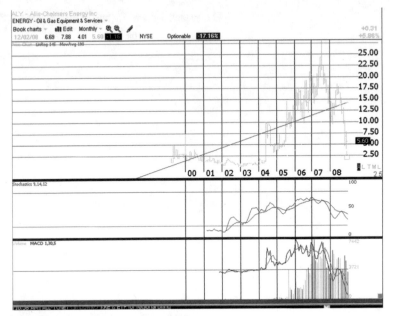

FIGURE 11.10   Allis-Chalmers Energy lately

Source: TCNet Telechart.

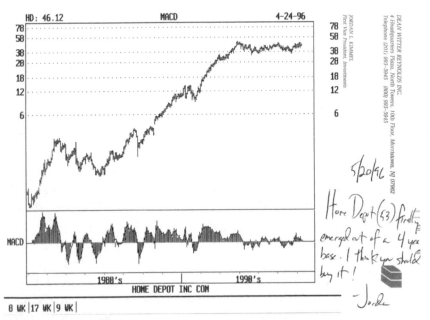

FIGURE 11.11   Home Depot's long run

Source: Telescan.

Following several years of consolidation, Home Depot had an explosive move to the upside. Once a quality stock breaks out of multiyear base, investors are often surprised by the magnitude of the move (Figure 11.12).

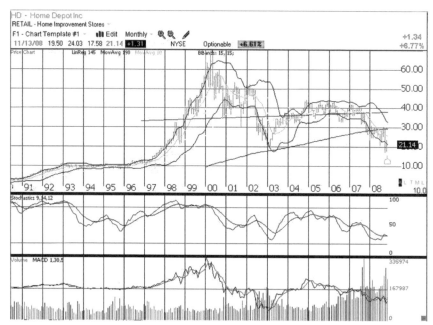

FIGURE 11.12   Home Depot lately

Source: TCNet Telechart.

A good company does not always make a good investment. Combining fundamentals with technicals is critical. Notice that, once this dramatic move was completed, the stock fell significantly again. Once an uptrend is broken, do not confuse a good company with a good investment.

Laboratory Corp of America (LH)

This is the point and figure (P&F) chart from Dorsey Wright I was reviewing in late 2000. I always review all trades, and you can see from my original note that I was disappointed we sold too soon. I like to keep a P&F chart for each stock we hold in our portfolios (Figures 11.13 and 11.14).

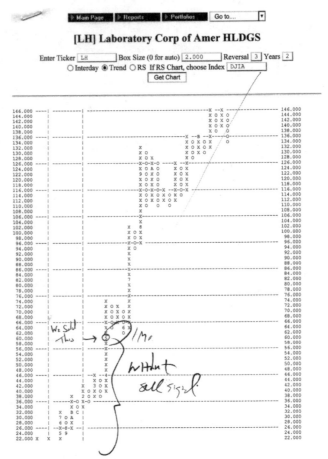

FIGURE 11.13   Laboratory Corp. of America's sell signal

Source: Dorsey Wright & Associates.

Southern Peru Copper (PCU)

This DailyGraphs chart shows the fundamentals that we look for in a Magnet stock. Note, in comparing it to the long-term chart that we show for the sell of PCU, that the stock had split a couple of times. Along with tremendous revenue and earnings growth, there were two dividend increases in the same year—a sign of real strength. This was a pure winner for us. We collected a tremendous amount of dividends and set a trailing stop-loss. When we were

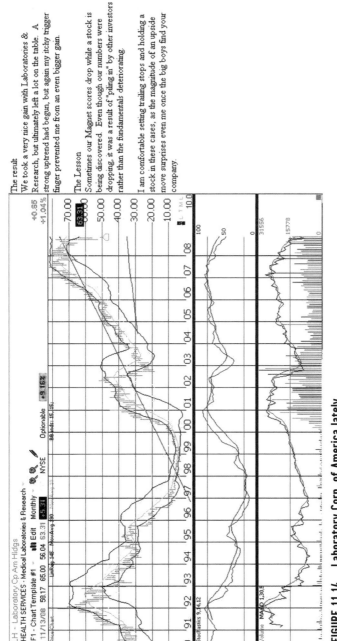

The result

We took a very nice gain with Laboratories & Research, but ultimately left a lot on the table. A strong uptrend had begun, but again my itchy trigger finger prevented me from an even bigger gain.

The Lesson

Sometimes our Magnet scores drop while a stock is being discovered. Even though our numbers were dropping, it was a result of "piling in" by other investors rather than the fundamentals deteriorating.

I am comfortable setting trailing stops and holding a stock in these cases, as the magnitude of an upside move surprises even me once the big boys find your company.

FIGURE 11.14 Laboratory Corp. of America lately

Source: TCNet Telechart.

ultimately stopped out, we were disappointed because it felt like we were losing an old friend (Figure 11.15).

After looking at the dramatic drop that PCU ultimately experienced once it stopped ranking, I have become more of a believer in our process than ever before. Never fall in love with a stock (Figures 11.16 and 11.17).

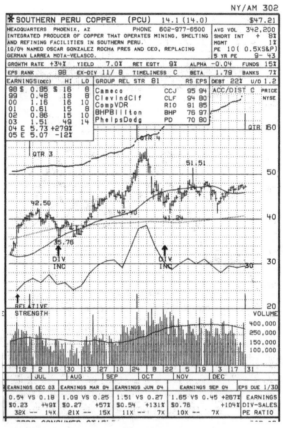

FIGURE 11.15   Southern Peru Copper fundamentals

Source: DailyGraphs, Inc.

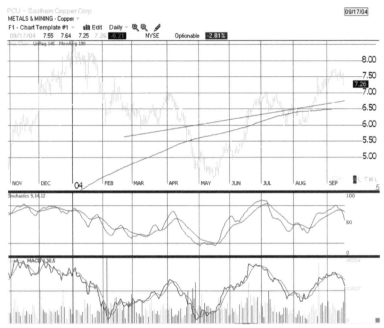

FIGURE 11.16   Southern Peru Copper buy signal

Source: TCNet Telechart.

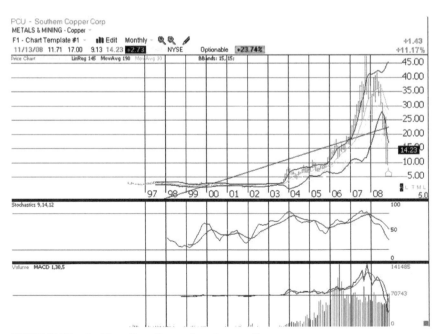

FIGURE 11.17   Southern Peru Copper long term, sell

Source: TCNet Telechart.

First Marblehead (FMD)

The set up and entry points for FMD looked almost perfect. It had one of the highest Magnet rankings at the time because the company was showing great earnings growth relative to its valuation, very high insider ownership, low debt, and strong relative strength. The series of insider sells highlighted at the bottom of the chart were troublesome to me, but the very high level of insider ownership was still impressive. What was unusual for a Magnet stock was that quarterly sales were declining (Figures 11.18 and 11.19).

FIGURE 11.18   First Marblehead buy signal

Source: DailyGraphs Inc.

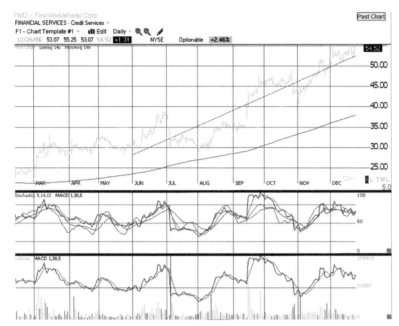

FIGURE 11.19   First Marblehead initial runup

Source: TCNet Telechart.

Only one earnings report later, the Magnet ranking on FMD had dropped significantly. Also, a further drop in revenue was accompanied by a drop in profit margins. Interestingly, the price-to-earnings ratio was lower, and the earnings estimates for next year were increased by the analysts. The stock price was virtually unchanged from our buy price; it was the sharp drop in the Magnet rank that compelled us to sell. This company was involved with the securitization of school loans and would go on to quickly lose over 90 percent in value within a short period after our sale. There was no way I could see the credit crisis that was just about to unfold. Luckily for us, by now I have learned to never stick with *any* stock when we see a large or sudden drop in the Magnet rank (Figures 11.20 and 11.21).

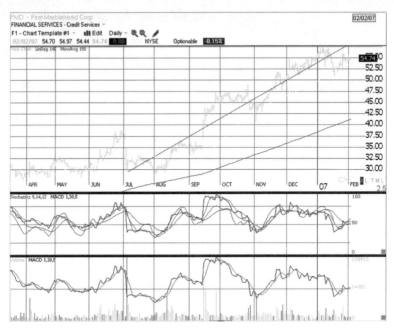

FIGURE 11.20   First Marblehead sell signal

Source: TCNet Telechart.

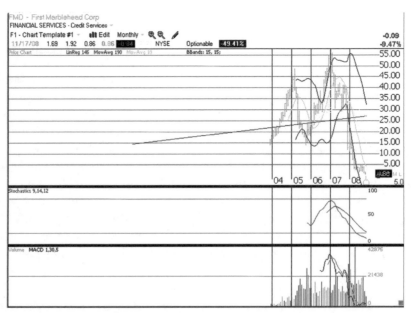

FIGURE 11.21   First Marblehead collapse

Source: TCNet Telechart.

Rick's Cabaret (RICK)

RICK was one of the most highly ranked companies on the Magnet ranking system in March 2008. The company was completely unfollowed by Wall Street. It had excellent sales, earnings, and margins, and each was accelerating. Even though much of the growth was occurring via acquisitions, as long as margins are increasing, usually the acquisitions are beneficial and accretive. Again, because I use stop-losses, once a company appears with a rank as high as RICK's had at the time, I trusted the system and start buying (Figure 11.22).

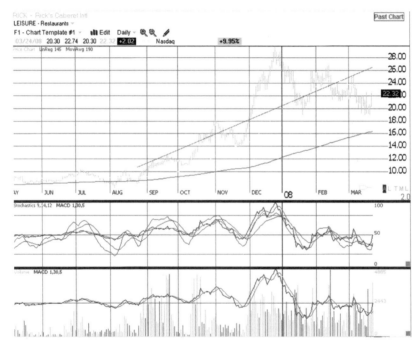

FIGURE 11.22   The chart for Rick's Cabaret

Source: TCNet Telechart.

Within a couple of weeks of buying RICK, the stock sold off on huge volume following a pretty good earnings report. Because of the very solid earnings numbers, despite the fact that the momentum factors in the Magnet system went lower, the overall Magnet rank stayed high. No difference: We were stopped out with a little more than a 20 percent loss. I use a fairly liberal 20 percent stop level because I do not want to get whipsawed and lose a stock position due just to minor price movements. Also, I use mental stops that I trigger myself instead of leaving a true stop with a market maker. The reasons are obvious to anyone with real experience in the market (Figure 11.23).

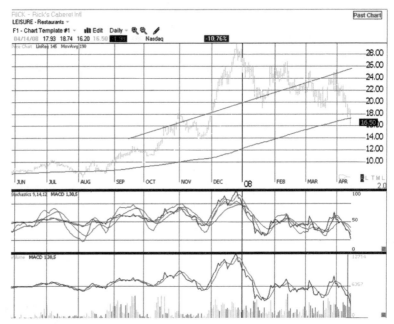

FIGURE 11.23   The selloff in Rick's Cabaret

Source: TCNet Telechart.

RICK stock stabilized soon after we were stopped out. By coincidence, I met the founder and CEO at a conference that I was speaking at and was impressed by him and what I heard and saw. Because RICK still ranked highly, I bought back in. Remember, just because you are stopped out, it does not mean you cannot go back in if the stock still has everything you are looking for. As it turns out, we were stopped out again! This time I set my stop a little closer, only because the previous selloff took place with such high volume.

The stock went much lower after we sold. As we go to print, I am not sure whether the problem was with the company or just an awful market environment, but it really does not matter. Large losses can result for 101 different reasons. I just want to avoid them, and stop-losses are there to prevent them (Figures 11.24 and 11.25).

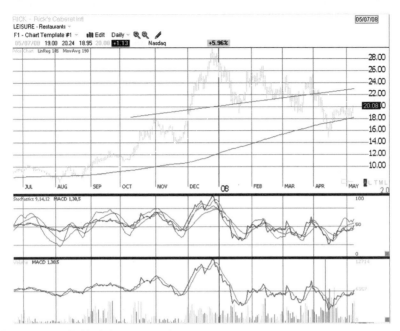

FIGURE 11.24   Rick's Cabaret repurchase

Source: TCNet Telechart.

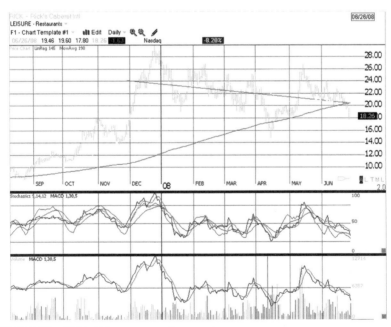

FIGURE 11.25   Rick's Cabaret stopped out again

Source: TCNet Telechart.

TOP-RANKED MAGNET STOCKS

Earlier in the book I exposed the problems and shortcomings of asset allocation and diversification. In this chapter I offer a solution: using a robust quantitative stock selection process like Magnet and being willing to hold fewer companies in your portfolio. My goal in this book follows the thought process of "teaching a man to fish" rather than "giving him a fish each day." However, my experience in the media reminds me that nobody wants me to leave the room without sharing the "top-ranked Magnet stocks of the day."

To conclude the book, I have included a list of the top 40 highest-ranked stocks according to the MSSP as we go to print. I have taken an additional step by conducting a secondary review and eliminating the top-ranked stocks that do not meet our relative strength standards, bringing the portfolio down to just 20 top Magnet stocks. As a student of the market, it will be interesting to me to see in the future if the 20-stock list (Figure 11.27) outperforms the 40-stock list (Figure 11.26). I expect it will. (Also see Louis Navellier's data from NavellierGrowth.com for his analysis of our Top-Ranked 20 Magnet Stocks as of April 15, 2009 in Figure 11.28.)

It is a particularly interesting time to build a portfolio. With the severe drubbing of a sharp bear market, very few stocks are showing any relative strength. We are in a state of deleveraging, and mass redemptions are taking place in mutual and hedge funds. Although it may be a great time to invest because valuations have fallen tremendously, a few companies will be overlooked simply because their relative strengths are so poor. As I encourage investors to research a stock or portfolio as comprehensively as possible before investing, I have also included an analysis of each company in our 20-stock portfolio provided by a few of the services that we subscribe to that have been generous enough to allow us to reprint their work (Figures 11.29 through 11.48).

These 40- and 20-stock portfolios were originally generated on December 1st, 2008. As we came to completion of the book in mid April of 2009, I wanted to update the portfolio with as fresh of a list as possible. Five stocks were replaced in the same way we would in managing active funds. The five stock symbols of the companies that were removed from the 20 stock portfolio were ISYS, CBST, FSYS, QCOR, and AFAM—they all ranked out at the time, but either dropped in ranking or lost relative strength and were replaced with currently higher ranking Magnet stocks. This portfolio, from December 1st, 2008 through April 15th, 2009, declined by roughly 1% while the S&P500 declined over 10%.

I remind you that this current list is not a set of recommendations or a buy list. Despite my experience, I am not an analyst, something compliance officers like to remind everybody. Markets change, and the Magnet rankings can change quickly. I would expect this list to do well, but I again remind you that rankings change frequently and there are no guarantees in any market. Finally, just as I eat my own cooking, the funds I manage will already be invested in many of the companies on this list. As time goes on, I will hold only the ones that continue to rank highly on the Magnet System. In practice, we allow The Magnet Stock Selection Process to deselect and reselect stocks within our portfolios each month. Do your own homework. Profitable investing lies ahead!

FIGURE 11.26 Magnet Investment Group's top-ranked 40 Magnet stocks (April 15, 2009)

Company	Ticker	Sector	Magnet Growth Ratio	Annual Sales Ratio	Quarterly Sales Ratio	OPM ACC	Price to Sales	Price to Earnings	% Held by Institution	Market Cap ($mil)	Total Magnet Score
Randgold Rsrcs	GOLD	Basic Matl	81.9	522.3	1898.7	12.1	1.77	33.0	67.2	2,914	797
Ebix Inc	EBIX	Tech	97.6	63.7	67.1	15.782	3.69	12.8	14.6	246	760
Soc Quimica Min	SQM	Basic Matl	141.1	43.0	79.1	12.283	3.53	13.9	11.7	5,935	710
Baytex Energy	BTE	Energy	110.7	147.2	165.9	4.9	1.28	5.8	27.5	1,466	655
Permian Bas Rt	PBT	Energy	N/A	79.8	90.2	0.289	7.26	N/A	14.1	816	645
Excel Maritime	EXM	Transport	216.5	273.8	435.6	7.325	0.20	0.6	85.0	114	610
Stepan Co	SCL	Basic Matl	254.0	23.4	27.7	0.584	0.28	18.7	71.0	436	610
Vse Corp	VSEC	Indus Prod	37.8	69.5	75.4	-0.028	0.18	9.4	45.6	170	593
Questcor Pharma	QCOR	Health	3688.1	259.9	57.5	46.362	5.95	11.9	71.3	568	590
Pricesmart Inc	PSMT	Retail/Whole	120.8	25.6	26.5	3.88	0.36	10.2	42.0	404	575
Vascular Solutn	VASC	Health	309.9	16.4	15.9	17.325	1.93	40.1	15.9	114	563
Terra Nitrogen	TNH	Basic Matl	N/A	55.0	83.1	26.458	2.13	6.8	9.3	1,868	561
Amer Caresource	ANCI	Health	196.9	211.4	124.9	N/A	2.37	53.1	26.2	120	558
Unibanco-Gdr	UBB	Finance	477.6	72.5	157.5	0.236	1.33	18.9	33.1	17,945	558
Insteel Inds	IIN	Indus Prod	82.5	18.3	42.5	3.734	0.48	3.9	85.6	171	558
Almost Family	AFAM	Health	27.9	46.3	81.2	3.563	1.96	23.3	60.2	357	553
Kearny Finl Cp	KRNY	Finance	105.6	-5.1	-1.5	-2.008	8.83	127.7	14.1	900	548
Compass Minerls	CMP	Basic Matl	125.8	47.3	68.5	3.894	1.64	14.7	94.8	1,815	548

Cal-Maine Foods	CALM	ConsStpl	136.4	42.1	15.2	9.582	0.64	4.1	98.7	600	545
Integral Sys/Md	ISYS	Tech	53.0	31.0	14.0	2.036	2.56	25.8	92.6	411	538
Brasil Telecom	BTM	Utilities	N/A	76.4	359.0	6.614	0.26	14.6	5.5	2,062	533
Vaalco Energy	EGY	Energy	64.1	80.8	57.5	1.93	1.93	9.5	65.2	367	530
World Fuel Svcs	INT	Energy	37.6	61.7	51.1	-0.06	0.05	10.9	88.1	1,062	528
Life Ptnrs Hldg	LPHI	Finance	N/A	60.7	35.9	10.692	4.91	20.7	24.4	424	510
Southwestrn Ene	SWN	Utilities	137.0	102.3	124.2	2.424	5.33	24.0	91.2	11,795	500
Bp Prudhoe Bay	BPT	Energy	N/A	18.1	40.5	0.029	6.93	N/A	12.5	1,511	497
Myriad Genetics	MYGN	Health	267.2	101.3	45.0	54.601	7.61	39.8	95.3	2,733	492
Mosaic Co/The	MOS	Basic Matl	400.0	85.9	114.7	14.326	1.11	4.6	33.7	13,483	490
Crawford & Co B	CRD.B	Business Serv	N/A	8.3	9.0	0.569	0.51	N/A	25.2	569	474
Potash Sask	POT	Basic Matl	238.7	84.6	134.5	18.984	2.09	6.4	83.0	18,798	470
Meadow Valley	MVCO	Construction	42.8	10.5	10.6	1.12	0.23	8.4	57.6	52	453
Take-Two Inter	TTWO	ConsDsry	192.6	57.0	109.6	10.344	0.63	8.1	91.4	943	453
Bp Plc	BP	Energy	85.2	41.5	43.6	1.398	0.44	5.0	19.6	170,269	448
Sabine Rlty Tr	SBR	Energy	N/A	39.2	62.9	1.305	7.21	N/A	7.4	614	445
Prospect Cap Cp	PSEC	Finance	65.1	97.3	128.9	8.004	3.73	5.4	29.3	373	445
Fisher Comm Inc	FSCI	ConsDsry	344.5	6.0	1.7	15.533	1.16	6.9	74.6	196	444
Axsys Tech Inc	AXYS	Tech	38.3	26.6	39.9	2.917	3.38	33.6	89.8	776	437
Allianz Ag-Adr	AZ	Finance	80.8	-28.4	4.3	2.346	0.39	0.5	2.6	37,274	436
Contango Oil&Gs	MCF	Energy	N/A	449.2	409.7	39.0	5.0	N/A	71.4	884	436
Telecommun Sys	TSYS	Tech	N/A	27.4	48.3	7.696	1.96	24.7	65.6	348	430

Source: The Magnet Investment Group.

157

FIGURE 11.27 Magnet Investment Group's top-ranked 20 Magnet stocks (April 15, 2009)

Company	Ticker	Sector	Magnet Growth Ratio	Annual Sales Ratio	Quarterly Sales Ratio	OPM ACC	Price to Sales	Price to Earnings	% Held by Institution	Market cap ($mil)	Total Magnet Score
Randgold Rsrcs	GOLD	Basic Matl	81.9	522.3	1898.7	12.1	1.77	33.0	67.2	2,914	797
Ebix Inc	EBIX	Tech	97.6	63.7	67.1	15.782	3.69	12.8	14.6	246	760
Soc Quimica Min	SQM	Basic Matl	141.1	43.0	79.1	12.283	3.53	13.9	11.7	5,935	710
Permian Bas Rt	PBT	Energy	N/A	79.8	90.2	0.289	7.26	N/A	14.1	816	645
Excel Maritime	EXM	Transport	216.5	273.8	435.6	7.325	0.20	0.6	85.0	114	610
Vse Corp	VSEC	Indus Prod	37.8	69.5	75.4	-0.028	0.18	9.4	45.6	170	593
Pricesmart Inc	PSMT	Retail/Whole	120.8	25.6	26.5	3.88	0.36	10.2	42.0	404	575
Vascular Solutn	VASC	Health	309.9	16.4	15.9	17.325	1.93	40.1	15.9	114	563
Terra Nitrogen	TNH	Basic Matl	N/A	55.0	83.1	26.458	2.13	6.8	9.3	1,868	561
Amer Caresource	ANCI	Health	196.9	211.4	124.9	N/A	2.37	53.1	26.2	120	558
Unibanco-Gdr	UBB	Finance	477.6	72.5	157.5	0.236	1.33	18.9	33.1	17,945	558
Compass Minerls	CMP	Basic Matl	125.8	47.3	68.5	3.894	1.64	14.7	94.8	1,815	548
World Fuel Svcs	INT	Energy	37.6	61.7	51.1	-0.06	0.05	10.9	88.1	1,062	528
Myriad Genetics	MYGN	Health	267.2	101.3	45.0	54.601	7.61	39.8	95.3	2,733	492
Mosaic Co/The	MOS	Basic Matl	400.0	85.9	114.7	14.326	1.11	4.6	33.7	13,483	490
Potash Sask	POT	Basic Matl	238.7	84.6	134.5	18.984	2.09	6.4	83.0	18,798	470
Bp Plc	BP	Energy	85.2	41.5	43.6	1.398	0.44	5.0	19.6	170,269	448
Allianz Ag-Adr	AZ	Finance	80.8	-28.4	4.3	2.346	0.39	0.5	2.6	37,274	436
Telecommun Sys	TSYS	Tech	N/A	27.4	48.3	7.696	1.96	24.7	65.6	348	430

Source: The Magnet Investment Group.

FIGURE 11.28 Louis Navellier's Portfolio Grader Pro top-ranked 20 Magnetic stocks, portfolio grade B (April 15, 2009)

Portfolio Grade	B	Total Stock Grade	Quant. Grade	Fund. Grade	Sales Growth	Operating Margin Growth	Earnings Growth	Earnings Momentum	Earnings Surprises	Analyst Earnings Revisions	Cash Flow	Return on Equity
American Careso	ANCI	A	A	B	A	C	A	B	F	D	B	A
Allianz SE (ADS)	AZ	C	C	C	D	D	D	D	D	D	B	B
BP PLC (ADS)	BP	D	D	C	F	C	D	D	B	D	C	A
CMP Compass Mineral	CMP	C	C	B	A	A	A	B	F	D	B	A
Ebix Inc.	EBIX	A	A	B	A	A	A	B	C	C	A	A
Excel Maritime	EXM	D	D	B	A	A	A	F	A	F	A	A
Randgold Resour	GOLD	B	A	C	D	C	C	D	B	A	C	C
World Fuel Serv	INT	A	A	B	F	A	A	B	B	A	A	B
Mosaic Co.	MOS	D	D	C	F	A	D	D	F	D	A	A
Myriad Genetics	MYGN	A	A	B	A	C	C	C	B	A	B	A
Permian Basin R	PBT	D	F	B	C	B	B	C	C	D	A	A
Potash Corp. of	POT	D	D	B	A	A	A	D	F	D	A	A

(Continued)

FIGURE 11.28   *(Continued)*

PriceSmart Inc.	PSMT	D	D	B	B	A	A	D	C	C	B
Sociedad Quimic	SQM	A	A	B	A	A	A	A	C	C	A
Terra Nitrogen	TNH	B	B	C	C	A	C	D	C	C	A
Tele Communicati	TSYS	A	A	B	A	A	B	F	B	A	B
Vascular Soluti	VASC	B	B	B	C	A	A	A	C	C	B
VSE Corp.	VSEC	A	A	B	A	B	B	B	C	A	A

Source: NavellierGrowth.com.

160

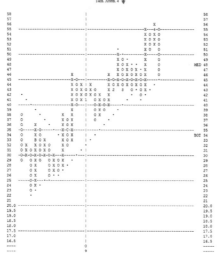

FIGURE 11.29A   Randgold Resources Limited

Source: Dorsey Wright & Associates.

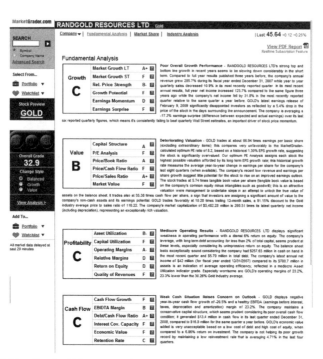

FIGURE 11.29B   Randgold Resources Limited

Source: MarketGrader.com.

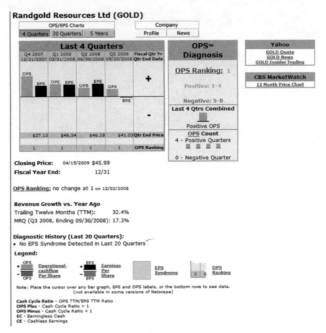

FIGURE 11.29C   Randgold Resources Limited

Source: StockDiagnostics.com.

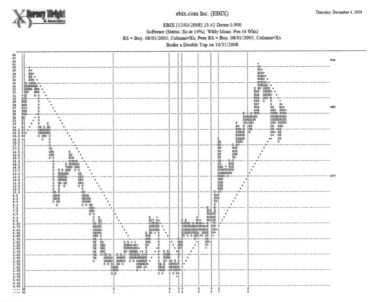

FIGURE 11.30A   Ebix Inc.

Source: Dorsey Wright & Associates.

FIGURE 11.30B   Ebix Inc.

Source: MarketGrader.com.

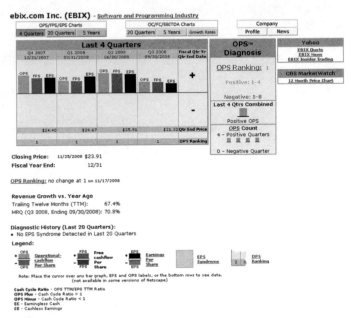

FIGURE 11.30C   Ebix Inc.

Source: StockDiagnostics.com.

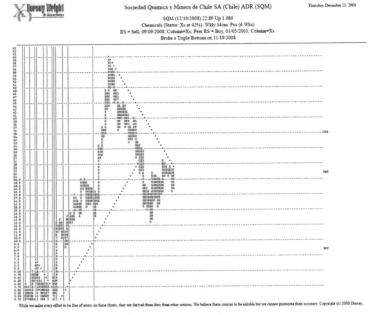

FIGURE 11.31A   Sociedad Quimica y Minera de Chile SA

Source: Dorsey Wright & Associates.

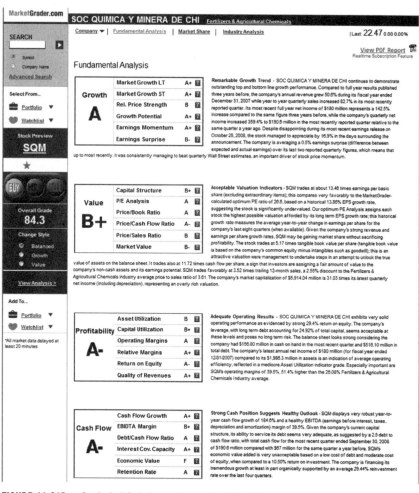

FIGURE 11.31B   Sociedad Quimica y Minera de Chile SA

Source: MarketGrader.com.

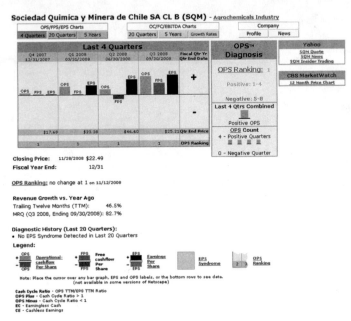

FIGURE 11.31C   Sociedad Quimica y Minera de Chile SA

Source: StockDiagnostics.com.

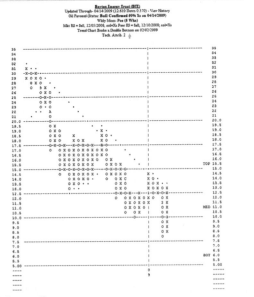

FIGURE 11.32A   Baytex Energy Trust

Source: Dorsey Wright & Associates.

FIGURE 11.32B   Baytex Energy Trust

Source: MarketGrader.com.

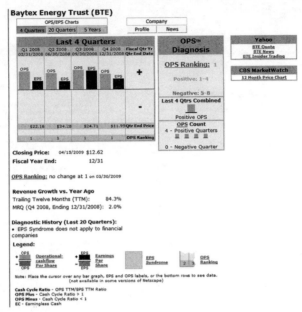

FIGURE 11.32C   Baytex Energy Trust

Source: StockDiagnostics.com.

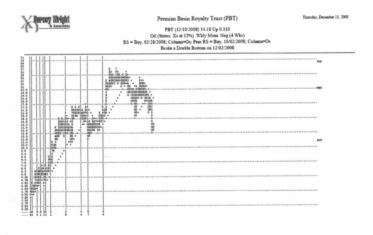

FIGURE 11.33A   Permian Basin Royalty Trust

Source: Dorsey Wright & Associates.

FIGURE 11.33B   Permian Basin Royalty Trust

Source: MarketGrader.com.

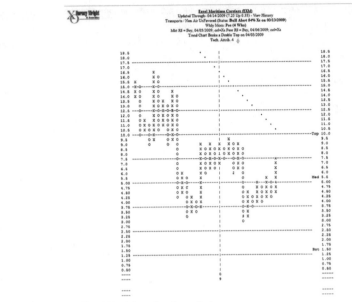

FIGURE 11.34A   Excel Maritime Carriers, Ltd.

Source: Dorsey Wright & Associates.

FIGURE 11.34B   Excel Maritime Carriers, Ltd.

Source: MarketGrader.com.

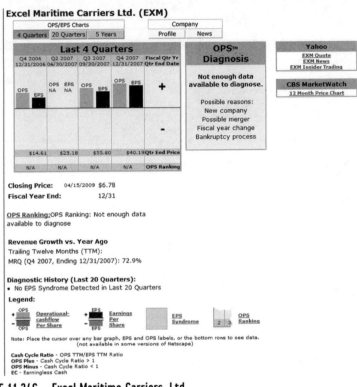

FIGURE 11.34C   Excel Maritime Carriers, Ltd.

Source: StockDiagnostics.com.

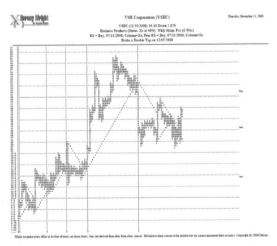

FIGURE 11.35A   VSE Corporation

Source: Dorsey Wright & Associates.

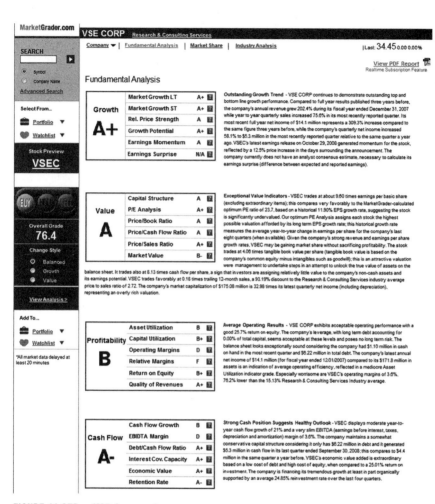

FIGURE 11.35B   VSE Corporation

Source: MarketGrader.com.

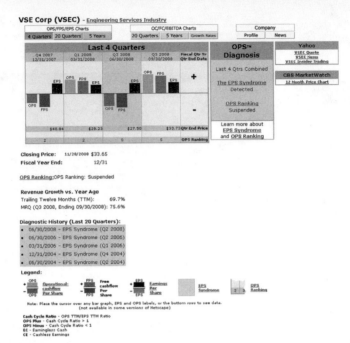

FIGURE 11.35C   VSE Corporation

Source: StockDiagnostics.com.

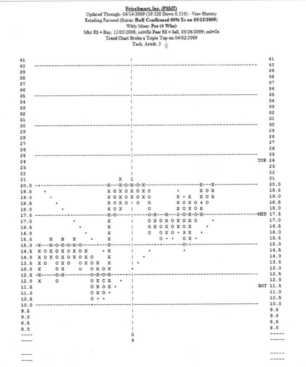

FIGURE 11.36A   PriceSmart Inc.

Source: Dorsey Wright & Associates.

FIGURE 11.36B   PriceSmart Inc.

Source: MarketGrader.com.

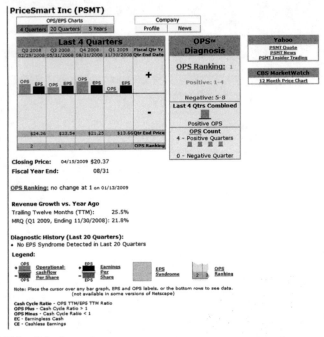

FIGURE 11.36C   PriceSmart Inc.

Source: StockDiagnostics.com.

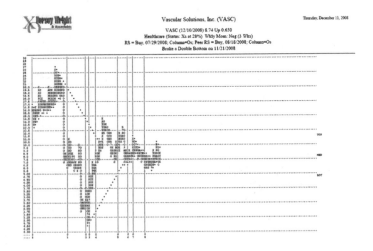

FIGURE 11.37A   Vascular Solutions, Inc.

Source: Dorsey Wright & Associates.

FIGURE 11.37B   Vascular Solutions, Inc.

Source: MarketGrader.com.

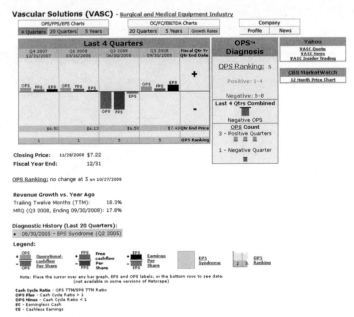

FIGURE 11.37C   Vascular Solutions, Inc.

Source: StockDiagnostics.com.

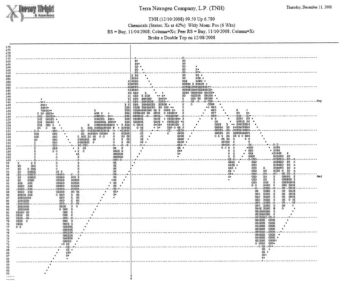

FIGURE 11.38A   Terra Nitrogen Company

Source: Dorsey Wright & Associates.

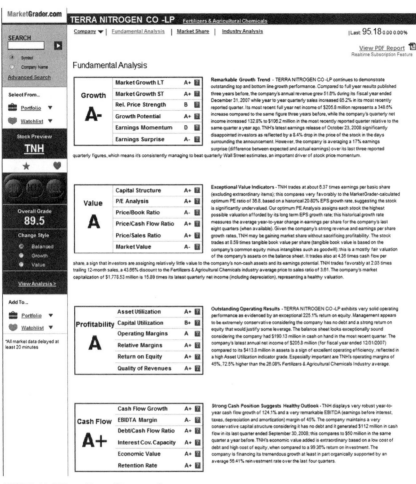

FIGURE 11.38B   Terra Nitrogen Company

Source: MarketGrader.com.

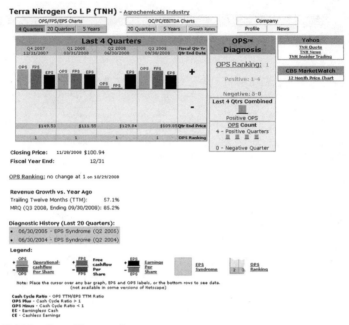

FIGURE 11.38C   Terra Nitrogen Company

Source: StockDiagnostics.com.

FIGURE 11.39A   American Caresource Holdings, Inc.

Source: Dorsey Wright & Associates.

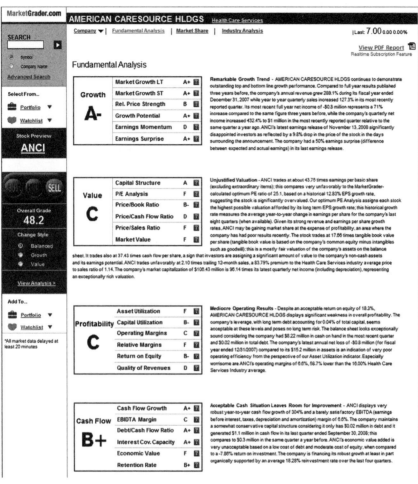

FIGURE 11.39B American Caresource Holdings, Inc.

Source: MarketGrader.com.

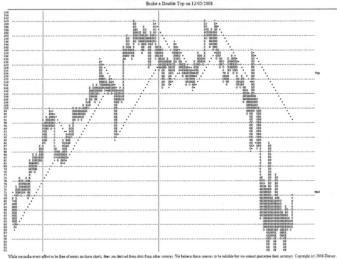

FIGURE 11.40A   Unibanco

Source: Dorsey Wright & Associates.

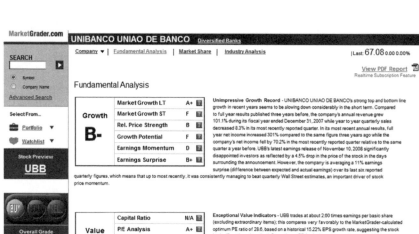

FIGURE 11.40B   Unibanco

Source: MarketGrader.com.

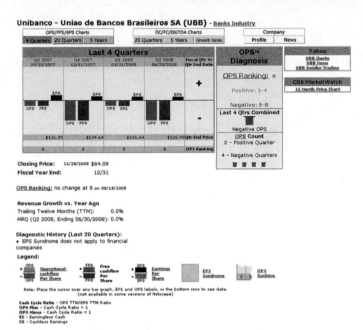

FIGURE 11.40C   Unibanco

Source: StockDiagnostics.com

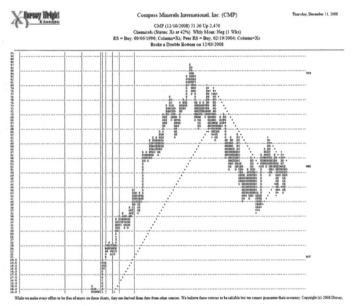

FIGURE 11.41A   Compass Minerals International, Inc.

Source: Dorsey Wright & Associates.

FIGURE 11.41B   Compass Minerals International, Inc.

Source: MarketGrader.com.

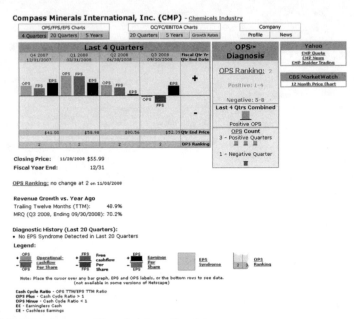

FIGURE 11.41C   Compass Minerals International, Inc.

Source: StockDiagnostics.com.

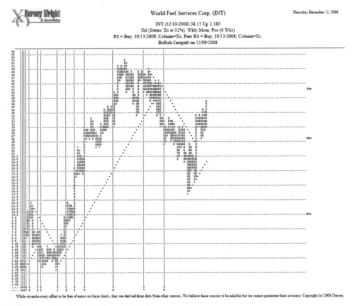

FIGURE 11.42A   World Fuel Services Corp.

Source: Dorsey Wright & Associates.

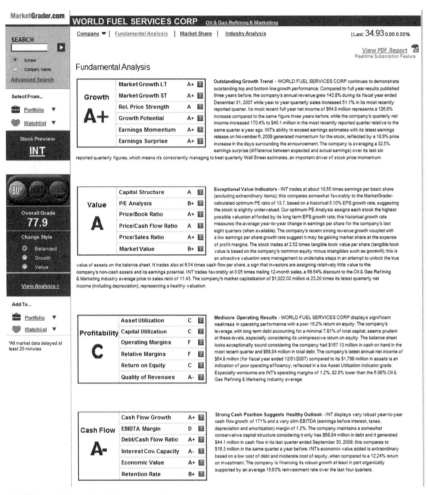

FIGURE 11.42B   World Fuel Services Corp.

Source: MarketGrader.com.

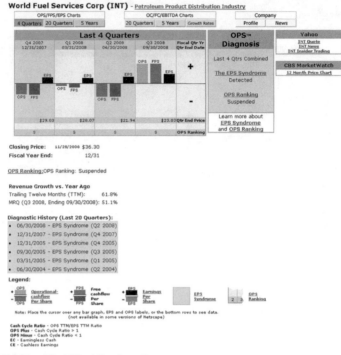

FIGURE 11.42C   World Fuel Services Corp.

Source: StockDiagnostics.com.

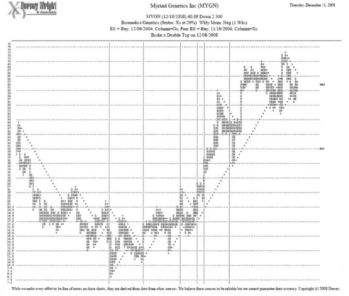

FIGURE 11.43A   Myriad Genetics, Inc.

Source: Dorsey Wright & Associates.

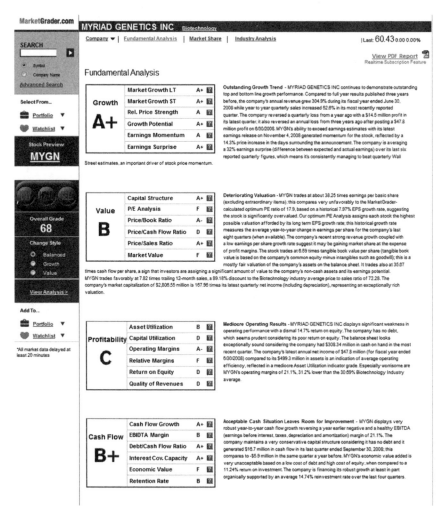

FIGURE 11.43B Myriad Genetics, Inc.

Source: MarketGrader.com.

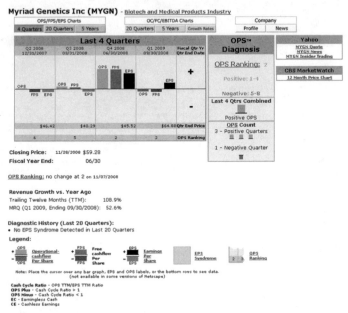

FIGURE 11.43C   Myriad Genetics, Inc.

Source: StockDiagnostics.com.

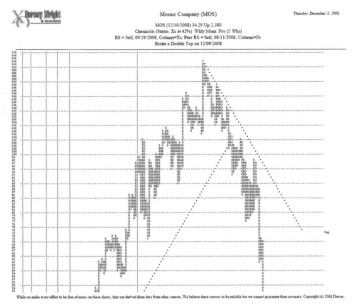

FIGURE 11.44A   Mosaic Company

Source: Dorsey Wright & Associates.

FIGURE 11.44B   Mosaic Company

Source: MarketGrader.com.

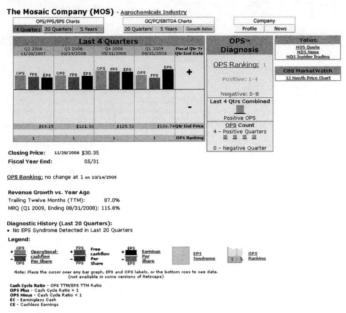

FIGURE 11.44C   Mosaic Company

Source: StockDiagnostics.com.

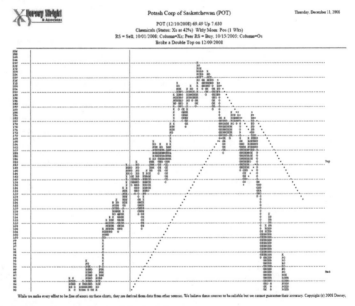

FIGURE 11.45A   Potash Corp. of Saskatchewan

Source: Dorsey Wright & Associates.

FIGURE 11.45B   Potash Corp. of Saskatchewan

Source: MarketGrader.com.

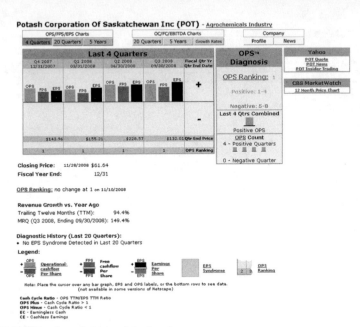

FIGURE 11.45C Potash Corp. of Saskatchewan

Source: StockDiagnostics.com.

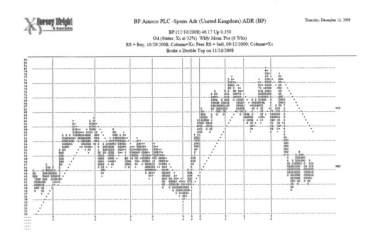

FIGURE 11.46A   BP Amoco PLC

Source: Dorsey Wright & Associates.

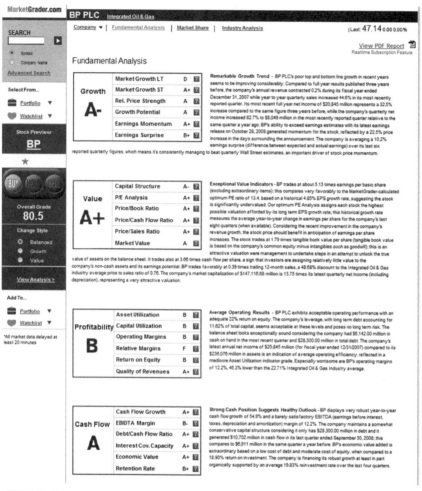

FIGURE 11.46B   BP Amoco PLC

Source: MarketGrader.com.

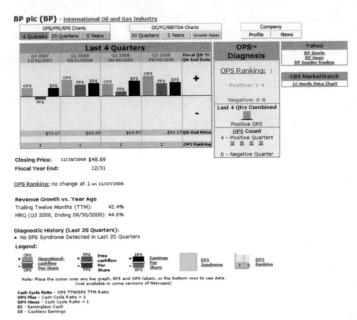

FIGURE 11.46C   BP Amoco PLC

Source: StockDiagnostics.com.

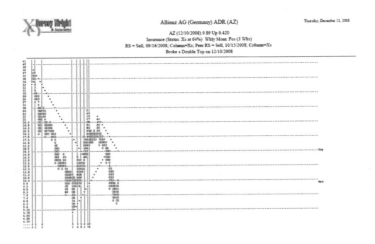

FIGURE 11.47A   Allianz AG

Source: Dorsey Wright & Associates.

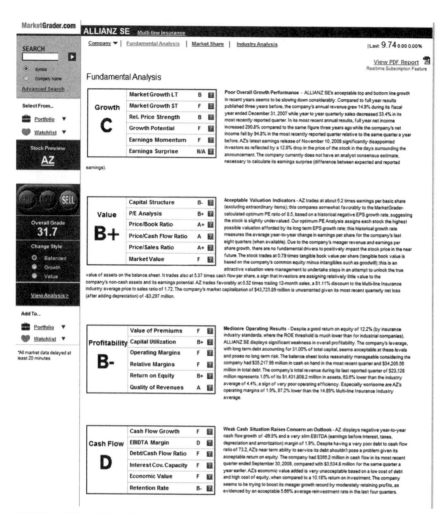

FIGURE 11.47B   Allianz AG

Source: MarketGrader.com.

197

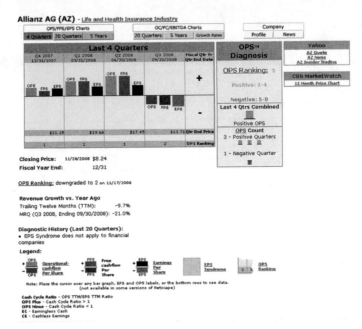

FIGURE 11.47C   Allianz AG

Source: StockDiagnostics.com.

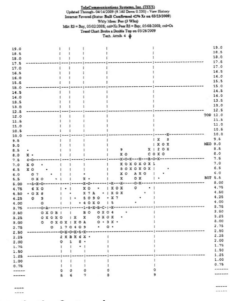

FIGURE 11.48A   TeleCommunication Systems Inc.

Source: Dorsey Wright & Associates

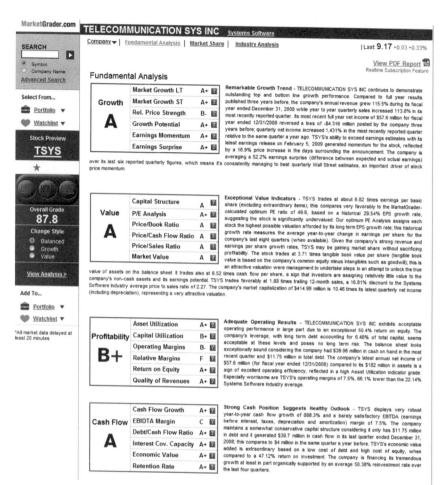

FIGURE 11.48B TeleCommunication Systems Inc.

Source: MarketGrader.com.

TeleCommunication Systems, Inc. (TSYS)

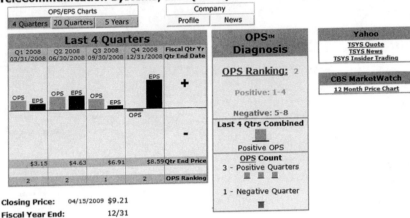

Closing Price: 04/15/2009 $9.21
Fiscal Year End: 12/31

OPS Ranking: downgraded to 2 on 03/09/2009

Revenue Growth vs. Year Ago
Trailing Twelve Months (TTM): 52.7%
MRQ (Q4 2008, Ending 12/31/2008): 113.8%

Diagnostic History (Last 20 Quarters):
- 06/30/2004 Remission

Legend:

Note: Place the cursor over any bar graph, EPS and OPS labels, or the bottom rows to see data.
(not available in some versions of Netscape)

Cash Cycle Ratio - OPS TTM/EPS TTM Ratio
OPS Plus - Cash Cycle Ratio > 1
OPS Minus - Cash Cycle Ratio < 1
EC - Earningless Cash
CE - Cashless Earnings

FIGURE 11.48C   TeleCommunication Systems Inc.

Source: StockDiagnostics.com.

12

Selected Articles and Interviews

Over the last several years I have been published in many magazines and newsletters. I include several articles and an interview here to reinforce my beliefs and show the major themes I have tried to share with investors over the years. My focus was always on demystifying the market and thinking about the stock market as a way to achieve wealth by identifying superior companies.

As a new bull market emerged following the Bear Market of 2000–2002, many of our top-ranked Magnet stocks were racing ahead while the market indexes were still struggling. In this *Financial Planning* article from 2005 (Kimmel 2005b), I discussed the need to stay on top of your portfolio and maintain a willingness to make changes when necessary. I also highlighted that the Magnet System was identifying several companies that were benefiting from the growth taking place internationally. A couple of years later we would be hearing of the emergence and importance of the BRICs.

STOCK SELECTION OR INDEXING?

While the frustration seems to be growing within the investment community, the stock market is doing better then the media portrays. While the major indexes are under water year-to-date, individual stocks are behaving much better. Close to 70% of all NYSE companies are trading above their 200-day moving averages, showing a very bullish tend. The advance/decline lines are strong and the new high list compared to new low list is also very constructive. So what is the problem? Clearly, too many investors have been schooled to dwell on the major market indexes. They are missing out on the opportunities presented by having a portfolio of the cream of the crop. Maybe it is time to reexplore the art of portfolio management!

Despite the positive action of the stock market below the major indexes, the public remains skeptical. The high-profile corporate and accounting scandals over the last several years have sent shell-shocked investors into their bomb shelters. In addition, the lack of international stability has added to the sharp drop in investor's confidence in recent years. Now even with consumer confidence returning following the recession in the United States of 2001–2, the distrust of Wall Street continues. With real estate taking center stage, people would rather put on an addition to their home than trust their money to the stock market. In light of the current back-lash against the stock market, the public needs to be reminded, that over time, investing in equities has generated significantly higher returns than real estate—especially if you can identify the right companies!

One of the big problems we have these days is the continued hangover from the dot.com bust. Companies in the commodity and basic material sectors have been shunned even though that is where the profits and action have been. The large-capitalization technology sector continues to receive too much attention and is producing too little returns. This only contributes to today's frustration. The reality is that a lot of companies in the technology sectors have been doing well—not just the largest and high-profile ones.

The reason people often gravitate to the larger companies is not only because they are better known—but they can be "traded" easily. In the late 1990s investors were "educated" in day trading. The result was a shift from true investing into technical trading. People's expectations and time horizons became their biggest enemies. Investors need to get away from instant gratification—stock market returns come over time. That is not to say we are advocating buy and hold—we are talking about buy and monitor your portfolio.

It is critical for investors to understand that they can regain their confidence and embrace individual stocks by isolating companies they can trust and feel comfortable with—for a while. The hardest concept to understand is that even most of the best companies do not stay good investments forever. Using our proprietary quantitative Magnet Stock Selection Process we rank all companies based on several criteria. Sorting and ranking by revenue growth, profit margin growth, free cash flow, and several proprietary ratios we created we attempt to identify the strongest companies at the moment. History, and our experience, tell us that our list of "Magnets" changes over time. When we can identify the companies that rank out on our model that have a high level of shares held by management, are still relatively underfollowed by Wall Street, and are underowned by the large mutual funds—that is when we feel most comfortable. Companies with these characteristics often attract capital and then pull in the institutional investors. Once companies get sufficiently large and have to live up to excessive expectations and valuations, that is when trouble often begins. Staying ahead of the curve can be difficult and requires a significant amount of work.

If you are willing to buy individual stocks, it is important to continue to monitor your holdings and make sure they continue to make progress from a fundamental basis. It is important not to fall in love with any holding no matter what industry they are in or how well you think you may know the company. Any company can decline significantly enough to ruin your overall investment results because no company is immune to going out of business. There are too many examples of former industry and stock market leaders that have gone belly up. It is hard to imagine, with the booming steel prices of today, that former market leader Bethlehem Steel is bankrupt. In another striking example, if you would have stuck to your guns and stayed with the former airline leader Pan Am, despite all the current air travel, you would have lost all your money.

Interestingly, the indexes continue to go higher over time precisely because they continue to change the components of the index. So while long-term investing in indexes has proven profitable, investing in the components has not worked out as well. There are fewer than 50 companies in the S&P 500 that were in the index over 30 years ago, and only a handful of these have actually outperformed the index itself. While several of the names that have been removed from the index were part of mergers the majority of the names were removed due to underperformance. New industries continue to be born and new market leaders show up unannounced. It is for the individual investor to find his own way to identify these industries and companies. It has been shown over bull market cycles that the leaders of the prior bull market are often not the leaders of the next.

Today's conditions are ripe for a strong bull market—everything is in place except investor confidence. Corporate profits as a percentage of the Gross National Product is the highest it has been in 38 years. The valuation of the S&P is the best it has been in several years. Corporations are buying back stock at record paces. Merger and acquisition activity has increased because corporations are flushed with cash. The largest investors are already moving money out of real estate, while the smaller investors are still more confident in the housing market than the stock market. The bond market offers very little competition to the stock market right now as rates are rising and there is very little interest income available at these still historically low rates. The last time we had this much uncertainty and negativity swirling around the stock market you were paid to wait, this time rates are too low to attract the big money. There is more money parked on the sidelines as a percentage of the total capitalization of the stock market than any time in history. This is the fuel that will propel the market higher once investor confidence is regained. Primarily, because many of the stagnant largest companies continue to hold back the major market indexes, the media has still not picked up on all the good news—and the relative attractiveness of the equity markets.

I see so many individual companies that rank up high on our Magnet model, and I continue to be amazed at the overall pessimism surrounding the stock market. Despite the unsettlingly international headlines, worldwide consumers will be coming on board in dramatic numbers. Billions of people will buy their first dishwasher and pair of sneakers soon. The demographics of an aging worldwide population points to tremendous opportunities in the healthcare industry while aging healthy baby boomers and their active lifestyle demands clearly offer opportunities in the leisure and travel industries; the challenge is to identify the companies most benefiting from these demographic shifts, not necessarily the biggest companies in those industries. Stock selection is the key. Opportunities abound, do not let the media or the major market indexes hold you back.

> This article was published by the *Dick Davis Digest* in 2005 (Kimmel 2005a). In it I highlighted how difficult it really is to be successful in the stock market. The real estate market was still red-hot at that time. I was highlighting the need to think independently and to ignore the negatively surrounding the stock market and focus on finding the few Magnet stocks worthy of accumulating. (Kimmel 2005, p. 1).

NOBODY SAID THE MARKET IS SUPPOSED TO BE EASY, BUT IT IS WORTH THE CHALLENGE!

For almost everybody, the stock market has been frustrating so far this year. Nobody really seems to be making money, neither the bulls nor the bears. Sectors are coming in and out of favor too rapidly for real gains to develop. Yet unfortunately, I continue to see the same commercials making stock market trading look easy. This focus on short-term trading, while good for the brokerage firms and the software companies that promise quick and easy profits, continues to foster the same-day trading mentality that gets investors in trouble. Only over longer-term time frames, and through considerable effort, can real wealth be generated in the stock market. This simple fact should be delivered to investors so we can rebuild the confidence the markets desperately need. Successful investing in the stock market takes considerable effort—but it is worth the challenge!

I believe the current market is in a great position to accumulate shares in the right companies. Valuations in many cases are excellent, corporate earnings are healthy, corporate cash flow is high. Companies are consolidating and buying back their own shares in record amounts. These are signs that management and CEO's see opportunity. But consumer confidence is at a 2-year low and analysts are afraid to raise estimates out of concern regulators will slap their hands if they are wrong. The general public's distrust of Wall Street continues to be the overriding issue.

Most investors today would rather place their hard earned money into a heated real estate market or leave it in the bank earning virtually no return—anything but put their assets in the hands of "the dirty rotten scoundrels in Wall Street." It is only periodically, every couple of generations, that this negative of a perception prevails—and that is exactly the time that astute longer-term investors sense the opportunities.

Making real money in the stock market requires everything you have. It is truly, a "Battle for Investment Survival," as Gerard Loeb says in his great book that was written many years ago. You have to read a lot. You have to study a lot. You need to dig to find the best individual companies to invest in—not day-trade around. You have to dedicate a few hours per week to monitor you holdings. I say this because, while I believe in long-term investing, I do not believe in long-term "buy and hold." My time frame is more like 2–5 years for most companies. Only rarely will a company rank out high enough on our quantitative model for more than a few years. When a company no longer ranks out high—that is when we sell.

Remarkably there are over 425 new names in the S&P 500 that were not there 25 years ago. While so much is made of long-term investing, even looking at the companies that have not been removed from the S&P, only a handful have outperformed the index. As the world economy continues to grow and change, new industries are created and new opportunities develop. You have to create a methodology to find the new younger faster growing companies that have the chance of being added to the major market indexes overtime and create real wealth for you.

We call our edge The Magnet® Stock Selection Process, a quantitative model that blends the best aspects of value, growth, and momentum investing. We have created several propriety ratios we use to screen the overall market to identify the best opportunities. Our process has been built around our philosophy of what makes a great company and a great investment at the same time. It is top-line revenue growth that leads our model, coupled with profit margin acceleration. We need to see our companies generating cash flow, while also trading at an acceptable valuation. We also need the market to be somewhat recognizing our companies creating some positive price momentum. When we find the "new Magnets" early, the management team tends to be receiving modest salaries and own a considerable amount of shares. It is at this time in a company's growth phase that management is truly focused on doing what is best for the company.

There are always new companies showing up using our model. Once our "short list" has been created using our quantitative screening model, considerable qualitative analysis is then done. We need to find out the factors that are actually driving the profit margin acceleration. Is a new product? Is it the company expanding into a new market? Understanding a company's business is the key, not a preoccupation with its stock chart. If this approach sounds like a lot of work—it is!

Success in the stock market does not come easy; however, the alternatives are unacceptable.

This next article I wrote for the April 2007 issue of the *Dick Davis Digest* (Kimmel 2007). In it, I reiterate the words of such greats as Nick Murray and John Templeton to further my point that the markets are more global and long term than most investors realize. So act as such!

EXPAND YOUR HORIZONS: THE MARKET ALREADY DID

It amazes me that, no matter how good the market conditions are, the public is still so easily put into a tizzy by the media and every little bump in the road. While it is common knowledge that wealth is created by ownership rather than lending (whether it is through real estate or equities), it is hard to stay the course when we are constantly hearing of another bubble bursting. Success in the stock market is a result of a combination of things—a strategy that works for you, good timing, and just plain old time. In the immortal words of Nick Murray, "I can't tell you which direction the next 10% move is—but I can tell you with certainty which direction the next 100% move is going." We are in a confirmed bull market that nobody believes in quite yet. Not only are we clearly in a bull market, but we are in a bull market that is bigger and more global than most people realize. Expand your horizons—the market already did!

In the early 1990s, the great investor and humanitarian, Sir John Templeton spoke impassionedly about the falling of the Berlin Wall and its tremendous significance in terms of opening the free market to Eastern Europe. He discussed the implications of 300 million new consumers coming on stream over a fairly short span. Looking back, did he ever hit the nail on the head! But that was just the beginning. Now, think in terms of our global economy—beyond the BRICs

(Brazil, Russia, India and China) that have caught everybody's attention. You can see a market far bigger than what short-term thinkers and traders can even fathom. There are new levels of trade and human talent now working together and just as importantly working separately, to address the opportunities and problems of the world.

As a result of increasing free trade, expanded earnings, and cash flow from operations, corporations have never been sitting on more cash than they are today. Cash has been building up not only for public corporations, but also in the pockets of private equity funds, asset management companies, and public hands as well. This helps to explain the torrent of mergers and acquisitions taking place with cash (not with shares—those mergers will take place at another temporary market top). In fact, relative to the total market capitalization of the market, there has never been a higher percentage of cash waiting to come in. This money continues to sit on the sidelines despite multiyear high readings in consumer confidence in the U.S. Why? The missing link is still a lack of investor's confidence stemming from the perfect storm that occurred since the broad market top back in early 2000; the rollover in technology shares, a recession, 9/11 and terrorism, accounting scandals of Enron/WorldCom, international hot spots flaring up . . . you name it.

The emotional cycle in the stock market is not new. Following previous bear markets, "operators" were always made out to be villains. Does anybody remember the mutual fund scandals of the early 1970s? Many said that nobody would ever invest in funds again! We recently went from a period in the 1990s when people were leaving work early to check their online accounts (or day-trade) to a time when the same people were not even opening their monthly statements. Now, the public is almost ready to come back, but it takes time.

Even with all of the negative headlines, we saw a bull market confirmed just last month according to the Dow Theory, registering simultaneous new all-time highs in the Dow Jones Industrials, Transports and Utilities. This is no small accomplishment by the market, which is always looking forward. Somehow the market sees things not seen by those looking at newspaper headlines or in the rearview mirror.

Despite our long-term bullishness, clearly not all companies are worth investing in. Through the use of The Magnet Stock Selection Process we rank all stocks by factors such as top-line revenue growth, profit margin acceleration, cash flow, debt levels, and a host of other proprietary fundamental indicators. Combining these factors in a unique way we identify our top prospects. If we see a group of companies within a given sector that score out highly for us, then we know that we have identified a sector currently experiencing pricing power—another major advantage. We have seen basic materials, construction, and the gaming sector score highly for some time already. These are groups that also just happen to fit in with the theme that is unfolding on every continent on the planet, a global build-out requiring vast quantities of cement, steel, and virtually all basic materials.

While our model helps us to control emotions and think long term, it is also essential to keep an eye on the short-term complexion of the market. Most investors focus on the major indexes like the Dow 30 or the S&P 500. We know that these indexes are price and capitalization weighted and are often misleading.

It is much more important for investors to keep an eye on the "internals" of the market. To us, the ratio of number of companies hitting new highs versus new lows, along with the overall advance/decline lines are the most important factors to be aware of. Prior to a bear market breaking out you will see clear deterioration within these two indicators. A current look at the ratio of new highs to new lows and the advance/declines lines shows a strong market that is simply taking a well deserved breather.

Up until a few weeks ago, the biggest complaint about the market was the lack of a correction for several months. We had gone a record period of time without a 2% decline in the daily prices of the Dow 30, too long without a 10% correction in the S&P 500, and this bull market was already considered too long in the tooth to be trusted (that is right—even if your portfolio does not reflect it— this bull market dates back to the fall of 2002). The new fear of the subprime loans derailing our economy reminds me of the early part of my career when the Resolution Trust Company was established to deal with the terrible real estate market that was going to bankrupt the country. Please, do whatever you need to do to help you think long term and not get caught up with the hysteria. Now that we are experiencing this long awaited pullback, the bears and the media have gone back to their, "This is the end!" rhetoric. Nonsense—this market is going much higher.

Lock and load—buy into the top companies and sectors within the market and be patient. Monitor your holdings and understand them to a point that news does not scare you because you know what you own. Only then will you be able to expand your time horizons and capture the rewards and profits available through the stock market.

The *Dick Davis Digest* has been one of my favorite newsletters for many years. I began contributing a cover "Prospective" piece each quarter back in 2005. These articles touched on my themes of having patience and being a disciplined investor. I also highlighted the importance of blocking out negative news and identifying Magnet stocks.

In this article for *Dick Davis Digest* (Kimmel 2008b, p. 1), I was reminding the readers to tune out the media's negative bias and just focus on finding the true winners: those on the right tip of the bell curve. I highlighted the difficulty of investing amid a deluge of negative news and also stressed the need to "Listen to the market and let it show you the winners," instead of having the ego to believe you can predict what will happen next.

FOCUS ON THE FEW TRUE SUPERLATIVES—AND JUST TUNE OUT THE REST . . .

As always, there is no shortage of bad news. These days the list is longer and scarier than usual. The plunging dollar, skyrocketing energy costs, accelerating food costs, recession, and stagflation—I will stop here. Yet with all the horrible headlines, try renting a crane or a tanker. Try locking in steel or cement prices. The reality is that the world economy is doing just fine, thank you. As an investor, you need to learn to filter the news and the headlines—read and listen, but always be on the lookout for what is going right and who is excelling. By nature, there can only be a few superlatives—finding the right industries, and the leaders in those industries is the key to successful investing.

Warren Buffett simplified economic forecasting and analysis. He said if you spend an hour per year thinking about the economy, you probably wasted 59 minutes. Through a dozen recessions Buffett instead focused on a few exceptional opportunities that meet his strict risk/reward calculations. By focusing at the company level, Buffett was able to navigate though all kinds of economic conditions and international events while piling up his outsized returns.

While Buffett's patience is certainly greater than most other investors', if you can maintain the same focus on individual companies you probably will improve your investment results. Foundations have been created with the wealth attained by those individuals that identified, concentrated, and profited with the true superlatives.

At a recent financial television network I was baited into agreeing that the world was basket case. As the argument was presented, "if the world conditions are not terrible, at least you could agree the United States is a mess and our economy is worse." I did not take the bait and I could not agree less with those statements. Instead, I changed the subject to "five things going really well right now!"

Right now there are a few industries that are in full blast bull markets. In these sectors—basic materials, energy, solar and other alternative energy, construction, steel, coal, and natural gas—new millionaires and billionaires are being minted daily. A lot of people have made a tremendous amount of money in these companies over the last several years. Investors in the right ones continue to make huge profits. Unfortunately, many investors remain captivated by the headlines in the financial sector. Guesses are made trying to pick the bottom or isolating the few healthy ones that will not get caught up in the contagion. If you are really patient, and lucky, you may buy near the low in financials and do well over time. All of the benefits of the global build-out will eventually be felt in the financial sector, the group just has to stabilize and recover—it will take time, though. By focusing on what is going right now, and isolating the few true superlatives, your emotions are held in check and your profits accumulate.

Why is it that so many smart individuals make such poor investors? Often the answer is overindulgent egos that believe they can be good at everything. We have all heard the expression "a little bit of knowledge can be dangerous." One of the problems with investing in the stock market is that so much misinformation is placed in the public's hands to get them to do the wrong things. Bad news regarding a company is often leaked by someone that has gone short that stock and wants to profit when the shares fall. Sometimes bad news is even generated by someone looking to buy in at lower prices. Another big problem is that too many investors spend too much time thinking and reading about the economy and do not realize the lag between the market and the macroeconomic conditions. When conditions look great and the mood is generally optimistic, people get fully invested and good values are hard to find. Conversely, when the economic news is awful and people are pessimistic like now, better valuations create opportunities to profit. "You pay a dear price for a rosy scenario" and "You need to buy when there is blood in the streets" are two age-old quotes that come to mind.

In addition to trying to figure out "what's next?" it is critical to know what is. Trends can stay in place for long periods of time or have quick traps and reversals. It is up to the investor to recognize the trends and not ignore or fight them. Our unbiased unemotional Magnet Stock Selection Process simply researches and screens all public companies looking for "free earnings." When companies can produce free cash flow in excess of market perception they will continue to attract new capital. Oftentimes, when a large number of companies in one or more sectors rank highly on our model, a certain story develops in the market to even accelerate the momentum of these companies.

Having been in the market for so long and seeing cycles come and go, I stress the need to stay on top of your investments. Despite believing that certain trends are firmly in place, by carefully following certain balance sheet and financial data I do constant diagnostic checkups on our holdings. This is because when you understand the nature of global competition, you must realize that companies cannot stay on top indefinitely. While market leading companies gain the attention of investors, they are also being watched and copied by their competitors. To simply believe that a company can continue to earn higher margins than their competitors and maintain market share over time is to ignore history. Some may survive generations while others flame out more quickly.

The tough part for many investors is that market leadership invariably changes in each new bull market leg up. Without having a way to identify new market leaders there may be a tendency for a good market timer to identify exactly when a strong market period presents a good opportunity, only to invest in a company that does participate in the rally. It is not enough to decide to own stocks, you need to identify the right ones. By now most investors understand you cannot achieve long-term financial goals in fixed-income securities. Nor can you generate high returns by being overly diversified. Make sure to supplement your reading outside the narrow focus of financial periodicals. Remember, most economists do not make great investors. By focusing on current industry leaders you can tune out the noise of the market and focus on the few superlatives.

> I wrote this commentary as the market was topping out and confidence was beginning to fail. It was not published anywhere, I simply sent it by e-mail (Kimmel 2006b) to several of our relationships. I was pointing out the need to be alert and flexible, as well as the need to identify individual companies and not just think about "the market."

TOO MUCH CASH . . . NOT ENOUGH CONFIDENCE

The last several quarters have been frustrating for most investors. The major market indexes have done little to create any enthusiasm. Sector rotation has been the dominant theme. While we have seen big gains made in several sectors, pity those that stayed too long in any one sector. Be it the retail companies, home builders, or energy stocks—they all took turns leading the market—all were subject to severe downdrafts.

There is another severe problem that seems to be stepping into the forefront—real estate seems to be topping and rolling over. All of the signposts are showing up. Tricky mortgage plays are beginning to unwind leading to more inventory on the market that is moving more slowly. We have also seen the signs of many home building stocks rolling over. Who knows, an unwinding of the housing market runup could end up being a benefit to the stock market. There are those who feel real estate money will come back into the equity markets. More likely, a downturn in the housing market will represent more problems for the economy as cash-out refinancing comes to a halt leading to a further drop in consumer confidence.

Now, with all of these negative headlines providing a perfect smoke screen, all of the catalysts are also in place to launch a new bull market in 2006. Thinking about it, it is hard to believe with all the shocks to the system that the stock market has been as resilient as it has been. In fact, while everyone remains focused on the S&P 500 and the Dow Jones 30—the S&P 600 and the S&P 400 and the NYSE equally weighted composite have all hit all-time highs last month. Corporate earnings are strong and corporate cash levels as a percentage of their market capitalization are at 26-year highs. This is why mergers and acquisitions are at new record levels.

The enormous distrust toward Wall Street has lead to an enormous cash buildup of money on the sidelines. The closely watched Institutional Brokers' Estimate System (IBES) Valuation Model shows the stock market as undervalued relative to the bond market by 39%, the highest level ever recorded! The international markets have been stronger then ours all year. The U.S. dollar has begun to regain strength making our market more attractive to foreign investors. Long-term trends are in place that will lead to millions of new consumers for agile companies selling into new markets. The only missing ingredient to ignite a powerful bull market move remains investor confidence.

What will turn around the investment climate and bring the sideline money back into the stock market? Liquidity! It drives the stock market. While the Federal Reserve Board has raised the Fed funds rates and received a lot of media doing so—it also has increased the money supply by the fastest rate seen in several years. The new Fed chairman will start lowering interest rates by the middle of next year: [2007] Oil and gas prices will ease providing relief to consumers. Japan's economy, the world's second largest, continues to improve. Any positive news out of Iraq or the war on terrorism would obviously be a huge and welcome benefit. As soon as a couple of these events unfold and consumer and investor confidence returns, the stock market should begin a new advance that will again take most investors, and "experts," by surprise.

Despite my positive expectations, I am not always bullish on the stock market, nor am I bullish on all stocks. I have and continue to stress careful stock selection. We use our proprietary Magnet Stock Selection Process to isolate companies that are showing rapid revenue growth, rapid profit margin acceleration, and strong cash flow. When we can find companies like this that trade at a discount to their growth rate and are under accumulation it is easy to tune out the noise. The good news is—we see plenty of ideas right now!

Remember the stock market is an auction market. During pessimistic times like these, if you are in your accumulation phase, you need to be a buyer. The old Wall Street expression says, "You pay a dear price for a rosy scenario." Times like these only come around once in a while. Take advantage of looking around the corner while the foolish will not dare!

> This article was published in the February 2006 *Dick Davis Digest* (Kimmel 2006a, p. 1). In it, I urge investors to tune out the negative media and economists while focusing carefully on the positive factors coming together in the market.

MARKET ON LAUNCH PAD—2006 WILL BE BETTER THAN EXPECTED . . .

Consumer and investor confidence is on the rise. Corporate profits and balance sheets are the best they have been in U.S. history. There is a global economic expansion unfolding fueled by excess liquidity and demand. The "internals" of the stock market look great—a strongly positive advance/decline line and a very healthy new high/new low ratio.

Even with all these factors in place, it amazes me how low many investors' expectations are. After suffering through a bear market that has been followed by this seemingly never ending trading range market, most investors cannot see the underlying strength in the market. The reality is the stock market is on a launching pad and 2006 will prove to be better than most expectations. Even so, the key is being in the right sectors and ultimately in the right stocks. That is why, despite the loud debates over whether we are, in fact, in a bull or bear market—in the stock market it is important to remember to drill from the bottom up.

The one group that seems to understand the current environment is the corporate insiders. Those deeply knowledgeable of the balance sheets of their own companies are engaged in record-setting share buybacks and mergers and acquisitions. We see the private equity players taking public companies private at an unprecedented rate. All this is taking place while individual investors are still licking their wounds from a generational bear market. The multitude of events that took place from the 2000 top of the market through the fall of 2002 were so emotionally devastating that many investors have been unwilling to even consider putting new money into the stock market.

Despite the strength of the U.S. and world economies, do not look to the economists for positive guidance. Many economists are not only wrong about the magnitude of the interest rate cycle, they also are wrong about the direction of interest rates on a year-to-year basis. Throughout one of the strongest global expansions, the public has been kept off guard and in cash by warnings of a double dip recession. Another problem confronting the public is that too much time is spent by Wall Street analysts developing multiyear themes—often based upon faulty economic expectations. This approach, when used in the stock market, leads to a top-down approach of trying to identify the best sectors where money is expected to flow.

My belief is that in order to be successful you need to "listen to and observe" the market's behavior rather than predicting long-term cycles. By using a methodology I call The Magnet Stock Selection Process, I simply try to identify a certain breed of company. By quantitatively isolating those companies with the highest revenue growth, combined with the highest accelerating profit margins, we can identify where growth is truly coming from.

Then taking this universe of companies we see which of these companies trade at a discount to their current valuation and which ones are under accumulation highlighted by an improving relative price trend. This methodology will tend to identify clusters of companies within a given sector that are experiencing pricing power and are generating accelerated levels of cash flow. I call these companies "Magnets," as other investors cannot help but to be attracted to them. We continue to see several groups and many stocks that meet our criteria—therefore I remain solidly, but selectively bullish.

There are many who believe that the energy and basic materials sectors have come too far too fast, and currently contrarian investors are quick to dismiss these sectors. Two decades ago Sir John Templeton stated that the fall of the Berlin Wall was one of the single most important events in his lifetime. Templeton accurately suggested that the spread of democracy would lead to an increased population experiencing and embracing capitalism and consumerism. Clearly the recent emergence of the BRICs (Brazil, Russia, India and China) is fueling a global expansion beyond what any of us would have thought possible just a decade ago. This is not a simple or short-term case of sector rotation, but instead a long-term trend that is almost irreversible.

Here at Magnet we continue to search for prolonged growth trends. We then drill deeper into those sectors to find the individual companies that stand out according to our disciplined quantitative process. Another sector that shows up in our work is within the gaming industry. Across the globe new gaming megafacilities are being built to generate tourism and offset tax burdens of cities and states in the United States and in countries throughout the world. Companies in this industry are naturally thriving, casino operators and suppliers alike. This is not a trend we were able to predict, but instead a trend we are able to observe and profit from.

You need to tune out the seemingly always negative media. Allow yourself to see the very positive trends that exist in the global economy and in the stock markets around the world. The fuel is ready on the sidelines to lift this market. Relative to the size of the total capitalization of the U.S. stock market, there is the highest percentage of cash being held by individuals since this ratio has been followed. Cash is abundant throughout the world and flowing into our markets. Do not wait to buy great companies until the positive articles appear regarding the stock market or the economy. Keep drilling for the best ideas and be confident to invest when you find them.

In the March 24, 2008 issue of the *Dick Davis Digest* (Kimmel, 2008h, p. 1), I shared my conviction that Main Street would be fine even if Wall Street was imploding at the time. Although I was early in recognizing the recession, I was sharing the need to invest in companies, not overthink the economy.

WALL STREET HAS THE PROBLEMS—NOT MAIN STREET . . . AND THE PROBLEM IS SHORT TERM

Times like these can be really scary and it is hard to want to buy stocks when the short-term trends seem so clearly negative. There is no doubt that the U.S. economy is in a recession—the question is how deep and how long the slowdown will last. Anyone that follows technical analysis has got to be bearish and the pessimism is everywhere. The media is in its heyday—recession, inflation, stagflation, a technical bear market in most markets, and there are real, but temporary, short-term problems in the credit and lending arenas. However, even the most bearish investors are asking "when to get in" not "when to get out."

Wall Street has the problems—not Main Street. When polled, 84% of Americans say they are happy with their lives. 95% of all eligible and willing to work have a job. A great many people from a great many places would love to come to America. Populations are growing and being increasingly introduced to the free markets and the opportunities becoming available to them. Main Street is going to continue to do well in more and more places.

The money changers on Wall Street are a different story than Main Street today. Simply because there is so much liquidity, products were developed that were appetizing to anybody looking for a "little extra yield." Institutions were experiencing problems generating income because interest rates had declined. This creates serious problems to groups that are overexposed to fixed income while trying to run entities experiencing rising costs. Most of these loan packages were further repackaged and then had derivatives written against them. Only when the problems began to surface did the engineers of the products find out how illiquid they could become. As history repeats itself, the big money is coming in at very low levels and scooping up these "problems" and will profit handsomely when things stabilize. The collateral on most of the devolvement projects is sound. And while real estate has taken a hit, we must be careful to put everything in perspective. Currently 95% of all mortgages are current within 30 days. Foreclosures, while reportedly are "skyrocketing—up 40%" are still below 3%. Much of the collateral to these investments were solid and are solid today. The problems with the subprime loans are not the defaults occurring, but the liquidity problems with the products themselves. Once this mess is resolved—and it will be—growth will resume not only across America, but all over the world. A tremendous hit to Wall Street and the banking industry will no doubt have a large short-term effect on the economy—but growth in almost every other area continues unabated. What is missing now is the "wealth effect" domestically. People can no longer use refinancing cash back loans to overindulge beyond their means. In fact, families are scaling back and pulling in their spending. So yes—business cycles have not disappeared and neither have recessions or bear markets.

If we are expecting, or experiencing, a bear market and a recession—how can I be so bullish? For one, equity prices are already down 15–30% off the highs depending on which sector or individual company you are looking at. I believe we will see the recession end up being postdated back to the last quarter of 2007 and the bear market to have begun at the October 2007 highs. We are already through much of the damage. (In fact, I started this article a few days ago. As I sit down to finish it, the Fed has already announced some of the measures that they needed to take to resolve the credit issues overhanging the markets.) More importantly, there is another factor even bigger coming into focus that has me even more bullish long term.

A lot has already been said about the international global build-out taking place. For years we have heard from the self-indulgent baby boomers and marketers alike about how big this group was and how they changed the supply and demand equations entirely. Because of the advances in communication and the Internet, the free market is spreading like a wildfire. The administration in Washington wants to talk about the spreading of democracy—from the business side it comes down to free markets. The communist from China goes onto the Internet the same way the socialist does from Sweden. The result is what I call the "InterBoomer Generation." Everyone from everywhere desires a higher standard of living that they can see being enjoyed around the world. The growth in the size of the capital markets over the next decades is being ignored by today's investors thinking short term.

I will leave the dramatic "entertainment commentary" to others. I will let them waste their time trying to answer the questions: Are we in a bull or bear market? Recession? How deep will it be? I even answer these questions to the media myself—just because they ask.

But that is not what is important. Instead, I will continue to focus on the companies with the good ideas and the good management that continue to generate what I call "Free Earnings"—generating accelerating cash flow while trading at a discount. Our Magnet System is finding an abundance of them, as it always does, in good times and bad. In the meantime, the free market will continue to spread, Wall Street will find a cure for the current liquidity crisis, and an even greater number of investors will bid the markets significantly higher over time.

This interview in *The Wall Street Transcript* in July of 2008 touched on many topics including why I think so differently than most other money managers. I focus on the Magnet System, the need to go beyond reported earnings and look at cash flow, and why diversification makes no sense to me (*The Wall Street Transcript* 2008).

INVESTING IN SUPERLATIVES

TWST: We talked to you last year, it was right before the whole sub-prime collapse and the credit crunch, and I think it's been an incredible 12 months of turbulent times for you. Do you want to start by talking about what happened and how it impacted your selection process?

Mr. Kimmel: The last 12 months have been a lesson to almost everybody in Wall Street in terms of having preconceptions in terms of what is cheap, and what is expensive. It also just as importantly showed the hazards of sticking your money in a broadly diversified portfolio that mirrors S&P index. Specifically going into last year, the financials carried the highest weighting in the S&P and anybody who felt compelled to stay in financials, defend financials, or in fact think that they were cheap has learned a dramatic lesson in both market psychology and in market performance. We feel very fortunate right here. We want to remain humble, but for the last 12 months, we've been talking about being exposed to more of the free market, which has led us into the basic materials, the energy, the international, and helped us not only to basically avoid financials, but most of our involvement on the financials has been on the short side all year along.

TWST: Longs are out for the time being or are you seeing an end to this type of environment?

Mr. Kimmel: My most important comment here is the lesson that deteriorating balance sheets are never cheap and my best guess here is that looking back on history and looking back on prior market cycles, the financials have probably come close to running their course to the downside, but because we are very disciplined users of The Magnet Stock Selection Process, we are only interested in companies with accelerating cash flow and therefore no financials really show up on our model. There will be a time when they turn and they get healthy and I do believe they will eventually benefit from the same global macro growth that we see helping other sectors currently, but to guess the bottom in financials and to guess the bottom with their disturbing balance sheets right now is anybody's guess. It's actually proven hazardous, so we do not play that game.

TWST: Tell us about The Magnet Stock Selection Process because it's so different in many ways from the traditional selection process of money managers.

Mr. Kimmel: It is completely different than traditional money management's systems in many ways. First of all, we believe most investors are simply too lazy to go through the full balance sheet when evaluating companies and for some unbelievable reason still are focused on bottom-line-reported earnings despite years of finding out, they are actually the most engineered and often misleading indicators to a company's health. At Magnet, we start with top-line revenue growth as our first piece and work all the way through the balance sheet down to cash flow. We are also, like many others, very interested in valuation, but insist on a strong balance sheet and insist on current improvement in a series of financial metrics along with actual price momentum.

At the end of our analysis, we come up with a very small fraction of eligible companies for investment and simply do not adhere to the wide diversification strategies that continue to dominate Wall Street.

TWST: Are there any sectors that you are finding better balance sheet financials?

Mr. Kimmel: Clearly there are, but I want to say before I highlight them, we remain more diagnostic than predictive. While it's always easy to construct a story on what you think is taking place or what you think will take place, I find it much more important to put your ego in check and to simply ask the question, "What is" rather than "What you think should be."

As we see this very dramatic international global build-out taking place, the companies involved in enabling and creating this build-out have been the major, major beneficiaries. Whether it's the steel required to build buildings, or concrete for highways, or agricultural products and fertilizers to feed an improving global appetite and standard of living. As this trend has developed, people keep looking over their shoulder looking for a top and looking for rotation back into other groups. For the last couple of years the best solution and I believe the best solution going forward is to just simply follow a free market approach and let your portfolio be weighted in the companies that are experiencing the fastest cash flow that continue to trade at moderate valuations. Today, a year, and six months ago, we've seen the basic materials, energy, and select technology companies lead the way. Although I strongly believe that they will continue to lead the way for quarters and potentially years to come, we are going to remain very disciplined, follow the model, and let our disciplined system pull us into the right sectors.

TWST: What about international stocks? Do you invest in international stocks as opposed to domestic companies with international operations?

Mr. Kimmel: I think it's so important in this case to just follow the money and follow the earnings, follow the cash flow, and for us—follow our model. Clearly the strongest growth has come outside the United States for a number of years. There has also been a number of companies domestically that are actually generating more business outside the U.S. than they are domestically. When I hear others say, "Well you should have at least 10% of your money internationally"—I am amused. We have taken a different approach. We have taken the approach that we do not care where a company is from, we are more interested in how their business is executing. This has pulled us into [a position where] almost 45% of our portfolio is currently international companies that continue to show spectacular growth even while the U.S. economy is clearly moderate to downtrending. We will continue to look at opportunities domestically and internationally and follow the cash flow. Fortunately, the model has pulled us into some of the greatest growth stories taking place internationally.

TWST: One of the hazards of your process of course is, when you are shorting the companies on the negative side of the bell curve, you are taking the money to buy on the positive side of the bell curve, the superlative companies. What happens when the superlative companies to buy at this time(?)? 'Do you ever run out of money to buy the superlatives?'

Mr. Kimmel: Actually, by our offering documents, we approach the business fully invested. Only one of our funds even allows us to short. We prefer the long side in the market. Clearly there is a long-term upward bias through the market, but what is so interesting is that in any market environment you always find that there are companies delivering and executing. Whether it be in industries of the past where you saw technology leading the way, now you are seeing a humongous global build out that people continue to underestimate. While a lot of people will talk about how rough the market is, and in fact the market is difficult here, when you are involved in the companies that are experiencing increased cash flow, they actually stand out almost three dimensionally to me when you look at the mediocre returns and performance of most companies.

As your question was alluding to, we understand, just by the nature of things, 90% of all companies are just average. There are the underperformers and then there are, and there are only a few of them, "the superlatives," which will continue to show up in virtually any market environment. This has been the case for the last 100 years.

TWST: The superlatives are found by doing research on the balance sheet?

Mr. Kimmel: It all started for me back in graduate school when I first saw this bell curve. The question at that time was, if this is true that there are only a few superlatives, the question really begged itself, "Why would anybody buy the full list?" What that set off was a virtual 25-year study, analyzing all the top money managers, all the great authors of years ago to figure out what actually made a great investment. A great investment is a combination of a great company, and finding it at the right time. The most important thing that we do is have a broad-based set of proprietary ratios that we've developed that walk us right through the balance sheet and then determine the very healthiest, fastest growing financials. Not only revenues, not only cash flow, but also profit margin acceleration—those are the hallmarks of a "Magnet Stock." They have something I call "Free Earnings."

Now, when these things all show up together, there is either a new geographic area a company is selling into, it's often a brand-new product that a company has developed with limited competition. The other thing you've got to remember is that these names will continue to change. To simply fall in love with a company and stick with it even when the fundamentals begin to deteriorate because of competition, that is the biggest mistake most investors make. You need to keep your eyes open, your emotions in check, tune out all the noise of the marketplace, and focus on the very few superlatives that are excelling in the current market environment.

TWST: What about the smaller companies? Are they also possibly superlatives or are they usually the large cap?

Mr. Kimmel: There is no question that the large caps come from somewhere and so my whole career, I have always been fascinated with the early identification of the best of the smaller companies. Our model tends to find them significantly earlier than other managers. Then you just have to pay attention to how the market is responding and treating them.

For six years, we saw the small-cap market actually lead the large caps in performance. About a year ago, the large caps started to dominate and outperform the small caps. What we are now seeing for the first time, in the last month or so, is small-cap companies begin to act better in the marketplace. Interestingly, the leaders are coming from smack in the middle—it is the mid caps currently leading this market.

One of the things that we've struggled with as our business has grown and the attention to our process has grown, we can move small stocks just ourselves and we don't want to do that. A lot of the new assets we are managing are in the larger names. In the international side, our portfolio tends to gravitate toward the larger names. But just the same way it has been for the last 25 years, when I see a real small company that ranks high on Magnet that is still what excites me. We make sure we try to talk with management quickly to find out actually what is going so well for them.

TWST: In what type of market environments does The Magnet Selection Process work, perform better?

Mr. Kimmel: The single best performance we have seen over the last 25 years, and this kind of excites me, is at the end of a recession. Often times during a recession you will see the cyclical companies, the more defensive kind of names dominating the market. When we go back into a growth environment where health care and technology and innovation come about, these are often the companies with the exciting new products that really excite Wall Street. The companies that rank highly for us tend to do exceptionally well following a recession. We are clearly in a recessionary type of period right now.

The fortunate side for us is that we have been so overweight in the right sectors over the last year that we have not experienced the pain that most money managers have. When you have a market environment that is very highly emotional and sectors are coming in and out of favor very rapidly—and the market trading very emotionally rather than trending—Magnet has a more difficult time finding the true market leaders. Once a market begins to trend though, we find them very early, and because we are not aggressive traders, and we do believe so strongly in identification of those superlatives, when we find them, we will stick with them and often can make three, four times on our investment over a couple of years once a trend actually develops and is in place.

TWST: Approximately, what is the percentage of superlatives in the portfolio at this time compared with others?

Mr. Kimmel: If you think about how we work, our model only even considers, say 1% of the top 1% companies. There are approximately 14,000 eligible companies with data. When you break that down and start to look a little bit more carefully, we are going to narrow that down to the top 30 stocks in our private funds and 40 stocks in our mutual fund. You are dealing with the extreme tip of the bell curve, the real exceptional companies that are scoring high for us on value, growth, and momentum. That is where we actually came up with the name, the Exceptionator funds. There was an old Forbes article that profiled my methodology and described me as Kimmel the Unterrible. Most companies actually score out terribly on our model. We are looking to only isolate the rare breed that scores highly across the model. Just like tennis players or golfers or architects or violinists by nature, there can only be so many superlatives.

The mistake Wall Street keeps making, I believe, is trying to find a new investment every couple of weeks or months and not sticking with something that continues to work. Of course, the other mistake is sticking with a company simply because you are familiar or you had a good prior experience with them. The main objective to profitable investing is to remain completely unemotional and clearly remembering not to get emotional with stocks, but just to remain disciplined and diagnostic.

TWST: Your focus on the Exceptionators is so distinctive from 95% of money manager's portfolios that are so overdiversified and bringing in subpar returns.

Mr. Kimmel: Let me tell you, this is the most fun part about the business for me. I am currently in the later stages of writing a new book. My old book is already ten years old. The new book will be published in the beginning of next year. It is going to actually expose and debunk that awful process of diversification and asset allocation, which has come to dominate Wall Street speak for the last 25 years. Now interestingly, during my research, when you analyze and interview the top investors of all time, none of them embraces diversification. It is just that many of the asset firms are afraid to look different from the market and are afraid to take risk simply because, in my opinion, they have failed to properly define what risk actually means. Wall Street remains focused on standard deviation and day-to-day and week-to-week volatility. What they should be doing is asking the longer-term question, what does the end result look like and are their clients actually achieving their long-term goals? Had these questions been asked prior, we would not see the dramatic underfunding in pension plans, government, and individual accounts.

My goal with the new book is to actually have people soul-search and to reevaluate the mathematics behind the original diversification studies done 30 years ago and change investor behavior—and make the country ultimately stronger as a result.

TWST: What about the risk management techniques? How do you attempt to control risk in your Magnet process and your selection?

Mr. Kimmel: Most importantly to have high returns over long time, you have to avoid dramatic drawdowns and losses in your accounts. What I have learned over all these years of study and evaluations of other money managers, and mistakes myself along the way, is that there is no actual holy grail to investing in individual stocks. What that means, despite my tremendous confidence in Magnet's ability to identify superlatives, when a score changes and a company goes down in score, which can happen as a result of financial deterioration or simply price deterioration, we do not defend our ideas. We do not average down, instead we strongly believe in stop-losses. If you are willing to have a concentrated portfolio of superlatives, you must remember that the market changes, investor perception changes, and you have to remain diligent to only stay with the strongest and healthiest companies. We use our model, which helps us actually get out of companies that we may have thought were going to be market leaders as soon as they begin to deteriorate. Remember the old words of Will Rogers, the famous actor and also a great investor, "All stocks are bad, only buy those that go up and if they stop going up, remember to sell them." Well, we take a much more extensive approach. If we are in a company on the long side, that company must continue to show positive price momentum, while continuing to trade at a discount to the earnings and cash flow and rank out on all our other metrics. You see, that is why so few companies at any one time can rank out on our model. Again to make it easy, the best offense includes having the best defense and not letting your ego begin to dictate your portfolio management.

TWST: Many money management firms now have an unemotional quantitative investment process. Is it the ranking that you do that distinguishes your firm?

Mr. Kimmel: Yes. Clearly there is an increase and acceptance of quantitative rankings and the reason for that obviously is, we are all experiencing the reality that it works. The most important distinction between our model and others can be described by thinking in terms of a process of elimination. We put our hurdles up that much higher than others do and we have that many more hurdles over the elimination course for a company to finally get through. So, if you are evaluating companies and you do not have as strict of an elimination process as we have, you will still outperform the market, but probably not reduce your list down to the ultimate superlatives. Couple the top selection process with very disciplined portfolio management and I believe you have a recipe to outperform the market over time and through actually any cycle. So the increase in quantitative funds is actually something I view as an absolute confirmation that the process is valid and works. Additionally it eliminates that very critical problem of emotions affecting your decision making.

TWST: The Magnet theory and the process have evolved over the years from high-net-worth individuals and then into institutions and last time you said that you were evolving even further beyond that? Do you want to discuss that?

Mr. Kimmel: Sure. Let me mention . . . a good news, bad news story for everybody. About a year ago, there was an offer to acquire Magnet by a group that was focused on nonprofits exclusively and wanted to contain any potential limitation constraints we may experience over the years to just that select group of clients. As it turns out, the buyer had financing with the purchase and the buyout never was completed. So Magnet remains to this point independent. We continue to be in a position therefore to not limit our work to nonprofits; instead we are continuing to help the high-net-worth individuals. We are helping nonprofits and we are helping new institutions that have been exposed to our model. So there was never an intention on me to stop working, I love what I do. The good news here is that we will not have a limited application of Magnet. We will continue to help all the good people we come across.

TWST: Is there anything that we didn't touch on that you would like to add?

Mr. Kimmel: I think that I want to just remind everybody of this new metric that I am discussing called "Free Earnings." It is this great combination of accelerating cash flow with good valuation. More money has been lost in the market over the years by actually overpaying for good ideas. Some of the earnings models that are out there are not paying enough attention to the valuation side, the balance sheet side, and the debt side. What I would encourage investors to do is to spend more time understanding what is driving a company and also making sure you are not overpaying. If you could do those things, you can actually find the superlatives and stick with them for quarter after quarter and look for much higher returns and not get caught up in this awful media that wants you to believe that the world is actually flat and we are about to go off a cliff.

TWST: Thank you.

As we go to print, we are in a horrific bear market. This recent note (March 14, 2006) to my media relationships touches on the need for Wall Street and the media to regain public trust. I also address the fact that patience has been lost because investors are being sold short-term trading systems and have seemingly forgotten that investment returns sometimes take time to materialize.

A BULL IS WORRIED: THREE THINGS I AM WORRIED ABOUT

Let me make it clear right up front—one of the things that I am not worried about is the stock market. We are currently in a bear market and in a recession. These two facts do not worry me one bit. All bull markets are followed by bear markets, and all periods of expansion are followed by recessions. The good news is that we are probably somewhere near two-thirds, or more, of the way through this bear market and better times for the stock market are ahead. There are, however, three things that I am very worried about and each needs to be addressed soon so that the future is indeed a better place.

The first thing that I am worried about is that Wall Street will not regain respect. Unless the management at the top Wall Street firms show more respect to individual investors and their shareholders, they cannot expect the public to buy into the overall market. Recently, when the SEC isolated 16 financial stocks that could no longer be illegally shorted, they sent the wrong message. If naked shorting is illegal, why just enforce the rules on 16 companies—why not the whole market? The standards are easy—clear, transparent, and honest. Currently over a dozen countries that speak different languages are working effectively on the International Space Station (ISS). The standards are clear and so is the accountability. Wall Street needs to act as if lives are at stake and pretend they work on the ISS—they sure get paid enough!

The second thing that worries me is that the media will finally convince the public that whatever happens—90% of it is bad. We all understand that bad new sells—but isn't anybody else appalled at how the media tries to convince the public that the sky is falling? If you read enough bad news it becomes hard to see the good things happening all around us. People are living longer and the standard of living continues to rise for most people all around the world. I realize that there are real problems and the world is far from perfect. I would like to see a less ugly media—that is all I am asking for.

The third thing that worries me is that individuals will continue their absurd push toward shorter holding periods. Great investment results cannot occur overnight. If you find a real undervalued investment opportunity, how much sense does it make that overnight it will be discovered and increase to its proper valuation level? Warren Buffett likes to remind people that it still takes 9 months to make a baby. The investors that have taken investing horizons from 3 years to 3 months to 3 days—and now even 3 hours have created almost unacceptable volatility. I cannot personally change this insanity—but I can hopefully point out the folly and help others avoid it.

Yes—this bull is worried—just not about the market. Plenty of profitable companies continue to offer exceptional opportunities to those that can see beyond today's headlines.

As the global credit market freeze spread in 2008, I shared this article in *Equities Magazine* (Kimmel, October 2008a, p. 32) to reinforce the importance of the spreading of the global free market. At the time of the article, a growing fear of a severe global recession was weighing heavily on the market, and I wanted to share a longer-term view.

ALL ABOARD! THIS PROFIT SHIP IS SAILING!

Those talking about a tumbling economy haven't been down to the shipyard, where every aspect of the global shipping business is red-hot. The industry's future looks bright as companies transport record levels of merchandise globally. Though this profit ship has already set sail, there's still plenty of time to jump on board.

You're probably aware of the impacts of increased standards of living around the world, as a much larger consumer base is living better and consuming more. This has generated a tremendous increase in tonnage being transported worldwide and has been a boom to the entire shipping business.

Over the last five years, the gross tonnage shipped has increased anywhere from 30% for the dry bulk shippers to more than 50%

for the chemical and liquid gas carriers. For the biggest carriers, despite relatively stable shipping rates, this has led to significant increases in operating margins. This is one of the things the Magnet system looks for.

There seems to be a fixation around the growth of commerce regarding China in recent years. What's more, you're seeing the same kind of growth out of India, Brazil, and Russia, to name a few. On virtually every continent, volume and tonnage are at an all-time high with no signs of abatement.

Despite my strong long-term conviction for the transportation and shipping industry, I still believe in business cycles. But while the United States is still the No. 1 consumer in the world, you should not underestimate the spreading of the free market and what it means to global consumerism.

In fact, this is the very thing that has kept me bullish during the current domestic pessimism. Of course, rising oil costs can cut into margins, and a slowdown in emerging markets may cause selling in shipping stocks. But when the smoke clears, you will see even bigger boats carrying even more tonnage.

While a rising tide may lift all boats, it's always my approach to look for the best companies in a given industry. Using the proprietary measurements of our Magnet Growth Ratio and Free Earnings, I am able to identify the most profitable and best-valued companies. Often, our model finds the smaller and faster growing companies in an industry. But in the shipping sector, our model has been selecting the bigger and more established names. There are big, stable cash-flow cows in this sector, and we own shares in several of them.

Ranking high is DryShips Inc. (NASDAQ: DRYS), a bulk commodity shipping company based in Greece. Because of continued upgrades to its fleet and its ability to move more goods, its earnings have increased twenty-fold in just five years. The rapid ramp-up in revenues and operating margins brought the company to the top of our scoring model several quarters ago.

While the share price of the company has been volatile, it is essential to separate volatility from risk. The company's strength is in the transport of raw materials like iron ore and coal products, which are essential to the mass global build-out that will take decades to complete. With an extraordinarily high return on equity, I expect DryShips to stay on our list for some time.

Barriers to entry are another interesting facet of the shipping industry. An extremely capital-intensive industry, successful players are able to update their fleets and improve their margins through cash flow. This is not the kind of industry in which a newcomer with better technology suddenly makes other competitors obsolete. In investing, protecting your downside is just as important as identifying your upside potential. Identifying the leaders in the shipping industry, and giving them time to work, may help you to learn to develop a different view toward risk.

It's too easy to get caught up in the short-term nature of the stock market. Tempting as it may be to catch the bottom in underperforming sectors, it's a difficult task. Even harder is betting on a turnaround with a company that is executing poorly and hemorrhaging cash. Too many never turn around at all. I prefer to identify the cream of the crop in an industry that has the wind in its sails.

This next article was published in 2008 in *Equities Magazine* (Kimmel, September 2008g, p. 15). In it I tried to share the importance of a company's need to create positive cash flow to remain healthy. A whole generation had fallen into a trap of valuing Internet companies based on a variety of factors that led to disastrous investment results. I was trying to point out the sector was not the problem: It was the valuation method that needed addressing.

PROFITING FROM ONLINE BUSINESS

The Internet has undoubtedly transformed the way business is done. Sure, money has been lost on Internet companies lacking sound business models, and there's been a fair amount of skepticism about transactions being done in "thin air," but over the years, online business has become an important asset to many industries.

It's no longer a question of whether a company needs to have an online platform, but only of how to best integrate it. Businesses that understood early on the global reach of online sales have made great strides, and the rewards to come will spread as online business and sales applications continue to expand.

I distinctly remember the major brokerage firms' initial reaction to online trading: It would be for the little guy and of no interest to big clients. Quickly, however, consumer demand and the fear of lost business forced the hands of financial firms. It became a matter of figuring out a way for clients to have the choice between speaking with a representative and letting them trade online for themselves.

It's become the same for retailers: Invite them into your stores, but make sure they can "click and ship" if they prefer. Many businesses have seen profits explode and their customer base widen dramatically by offering online shopping. High prices at the gas pump will only fuel this trend.

Also a result of online capabilities, delivery services like UPS and FedEx have suddenly become global. This has had a profound effect on many industries and is helping to continue to spread the free market around the world. Dramatic cost savings are helping companies fill orders for products they were previously only buying locally.

By responding to international requests for proposals, business-to-business transactions are replacing the showroom salesperson and have knocked down geographic boundaries. The cost savings for buyers and expanded volume for sellers has been measured in the billions of dollars for many companies.

One of the more interesting developments that's taken place is in the area of excess inventory in the travel industry. We've previously been exposed to the dramatic price swings for airplane tickets depending on how long in advance a flight is booked. Once the plane takes off, it's another story: Each unsold seat on the plane drives the airlines crazy.

Understanding this love-hate relationship between the passengers and airlines, Priceline.com Inc. (NASDAQ: PCLN) created a great business model. Despite the poor reviews its initial advertisements received, Priceline had a solid idea and has since grown into a profitable cash cow. It figured out a way to benefit both the buyers and sellers in the transaction. A comparison of what Priceline was able to accomplish over less successful Internet businesses drives home the importance of what to look for in Internet-based companies.

A few years ago, investors and analysts developed new metrics to evaluate online businesses—we began to hear about "hits" and "clicks" as a measure of success. As we know now, these methods lost investors money while a focus on accelerating margins and cash flow continued to work. Cash flow can aid in making acquisitions, buying back shares, and expanding reach. This fact holds constant regardless of the type of business. Somehow people forgot that when investing in online companies, and they paid dearly for it.

The Internet is still in its commercial infancy. Over time, speed, and connectivity will be enhanced several times over. More applications will become available, and Web 2.0 will give way to newer ideas. Regardless of the new names or new ideas, remember that it still comes down to making money.

When investing in a stock, think about the most important question: "Would I like to own the whole business?" The answer can usually be found by looking at the cash flow, not counting eyeballs or page clicks. Don't get lost in "new era" talk. Yes, online profits are available, but don't forget: It's still business.

In early 2008, the financial sector was unraveling. Although the banking system was clearly out of favor, I was trying to look toward the horizon to highlight the reality that the financial industry was not going to collapse entirely and that the future of the financial markets would indeed be global in nature. Here is what I wrote in my article, "Banking on Growth" on page 32 of the summer 2008 issue of *Equities Magazine* (Kimmel 2008c).

BANKING ON GROWTH

Today, a combination of falling home prices and a liquidity crunch for the myriad of securitization products has wreaked havoc on banks, mortgage companies, home builders, and the brokerage firms that issued and traded these mortgage-related products. A new bear market has developed, engulfing every industry in the financial sector, and most bank stocks have fallen by 60% to 80%.

Of course, now the question is: Do we take advantage of the already fallen prices or stay clear of another shoe yet to drop?

The biggest issue is trying to get a handle on how big the problems really are. The initial estimates were for $100 billion in write-downs and losses among the brokerage firms and banks. But that estimate was soon increased to $250 billion, and some say the total losses now range as high as $1 trillion. We now have worry mongers projecting a recession, deflation, and years of decline.

While real estate has taken a hit, we must be sure to put everything in perspective. Right now, 95% of mortgages are current within 30 days. Foreclosures, while reportedly skyrocketing to a rate of 40%, are in fact still below 5%. Much of the collateral in these investments was solid and remains solid today. The problems with the subprime loans are not the defaults occurring but the liquidity problems with the products themselves. Once this mess is resolved—and it will be—growth will resume not only across America but also worldwide.

It is important to note that the worldwide equity markets exceed a market capitalization of more than $60 trillion, and the global bond market is significantly larger than the equity market. To get a handle on the size of the overall world economy, you would have to include the cash markets, the real estate markets, and the commodity markets. The bear market reaction to the credit crisis has resulted in a $6 trillion loss in the global equity markets. The losses we hear about on an individual company level are huge, and Wall Street will continue to struggle for a while. But the losses are sustainable and the capital markets are large enough to handle them. Remember, a balance sheet should be looked at for both the debt and credit side, and the total net worth of Americans exceeded $50 trillion just last year.

To profitably navigate today's financial sector, it is necessary to look forward rather than in the rearview mirror. By the same token, it's important to think globally, not domestically. The current global build-out is far larger and more complex than most people realize. America's No. 1 export is the free market. As a result of the Internet and mass communication, economic landscapes are changing rapidly and the development of the world population into consumers is taking place on a global scale.

While politicians talk democracy, the real issue lies in the opening of the free market. Global populations are increasingly participating in the higher standard of living they see being enjoyed around the world. Short-term-focused investors are ignoring the inevitable growth in the size of the capital markets over the next few decades.

Just 40 years ago, the NYSE was closed to celebrate surpassing 1 million traded shares in a single day. Now, we routinely see 2.5 billion shares per day on both the NYSE and the NASDAQ, and the time will soon come when 10 billion shares trade per day—imagine the profits of the financial service firms.

Plus, over the next few decades, innovative new industries will emerge. Financial firms will underwrite these new issues and collect fees. The earnings from those new companies—companies that do not even exist yet—will help drive the economy.

While there is certainly more bad news to come, the bottom may be near, if it hasn't already passed in the U.S. banking and financial sector. As a result of the negative sentiment, everything is already on sale in the financial industry, and if you can buy and hold for a few years, you may be very profitable.

My approach is to use the Magnet System, which means letting the bottom pass and buying domestic banks another time, once they've passed the bottom and are entering a period of strength. I'll continue to focus on the companies with the good ideas and management that continue to generate "free earnings," accelerating cash flow while trading at a discount.

We're finding a host of banks in the international banking sector that are scoring highly on our model, including Banco Itau Holdings (NYSE: ITU), Credicorp Ltd. (NYSE: BAP), and Oriental Financial Group (NYSE: OFG).

If you want to make money in the stock market, think long term and pay less attention to the rearview mirror. Tune out the doomsday nonsense. Look for the free market to continue to spread. Wall Street will find a cure for the current liquidity crisis, and a far greater number of investors will bid the markets significantly higher over time. You can bank on it.

In this article published in *Equities Magazine* in early 2008 (Kimmel 2008e, p. 27), I wanted to focus on two major themes: (1) The global markets were growing even while the short-term conditions were weakening. (2) I also wanted to share the concept of investing in a provider of equipment to an entire industry, rather than trying to figure out the best positioned company in a given sector.

PICKS AND SHOVELS

There are clear signs that the U.S. economy is in a slowdown. The media is fixated on how long and deep the upcoming recession will be, but while we have seen a definite slowdown in U.S. consumerism, the international picture is drastically different. The global build-out is actually larger and more sustainable than most people can imagine. While everybody continues to look over his or her shoulder for signs that the commodity sector will roll over, the signs are not there. In fact, if you look for the pockets of strength in the stock market, you'll see that the mining and basic material groups remain the strongest. While it's hard to say which mineral or metal will outshine the others in price appreciation or the duration of their move, there are easy ways to profitably play this sector. One suggestion is to invest in the picks and shovels.

Over the last several quarters, despite the seemingly relentless moves in most commodity prices, we have seen several violent shakeouts. In fact, we are experiencing another as of this writing. But despite the slowdown in the activity of the domestic consumer, the spreading of the free market is generating an almost insatiable demand for almost every commodity you can think of. Back in the early 1990s, Sir John Templeton gave a tremendous presentation in which he discussed the impact of the fall of the Berlin Wall. He said it would have the single biggest impact on investments of any event that had occurred in his lifetime. And how right he was. But that event is now dwarfed by the explosion in the growth taking place around the world today. While there is a focus on China—which currently accounts for 50% or more of the worldwide demand for copper, aluminum, zinc, lead, and steel—growth is taking place on every continent.

My focus with investments is to avoid being "too predictive" and to instead listen to the market. Although I have a degree in economics, I try to forget about it altogether. Experience and history will show that too much focus on economics will lead to faulty analysis. For starters, not a single recession has been correctly forecasted by the economists in the government or on Wall Street. Often, money is lost by individuals who think they can forecast complicated cause-and-event scenarios that will take place over a number of years. A more profitable way of investing is to put your ego aside and allow the market to tell the story. Once in a while, a group of stocks in a given sector will cluster to the top of one's quantitative best ideas list. Ideally, one will find a company within a favorable sector that dominates its niche.

One clear example of this can be seen with Bucyrus International (NASDAQ: BUCY). A quick look at a three-year chart shows a dramatic rise in the shares. While the share price has more than quadrupled, there have been several sharp and sudden drops that would have shaken out most investors. Anybody that believes in tight stops could not have stayed in the stock despite the company's tremendous fundamental competitive advantage within its niche business. The extreme volatility seen in some of these smaller but dynamic companies makes it very hard to maintain one's long-term perspective.

During the sharp sell-off in January 2008, I spoke with management at BUCY. At the time, it was down more than 30% in price from just a month before. What was striking in the conversation was the comment by management that there are only two companies in the world—BUCY being one of them—that make a particular type of shovel required in all mining endeavors. Margins were still accelerating, and the current backlog was at an all-time high. In this case, it was not management "explaining away" a bad quarter or slow down in business; it was a clear example of the market's short-term volatility opportunity.

Of course, when it comes to picks and shovels, we are also talking about the equipment used in the expanding agriculture markets. We are now seeing a lot of attention in this area for good reason. As development continues to spread around the globe, a greater number of people are in a position to improve their diets. The same yield improvements within the farming industry that took place in the U.S. are just taking place now overseas. With the world's increase in population and the constant improvement of the general standard of living, when do you see the demand for large machinery going out of favor?

APPENDIX

Testing the Magnet Approach: The Investment Performance of the Superlatives

As part of my continuing efforts to improve and maximize my Magnet® Stock Selection Process, in 2006 I employed the back-testing analytical prowess of HedgeMetrics to help confirm or deny the efficacy and superior performance capability of my system. After the first back-test was complete, several other questions about the finer points of the system came up. So we ran those through a back-test as well. Presented here in their entirety are the results of the two back-tests with commentary from C. Michael Carty, from New Millennium Advisors, and Edward Matluck, PhD, from HedgeMetrics.

BACK-TEST OF THE MAGNET INVESTMENT STRATEGY (HEDGEMETRICS): OCTOBER 19, 2006, BY C. MICHAEL CARTY AND EDWARD MATLUCK, PHD

I. Introduction and Summary

The primary purpose of this study is to back-test the performance of the scientifically based, proprietary Magnet Investment Strategy. This Strategy uses conventional technical and fundamental factors within a theoretically sound framework and a clear set of heuristic rules to select a limited number of stocks expected to outperform the Russell 2000 and S&P 500.

The theory underlying the Magnet Investment Strategy holds that stocks with large and rapidly growing sales which are reasonably priced according to metrics such as their price-to-earnings multiples and earnings growth, having above average relative strength, are undervalued and, therefore, likely to outperform the Russell 2000 and S&P 500. Empirical evidence, developed in this study, based on extensive back-testing indicates that the strategy would have produced superior returns relative to the Russell 2000 and S&P 500 between February 1987 and April 2006, a period of 231 months, equivalent to nineteen years and three months.

This study discusses the principal criteria used in selecting stocks and the heuristic rules used to eliminate some stocks from consideration. It then uses those criteria and rules to select portfolios, and compares their performance to the indexes. The study back-tests the Strategy using portfolios of varied sizes: i.e., 20, 25, and 30 stocks.

We found that each of the Magnet portfolios produce greater returns than the Russell 2000 and S&P 500 by substantial margins. In addition, although the Magnet portfolios have higher standard deviations than the Russell 2000 and S&P 500, their risk-adjusted returns and Sharpe ratios are superior to those of the indexes. Moreover, all Magnet portfolios have lower maximum drawdowns and shorter drawdown durations.

On the basis of this evidence, we conclude that the Magnet Strategy is theoretically sound, and that portfolios constructed using its selection criteria and rules offer significant prospects for outperforming the Russell 2000 and S&P 500. We have been involved in back-testing various strategies over many years. The back-test of the Magnet strategy has produced some of the highest un-leveraged returns of any model that we have tested to date. These results are consistent with results obtained by other researchers and reflect methodologies used by a number of "Best of Breed" money managers in major U. S. institutions.

II. The Magnet Investment Strategy

The Magnet Investment Strategy is a disciplined system for selecting stocks that have the greatest potential for monthly capital appreciation. It is implemented in two steps. The first step is to rank all stocks in the Zacks universe having earnings estimates (The Zacks universe consists of all U.S. equities traded on the NYSE, AMEX, and NASDAQ exchanges for which earnings estimates are available, currently 4,700), based on fundamental, valuation, and technical criteria, which research has shown, is shared by stocks that have performed well historically. The second step is to eliminate certain stocks from consideration based on a set of rules that limit sector exposure and promote diversification.

The first step in back-testing the Strategy is to rank all stocks in the Zacks universe meeting its criteria from 1 to 4,700 and select the top 20, 25, or 30 best for each of the three portfolios. Among the fundamental criteria considered are those related to sales and earnings, favoring companies with superior growth over others with average or below average growth. The valuation criteria consider a company's market value relative to its sales and earnings, favoring companies that appear to be undervalued at current prices. The technical criteria consider a company's stock price momentum relative to others, favoring those with the greatest momentum. The specific measures and ranking algorithm are proprietary.

The second step in back-testing the Strategy is to compare the stocks selected in the first step with Magnet rules. Among these rules is one that limits sector exposure to 25% of the portfolio in order to ensure adequate diversification, thereby avoiding the potential for catastrophic losses in any one sector. Another rule places stop-loss limits on holdings to limit downside losses at 20%, and partially pares back positions on stocks, which have appreciated 40% to lock in a portion of the gain. Also, each stock must be liquid and have a minimum daily trading volume of 35,000 shares.

III. Methodology Used in the Back-Test

This study uses only data that would have been known at the time stocks are selected. Some fundamentals become available with a one-quarter delay; e.g., sales and earnings per share are reported at the end of March having fiscal years corresponding to a calendar year. Price data are available daily, so that a price-to-earnings multiple based on March's non-adjusted trailing 12-month earnings per share uses June's month-end stock price. Stocks are eliminated from consideration if they have negative or undefined earnings.

The Magnet stock selection criteria and rules are used to rank each stock from one to the number of stocks in the universe. The highest ranked stocks in the ranking are selected for the portfolios in descending order. Once a stock in a particular sector is selected, another lower ranked stock also in the same sector is eliminated from consideration. The same selection process is used for the 20-, 25-, and 30-stock portfolios.

The three Magnet portfolios are selected and subjected to rules using limits to stop losses and harvest gains. The stop-loss rule sells any stock if it falls 20% from its purchase price. When sold it is replaced with the stock that had the next highest rank in the most recent ranking period. Stocks are ranked each month and new portfolios formed.

IV. Analysis of Magnet Strategy's Performance

Table A.1 contains summary statistics of the Strategy's performance using stop limits in portfolios with 20, 25, and 30 stocks. In all cases, the portfolios outperformed the Russell 2000 and S&P 500 by significant margins. The 30-stock portfolio achieved 38.6%, the 25-stock portfolio, 37.4%, and the 20-stock portfolio, 36.1%.

TABLE A.1 Summary of the Back-Test Results

Performance	20 Stocks	25 Stocks	30 Stocks	Russell 2000	S&P 500
Compound Annual Return (%)	36.07	37.35	38.64	8.86	8.47
Annual Standard Deviation (%)	30.61	29.76	28.95	19.19	14.82
Sharpe Ratio	1.02	1.09	1.17	0.21	0.24
Maximum Drawdown (%)	−35.18	−33.03	−33.53	−37.68	−46.28
Max Drawdown/ Average Return. (Years)	0.98	0.88	0.87	4.25	5.46
Avg. Monthly Turnover (%)	14.9	17.96	20.94	N/A	N/A

Source: HedgeMetrics, Inc.

TABLE A.2 Comparative Annual Returns of MAGNET Strategies vs. the Indexes Over 1, 3, 5, and 10 Years

With Stops	20 Stocks	25 Stocks	30 Stocks	Russell 2000	S&P 500
1 Year	93.4%	95.5%	90.4%	24.0%	10.0%
3 Years	52.7%	50.8%	45.8%	20.1%	10.8%
5 Years	32.2%	31.6%	30.9%	9.0%	0.9%
10 Years	36.0%	36.8%	37.3%	7.7%	7.0%

Source: HedgeMetrics, Inc.

Importantly, Magnet portfolios are consistent and have consistently higher returns than the indexes (Table A.2). The 30-stock portfolio has greater returns than the Russell 2000 every year and the S&P 500 in sixteen years. The 25-stock portfolio has greater returns than the Russell 2000 in seventeen years and greater returns than the S&P 500 in sixteen years. The 20-stock portfolio has greater returns than both indexes in sixteen years.

The Strategy's consistency is reflected in its performance over 1, 3, 5, and 10 years ended April 2006. As shown in Table A.2, its compound annual returns are significantly above the Russell 2000 and the S&P 500 by multiple factors in each period.

The Magnet portfolios are more volatile than the Russell 2000 and S&P 500, but not to the same degree as their excess returns. The 30-stock portfolio has an annual standard deviation of 29.0%, the 25-stock portfolio, 29.8%, and the 20-stock portfolio, 30.6%.

Yet, the return-to-risk trade-offs of the Magnet portfolios have better Sharpe ratios than the indexes, the 30-stock portfolio has a 1.17 ratio, the 25-stock portfolio a 1.09, and the 20-stock portfolio, 1.02. Sharpe ratios for the Russell 2000 and S&P 500 are significantly smaller, 0.21 and 0.24, respectively.

Monthly roundtrip turnover rates are 20.9% for 30 stocks, 18.0% for 25 stocks and 14.9% for 20 stocks.

Assuming initial investment of $1.00 is made in the three Magnet strategies and two indexes on February 28, 1987, the terminal values of those investments on April 30, 2006 appear in Table A.3.

Figure A.1 compares the growth in the value of $1.00 in the 30-, 25-, and 20-stock strategies versus the Russell 2000 and S&P 500. The

TABLE A.3 Values of an Initial $1.00 Investment*

	Terminal Value
30 Stocks	$544.21
25 Stocks	$445.21
20 Stocks	$371.98
Russell 2000	$5.12
S&P 500	$4.78

*February 1987 to April 2006

Source: HedgeMetrics, Inc.

30-stock strategy has the greatest terminal value, $544.21, followed by the 25-stock strategy's $445.21, and the 20-stock strategy's $371.98. The Russell 2000 and S&P 500 shown in the legend are, in fact, lying on the horizontal scale since their appreciation is too small to be shown on the same scale as the Magnet strategies, being $5.12 and $4.78, respectively.

One might assume that a strategy utilizing the top 20 ranked stocks should outperform another using the top 30 ranked stocks

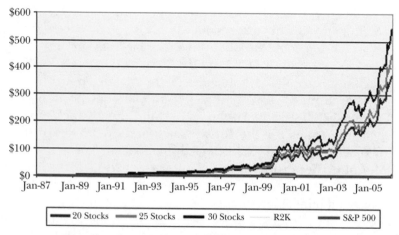

FIGURE A.1   Growth in the value of $1.00 in the 30-, 25-, 15-, and 20-stock strategies, the Russell 2000 and the S&P 500—February 1987 to April 2006

Source: HedgeMetrics, Inc.

because the 30-stock strategy contains 10 lower ranked stocks. However, the empirical evidence suggests that the ranking system does not sufficiently discriminate the next month's performance of the top 20 from the top 30 stocks, and that a 30-stock strategy provides 10 more chances of picking stocks that will outperform in the coming month. By being more diversified it also limits the impact of losses from stocks that do go down. It is also possible that some stocks achieve the highest ranks by virtue of their exceptional price momentum, which may be about to wane, in contrast to those occupying ranks from 21 to 30 continuing to gain momentum.

Magnet portfolios are also superior to the Russell 2000 and S&P 500 in perhaps the most relevant measure of risk, the maximum drawdown. The 30-stock portfolio's maximum drawdown is −33.5%, the 25-stock portfolio's −33.0%, and the 20-stock portfolio's −35.2%. The maximum drawdown for the Russell 2000 is slightly deeper at −37.7%, but much deeper for the S&P 500 at −46.3%.

Table A.4 contains the five greatest drawdowns for the Magnet portfolios, the Russell 2000 and the S&P 500 over the period from February 1987 through April 2006. Their average time to recovery varies from 5 to 8 months, which is shorter than the average 12-month recovery period for the Russell 2000 and 16 months for the S&P 500. The average drawdowns of the Russell 2000 and the S&P 500 are less deep than Magnet portfolios but their time to recover is longer.

V. Summary and Conclusions

The Magnet Strategy appears to have sound theoretical, fundamental, and technical underpinnings. The empirical evidence compiled between February 1987 and April 2006, a period of 231 months, suggests that portfolios constructed using Magnet selection criteria and rules offer significant prospects for outperforming the Russell 2000 and S&P 500. Stocks with large and rapidly growing sales which are reasonably priced according to their price-to-earnings multiples and earnings growth, having above average relative strength, are possibly undervalued and likely to outperform the indexes the following month. Annual returns of the Magnet Strategies are contained in Table A.5.

TABLE A.4   The Five Greatest Drawdowns and Recovery Periods for MAGNET Strategies and the Indexes*

MAGNET Portfolios	Max DD Date	Max DD	# Mos to Max DD	# Mos to Recover
20 Stocks	9/30/87	−35.2%	2	7
	5/31/01	−34.7%	4	20
	5/31/90	−31.2%	5	4
	6/30/98	−29.9%	2	5
	8/31/00	−25.8%	3	5
Average		−31.4%	3	8
25 Stocks	9/30/87	−33.0%	2	7
	5/31/01	−32.1%	4	20
	5/31/90	−31.8%	5	4
	6/30/98	−28.4%	2	4
	2/29/92	−26.3%	4	5
Average		−30.3%	3	8
30 Stocks	5/31/01	−33.5%	4	6
	9/30/87	−32.2%	2	5
	6/30/90	−31.9%	4	4
	6/30/98	−30.2%	2	4
	8/31/00	−24.6%	3	5
Average		−30.5%	3	5
Russell 2000	2/29/00	−37.7%	36	11
	8/31/87	−35.8%	3	21
	9/30/89	−33.1%	13	7
	4/30/98	−30.1%	4	16
	5/31/96	−12.7%	2	5
Average		−29.9%	12	12
S&P 500	8/31/00	−46.3%	25	44
	8/31/87	−30.2%	3	20
	5/31/90	−15.8%	5	4
	6/30/98	−15.6%	2	3
	1/31/94	−7.8%	5	8
Average		−23.1%	8	16

*From February 1987 to April 2006

Source: HedgeMetrics, Inc.

TABLE A.5   Annual Returns of Magnet Strategies

	20 Stocks	25 Stocks	30 Stocks	Russell 2000	S&P 500
1987*	−4.7%	−2.0%	3.4%	−19.5%	−9.9%
1988	38.2%	35.1%	33.3%	22.4%	12.4%
1989	63.3%	62.1%	69.5%	14.2%	27.3%
1990	−5.6%	−5.6%	−0.7%	−21.3%	−6.6%
1991	103.2%	110.1%	99.1%	43.4%	26.3%
1992	63.5%	50.5%	52.4%	16.5%	4.5%
1993	12.5%	21.9%	22.4%	17.3%	7.1%
1994	13.7%	16.2%	21.3%	−3.3%	−1.5%
1995	48.8%	52.9%	57.5%	26.5%	34.1%
1996	44.9%	51.7%	58.8%	14.8%	20.3%
1997	33.7%	33.0%	31.1%	20.7%	31.0%
1998	19.0%	19.3%	22.6%	−3.8%	26.7%
1999	100.1%	100.8%	96.2%	19.6%	19.5%
2000	9.7%	14.7%	20.4%	−4.3%	−10.1%
2001	34.7%	34.4%	32.5%	1.0%	−13.0%
2002	−10.8%	−5.1%	−0.8%	−21.6%	−23.4%
2003	123.3%	108.1%	109.2%	45.4%	26.4%
2004	11.0%	8.2%	5.5%	17.0%	9.0%
2005	47.1%	51.3%	42.8%	3.3%	3.0%
2006†	30.9%	33.2%	32.4%	13.6%	5.0%

*Average returns over 11 months beginning in February 1987

†Average returns over 4 months ending in April 2006

Source: HedgeMetrics, Inc.

BACK-TEST OF THE MAGNET INVESTMENT STRATEGY (HEDGEMETRICS): APRIL 6, 2007, BY C. MICHAEL CARTY AND EDWARD MATLUCK, PHD

I. Introduction and Summary

This study seeks to determine: (1) whether the Magnet Investment Strategy's performance would be enhanced by adding a variable measuring the number of analysts covering a company to its selection criteria, (2) whether the sales growth acceleration and margin acceleration-related factors should continue to be more heavily weighted than other factors, (3) whether stocks selected by the Strategy from the S&P 500 universe might be used to outperform it, and (4) whether the Strategy should use stop-loss limits on holdings to limit downside losses to 20%, and partially pare back positions on stocks which have appreciated 40% to lock in a portion of the gain.

The theory underlying Magnet's Investment Strategy holds that stocks with large and rapidly growing sales which are reasonably priced according to fundamental factors (i.e., profit margins, price-to-earnings multiples and earnings growth, etc.), having above average relative strength, are undervalued and, therefore, likely to outperform the Russell 2000 and S&P 500. The empirical evidence developed in an earlier study was based on extensive back-testing which indicated that the Strategy would have produced superior returns than the Russell 2000 and S&P 500 between February 1987 and April 2006, a period of 231 months, equivalent to nineteen years and two months.

This study reviews the principal criteria used in selecting stocks and the heuristic rules used to eliminate some stocks from consideration. We then use those criteria and rules to select stocks from the Zacks universe of 4,700 stocks to create 20-, 25-, and 30-stock portfolios in order to use their performance as a Base Case against which to judge whether attempts to change the Strategy by adding new factors, or changing the weighting scheme of existing factors is likely to improve its performance. Finally, we test the Strategy's efficacy by selecting 20-, 30-, and 40-stock portfolios from the S&P 500's universe to determine if they can outperform it.

In the earlier study, we found that the Strategy produced greater returns than the Russell 2000 and S&P 500 by substantial margins. In addition, although the MAGNET portfolios have higher standard deviations than the Russell 2000 and S&P 500, their risk-adjusted returns and Sharpe ratios are significantly superior to those of both indexes.

This study builds on the earlier study with additional findings:

> Adding the number of analysts covering a company increases annual returns to 20-, 25-, and 30-stock portfolios by incremental amounts of from 0.9% to 4.7%, and that tripling the weight of that factor increases incremental annual returns by as little as 3.3% and as much as 5.2%.

Increasing the weights to certain sales-related factors does not enhance, but, instead, reduces annual returns by as little as 0.5% or as much as 6.6% depending on the number of stocks included in the portfolio.

The 20-, 30- and 40-stock portfolios selected from the S&P 500 universe have substantially better performance than the S&P 500 with incrementally greater annual returns of 6.3% to 8.3% and only modestly higher standard deviations.

The Strategy's performance may be improved by eliminating tactics such as stop-loss limits and partially paring back positions on stocks that have appreciated. This result was unanticipated. It turned out that stocks up 40% continued up for the next month and ultimately were dropped by the ranking system. Similarly stocks that were stopped out ended up being dropped by the ranking system in the next month anyway. In some cases reversion to the mean in future months helped limit initial losses.

On the basis of this evidence, we continue to conclude that the Magnet Strategy is theoretically sound, and its selection criteria and rules offer significant prospects for outperforming benchmarks such as the Russell 2000 and S&P 500. We have been involved in back testing various strategies over many years. Back-tests of the Magnet Strategy have produced some of the highest un-leveraged returns of any model we have tested to date. These results are consistent with results obtained by other researchers and reflect methodologies used by a number of "Best of Breed" money managers in major U.S. institutions.

II. The Magnet Investment Strategy

The Magnet Investment Strategy is a disciplined system for selecting stocks that have the greatest potential for monthly capital appreciation. It is implemented in two steps. The first step is to rank all stocks in the Zacks universe having earnings estimates according to certain fundamental, valuation, and technical criteria which research has shown is shared by stocks that have performed well historically. (The Zacks universe consists of all U.S. equities traded on the NYSE, AMEX, and NASDAQ exchanges for which earnings estimates are available, currently 4,700). The second step is to eliminate certain stocks from consideration based on a set of rules that limit sector exposure, promote diversification, harvest gains, and cut losses.

Among the fundamental criteria the Strategy considers are those related to sales and earnings, favoring companies with superior growth over others with average or below average growth. The valuation criteria consider a company's market value relative to its sales and earnings, favoring companies that appear to be undervalued at current prices. The technical criteria consider a company's stock price momentum relative to others, favoring those with the greatest momentum. The specific measures and ranking algorithm are proprietary.

The final step in selecting a Magnet portfolio is to subject the initially selected stocks to a set of heuristic rules. Among these rules is one that limits sector exposure to 25% in order to ensure adequate diversification, thereby avoiding the potential for catastrophic losses in any one sector. Also, each stock must be liquid and have a minimum daily trading volume of 35,000 shares.

III. Methodology Used to Determine the Value of Analysts' Coverage

It is widely believed by proponents of Efficient Markets Theory that stocks followed by a large number of analysts are more efficiently priced than those followed by few or no analysts. It is also believed that the lack of information in inefficient markets gives any additional information a disciplined investment process can provide considerable value. Therefore, if market efficiency is inversely correlated to the number of analysts following a particular stock, then the Magnet Strategy might improve its returns by favoring stocks with less analysts' coverage.

To test this hypothesis, a Base Case of 20-, 25-, and 30-stock portfolios are selected using the Strategy. Then, 20-, 25-, and 30-stock portfolios are selected adding analysts' coverage to the criteria, and weighting it in subsequent tests by one, two, and three times the weights accorded other factors. The results are shown in Table A.6.

As illustrated in Table A.6, and noted in the earlier study, portfolios selected using the Magnet Strategy produce significant returns above the Russell 2000 and S&P 500. Despite their greater volatility, these portfolios have Sharpe ratios approximately four times greater than the indexes.

TABLE A.6   Performance of the Magnet Strategy Without and With Analysts' Coverage

Back-Test Description	Performance Metric	30 Stocks	25 Stocks	20 Stocks	Russell 2000	S&P 500
Base Case	Ann. Ret. (%)	38.6	37.4	36.1	9.5	9.1
	Std Dev. (%)	29.0	29.8	30.6	19.3	15.1
	Sharpe Ratio	1.17	1.09	1.02	0.23	0.28
	Max DD (%)	−33.5	−33.0	−35.2	−37.7	−46.3
	Max DD Dur (Yr)	0.87	0.88	0.98	3.96	5.07
	Turnover (%)	20.9	17.9	14.8	N/A	N/A
Analyst Wgts.= 1	Ann. Ret. (%)	39.5	42.1	38.8	9.5	9.1
	Std Dev. (%)	27.6	29.2	31.1	19.3	15.1
	Sharpe Ratio	1.25	1.28	1.09	0.24	0.28
	Max DD (%)	−36.4	−34.3	−33.1	−37.7	−46.3
	Max DD Dur (Yr)	0.92	0.82	0.85	3.96	5.07
	Turnover (%)	27.0	21.0	14.9	N/A	N/A
Analyst Wgts. = 2	Ann. Ret. (%)	41.4	42.6	39.3	9.5	9.1
	Std Dev. (%)	27.7	28.7	31.5	19.3	15.1
	Sharpe Ratio	1.32	1.31	1.09	0.24	0.28
	Max DD (%)	−36.5	−32.6	−36.5	−37.7	−46.3
	Max DD Dur (Yr)	0.88	0.76	0.93	3.96	5.07
	Turnover (%)	27.1	21.1	15.0	N/A	N/A
Analyst Wgts. = 3	Ann. Ret. (%)	41.9	42.2	41.3	9.5	9.1
	Std Dev. (%)	27.5	28.8	31.5	19.3	15.1
	Sharpe Ratio	1.35	1.30	1.15	0.24	0.28
	Max DD (%)	−36.5	−34.2	−34.6	−37.7	−46.3
	Max DD Dur (Yr)	0.87	0.81	0.84	3.96	5.07
	Turnover (%)	27.3	21.2	15.0	N/A	N/A

Source: HedgeMetrics, Inc.

As shown in Table A.6 the addition of analysts' coverage gives the 25-stock portfolio annual returns of 42.1% versus the 37.4% of the Base Case, a difference of 4.7%, with a slight reduction in standard deviation. The incremental improvement in the 20- and 30-stock portfolios' returns is less dramatic, being 2.7% and 0.8% above the Base Case, respectively. Also noteworthy is the significant increases in the returns and Sharpe ratios of all three portfolios as the weights given the analysts' coverage factor are increased.

Adding the analysts' coverage factor increases by only small amounts the maximum drawdowns but generally reduces drawdown durations (defined as the maximum drawdown divided by the average annual return) of all three portfolios irrespective of whether that factor is weighted one, two, or three times.

Analysts' coverage, however, significantly increases the monthly roundtrip turnover in the 25- and 30-stock portfolios. Turnover increases from 17.9% in the Base Case's 25-stock portfolio to between 21.0, and 21.2% in the 25-stock portfolio. It is further increased from 20.9% in the Base Case's 30-stock portfolio to 27.3% as the weight of analysts' coverage increased by a multiple of three.

IV. Methodology Used to Test Weights Given the Sales-Related Factors

Several sales-related factors (sales growth, sales acceleration and operating margins) are currently given additional weights in the selection process. In order to determine whether the increased weighting of these factors is justified, we compared the performance of the Base Case 20-, 25-, and 30-stock portfolios against those resulting from a selection process which equal-weighted all factors.

As illustrated in Table A.7, all three portfolios using Equal Factor Weights have higher returns than those of the Base Case. The Equal Factor Weighted 20-stock portfolio has an annual return of 42.7% versus the 36.1% of the Base Case 20-stock portfolio, a difference of 6.7% with no change in volatility. The Equal Factor Weighted 25-stock portfolio return of 40.4% is 3.1% greater than the 37.4% achieved by the Base Case 25-stock portfolio, with 1.2% less standard deviation. There is minor 0.5% difference in the returns to the 30-stock portfolios, but the Equal Factor Weighted portfolio has a 1.5% lower standard deviation (see Table A.7).

Despite minor differences in the maximum drawdowns between the Equal Factor Weighted and Base Case portfolios, there are

TABLE A.7   Comparative Performance of the Base Case Magnet Strategy vs. an Equal Factor Weighted Strategy

Test Description	Performance Metric	30 Stocks	25 Stocks	20 Stocks	Russell 2000	S&P 500
Equal Factor Wgts.	Ann. Ret. (%)	39.1	40.4	42.7	9.5	9.1
	Std Dev. (%)	27.5	28.6	30.6	19.3	15.1
	Sharpe Ratio	1.25	1.24	1.24	0.23	0.28
	Max DD (%)	−31.1	−33.1	−32.4	−37.7	−46.3
	Max DD Dur (Yr)	0.80	0.82	0.76	3.96	5.07
	Turnover (%)	27.2	21.1	14.9	N/A	N/A
Base Case	Ann. Ret. (%)	38.6	37.4	36.1	9.5	9.1
	Std Dev. (%)	29.0	29.8	30.6	19.3	15.1
	Sharpe Ratio	1.17	1.09	1.02	0.23	0.28
	Max DD (%)	−33.5	−33.0	−35.2	−37.7	−46.3
	Max DD Dur (Yr)	0.87	0.88	0.98	3.96	5.07
	Turnover (%)	20.9	17.9	14.8	N/A	N/A

Source: HedgeMetrics, Inc.

significant differences in their drawdown durations due to differences in their annual returns. For example, the maximum drawdown duration associated with the Equal Factor Weighted 20-stock portfolio drops to 0.76 years from 0.98 years with Base Case's 20-stock portfolio, a reduction of nearly 3 months.

V. Analysis of the Magnet Strategy Selecting Stocks from the S&P 500

The Magnet Strategy produces greater returns than the S&P 500 when selecting stocks from a large population such as the Zack universe (see Table A.8). If the Strategy can reliably outperform the S&P 500 using large cap stocks, it might serve as the basis for an enhanced S&P 500 indexed product. The question we investigated is, "whether it can outperform the S&P 500 when stocks are drawn from the population of large cap stocks in the S&P 500 universe?"

TABLE A.8   Comparative Performance of the Base Case Magnet Strategy Drawn from the S&P 500 Universe

Back-Test Description	Performance Metric	40 Stocks	30 Stocks	20 Stocks	S&P 500
Base Case 500	Ann. Ret. (%)	17.0	17.5	15.4	9.1
	Std Dev. (%)	18.3	18.7	19.7	15.1
	Sharpe Ratio	0.67	0.67	0.53	0.28
	Max DD (%)	−29.1	−28.9	−31.9	−46.3
	Max DD Dur (Yr)	1.71	1.65	2.07	5.07
	Turnover (%)	13.82	11.10	7.48	N/A

Source: HedgeMetrics, Inc.

The information contained in Table A.8 partially answers that question. It contains summary statistics of the Strategy's Base Case performance of 20-, 30-, and 40-stock portfolios drawn from the S&P 500 universe. In all three cases, their average annual returns are greater than the S&P 500's. The 40-stock portfolio achieved a 17.0% annual return, the 30-stock portfolio, 17.5%, and the 20-stock portfolio, 15.4% versus the S&P 500's 9.1%. Moreover, Base Case 500 portfolios' individual annual returns are greater than the S&P 500's in most years. (Supporting evidence is contained in the Appendix.) The 30-stock portfolio outperformed the Index in 18 of 20 years, the 40-stock portfolio in 16 years, and the 20-stock portfolio in 15 years.

The Base Case 500 portfolios, however, are more volatile than the S&P 500's 15.1%, but their standard deviations diminish as the number of stocks contained in the portfolios increase. The 20-stock portfolio's standard deviation of 19.9% is the highest of the three; the 30-stock portfolio's is second with 18.7% and the 40-stock portfolio's is 18.3%, or only 3.2% greater than the S&P's. Despite their higher volatility, the Base Case 500 portfolios' greater returns produce Sharpe ratios that are 1.9 and 2.4 times superior to S&P's (see Table A.9).

The Strategy's consistency is further demonstrated in its performance over 1, 3, 5, and 10 years ended December 2005. As shown in Table A.4, its average annual returns are significantly greater than the S&P 500's in each period.

Table A.9 Comparing the Annual Returns of Base Case 500 Portfolios vs. the S&P 500 Over 1, 3, 5, and 10 Years*

Time Period	20 Stocks	30 Stocks	40 Stocks	S&P 500
1 Year	19.3%	20.7%	24.5%	3.0%
3 Years	26.0%	27.2%	29.4%	12.4%
5 Years	10.4%	10.8%	12.3%	–1.1%
10 Years	14.4%	14.6%	12.7%	7.3%

*For the years ended December 31, 2005

Source: HedgeMetrics, Inc.

Figure A.2 compares the growth in the value of $1.00 invested in the Base Case 500 portfolios and S&P 500 starting in early February 1987 and held through April 2006. The 30-stock portfolio has the greatest terminal value at $22.03, followed by the 40-stock portfolio's $20.59, and the 20-stock portfolio's $15.90. In contrast, the terminal value of the S&P 500 is $5.35, less than one-fourth the value of the 30-stock portfolio.

As illustrated in Tables A.3 and A.6, the Base Case 500 portfolios are superior to the S&P 500 in perhaps the most relevant measure of risk, the maximum drawdown. The 40-stock portfolio's maximum drawdown is –28.2%, the 30-stock portfolio's is –28.8%, and the 20-stock portfolio's is -37.4%. The maximum drawdown for the S&P 500 is much a deeper, –46.3%.

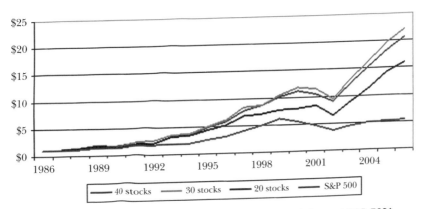

FIGURE A.2   Growth in the value of $1.00 in the Magnet Portfolios and S&P 500*

Source: HedgeMetrics, Inc.

Table A.6 contains the five greatest drawdowns for the Base Case 500 portfolios and the S&P 500. Their average drawdowns, however, are greater than the S&P 500's 23.1%. However, because their average returns are greater than the S&P 500, their average drawdown recovery periods vary from 8.8 to 10.8 months versus 15.6 months for the Index.

VI. Analysis of Tactics Using Stop-Loss Limits and Reducing Profitable Positions

Investors searching for profits seek to avoid losses. One common strategy is to use stop-loss limits, and another is to reap profits by selling part of a position that has had significant appreciation. In order to determine whether the Strategy would benefit from using these tactics, we conducted a test, called the "Stop Strategy" which imposed stop-loss limits of 20% on holdings and pared back positions on stocks which appreciated 40%. We then compared this strategy to another, the "No-Stop Strategy," that used no stops and did not pare back gains. The results of this test on 20-, 30-, and 40-stock portfolios are shown in Table A.10 and Figure A.2.

TABLE A.10   Five Greatest Drawdowns and Recovery Periods for the Base Case 500 Portfolios and the S&P 500*

Magnet Portfolios	Date	Maximum DD (%)	No. of Mths to Max DD	No. of Mths to Recover
40 Stocks	9/30/87	−29.13	2	14
	8/31/00	−26.96	30	9
	4/30/98	−22.28	4	5
	8/31/89	−21.92	14	7
	1/31/94	−10.52	5	10
Average		−22.2	11.0	9.0
30 Stocks	5/31/01	−28.86	21	10
	9/30/87	−27.73	2	7
	9/30/89	−24.44	13	14
	4/30/98	−23.63	4	8
	8/31/00	−14.63	3	5

TABLE A.10   Five Greatest Drawdowns and Recovery Periods for the Base Case 500 Portfolios and the S&P 500*

Average		−23.9	8.6	8.8
20 Stocks	4/30/01	−31.91	22	10
	9/30/89	−28.81	13	24
	9/30/87	−28.02	2	7
	3/31/98	−21.71	5	8
	4/30/00	−20.61	7	5
Average		−26.2	9.8	10.8
S&P 500	8/31/00	−46.28	25	43
	8/31/87	−30.17	3	20
	5/31/90	−15.84	5	4
	6/30/98	−15.57	2	3
	1/31/94	−7.75	5	8
Average		−23.1	8.0	15.6

*From February 1987 to April 2006

Source: HedgeMetrics, Inc.

It is evident that the Magnet Strategy's performance may be improved by eliminating the use stop-loss limits and paring back positions on stocks that have appreciated. The three portfolios without stops have higher returns and equivalent risk than those using stops. The No-Stop 20-stock portfolio has an annual return of 46.1% versus the 41.2% of the Stop 20-stock portfolio, an improvement of 4.9%. Table A.11 compares the returns using the stop and nonstop strategies. The No-Stop 30- and 40-stock portfolios also had higher returns by 4.4% and 3.2%, respectively. The enhanced returns are also evident in their significantly superior Sharpe ratios. Further, the No-Stop 30- and 40-stock portfolios have lower maximum drawdowns, while all have lower maximum drawdown durations and turnover rates.

VII. Summary and Conclusions

This study sought to determine: (1) whether the Magnet Investment Strategy's performance could be enhanced by adding the number of analysts covering a company to its selection criteria, (2) whether the

TABLE A.11   Comparing the Stop and No-stop Strategies

Back-Test Description	Performance Metric	40 Stocks	30 Stocks	20 Stocks	Russell 2000	S&P 500
Stop Strategy	Ann. Ret. (%)	41.9	42.2	41.2	9.5	9.1
	Std Dev. (%)	27.5	28.8	31.5	19.3	15.1
	Sharpe Ratio	1.35	1.30	1.15	0.23	0.28
	Max DD (%)	−36.5	−34.2	−34.6	−37.7	−46.3
	Max DD Dur (Yr)	0.87	0.81	0.84	3.96	5.07
	Turnover (%)	27.3	21.2	15.0	N/A	N/A
No-Stop Strategy	Ann. Ret. (%)	45.1	46.6	46.1	9.5	9.1
	Std Dev. (%)	27.6	28.6	31.3	19.3	15.1
	Sharpe Ratio	1.46	1.46	1.32	0.24	0.28
	Max DD (%)	−32.6	−33.9	−34.5	−37.7	−46.3
	Max DD Dur (Yr)	0.72	0.73	0.75	3.96	5.07
	Turnover (%)	19.2	15.1	10.7	N/A	N/A

Source: HedgeMetrics, Inc.

sales-related factors should be more heavily weighted than other factors, (3) whether the Strategy could select stocks from the S&P 500 universe that would outperform the Index, (4) and whether the Strategy's performance might be improved by using tactics such as stop-loss limits and partially paring back positions on stocks that have appreciated.

We reviewed the principal criteria the Magnet Strategy uses to select stocks and the heuristic rules to eliminate some from consideration. We also used those criteria and rules to select and screen stocks from the Zacks universe of 4,700 stocks to create 20-, 25- and 30-stock Base Case portfolios against which to judge the efficacy of adding new factors, or changing the weighting scheme of existing. We further tested the Strategy by selecting a Base Case of 20-, 30-, and 40-stock portfolios from the S&P 500's universe to compare their performance against the Index (see Table A.12). Finally, we compared the Strategy's performance with and without using stop-loss limits and capturing profits.

TABLE A.12   Annual Returns of Magnet Strategies Selected from the S&P 500 Universe

Year	40 Stocks	30 Stocks	20 Stocks	S&P 500
1987*	17.20	17.09	12.15	2.03
1988	18.38	21.21	16.81	12.40
1989	33.22	33.92	32.72	27.25
1990	–8.26	–11.26	–15.70	–6.56
1991	35.65	33.61	27.71	26.31
1992	15.58	17.38	16.24	4.46
1993	32.81	34.18	47.98	7.05
1994	–2.12	3.53	6.90	–1.54
1995	37.74	37.20	24.81	34.11
1996	22.38	22.69	18.89	20.26
1997	32.92	34.96	33.28	31.01
1998	13.42	4.61	4.31	26.67
1999	16.02	19.73	10.04	19.53
2000	8.99	12.74	1.52	–10.14
2001	–5.02	–2.28	5.40	–13.04
2002	–13.71	–16.93	–21.92	–23.37
2003	35.92	38.26	37.61	26.38
2004	23.49	23.34	26.57	8.99
2005	19.31	20.65	24.47	3.00
2006†	12.96	11.88	12.38	3.73

*Monthly from February through December
†Monthly from January through April
Source: HedgeMetrics, Inc.

Based upon our analysis, the following conclusions appear to be valid:

Adding the number of analysts covering a company to the Strategy is likely to increase annual returns of Magnet selected portfolios whether it is equally-weighted with other factors, or given addition weights.

Giving certain sales-related factors additional weights does not increase, but instead, serves to reduce returns by amounts which depend on the number of stocks contained in the portfolio.

The Base Case 500 20-, 30-, and 40-stock portfolios chosen from the S&P 500 universe have greater returns with only slightly higher risk, better Sharpe ratios, lower maximum drawdowns and shorter drawdown durations than the S&P 500.

The Strategy's returns, Sharpe ratios, drawdowns, drawdown durations and turnover rates are likely to improve by eliminating tactics such as stop-loss limits and partially paring back positions on stocks that have appreciated.

REFERENCES

Altman, Stan. "The Dilemma of Data Rich, Information Poor Service Organizations," *Journal of Urban Analysis and Public Management* Vol. 3 (December 1975): 61–75.

Aronson, David. *Evidence Based Technical Analysis: Applying the Scientific Method and Statistical Inference to Trading Signals.* Hoboken, NJ: John Wiley & Sons, 2006.

Bass, Thomas. *The Predictors: How a Band of Maverick Physicists Used Chaos Theory to Trade Their Way to a Fortune on Wall Street.* New York: Henry Holt, 2000.

Boik, John. *Lessons from the Greatest Stock Traders of All Time: Proven Strategies Active Traders Can Use Today to Beat the Markets.* New York: McGraw-Hill, 2004.

Boik, John. *How Legendary Traders Made Millions: Profiting from the Investment Strategies of the Greatest Traders of All Time.* New York: McGraw-Hill, 2006.

Boik, John. *Monster Stocks: How They Set Up, Run Up, Top, and Make You Money.* New York: McGraw Hill, 2007.

Brown, David, and Kassandra Bentley. *Cyber Investing: Cracking Wall Street with Your Personal Computer.* Hoboken, NJ: John Wiley & Sons, 1997.

Buffett Partnership Ltd. "Our Performance in 1965," http://www.ticonline.com/buffett.partner.letters/1966.01.20.pdf (accessed January 19, 2009).

Buffett, Warren. "Chairman's Letter—1993," Berkshire Hathaway Inc., http://www.berkshirehathaway.com/letters/1993.html (accessed March 20, 2008).

Buffett, Warren. "Chairman's Letter—1966," Berkshire Hathaway Inc., http://www.berkshirehathaway.com/letters/1966.html (accessed March 20, 2008)

Burton, Jonathan. "Revisiting the Capital Asset Pricing Model," *Dow Jones Asset Manager* (May/June 1998): 20–28.

Dent, Harry S. *The Next Great Bubble Boom: How to Profit from the Greatest Boom in History.* New York: Simon & Schuster, 2004.

Ellis, Charles. *Investment Policy: How to Win the Loser's Game,* 2nd ed. Chicago: Irwin, 1993.

Ellis, Charles, and James Vertin. *Classics: An Investor's Anthology.* Homewood, IL: Dow Jones, 1989.

Fabrikant, Geraldine. "Humbler, After a Streak of Magic," *New York Times,* Finance Section (May 11, 2008).

Gleick, James. *Chaos: Making a New Science.* New York: Penguin, 1987.

Greenblatt, Joel. *You Can Be a Stock Market Genius: Uncover the Secret Hiding Places of Stock Market Profits.* New York: Fireside/Simon & Schuster, 1997.

Graham, Benjamin. *The Intelligent Investor.* New York: Harper & Row, 1972.

Greenwald, Bruce. *Value Investing: From Graham to Buffett and Beyond.* Hoboken, NJ: John Wiley & Sons, 2001.

Hagstrom, Robert G. *The Warren Buffett Way: Investment Strategies of the World's Greatest Investor.* Hoboken, NJ: John Wiley & Sons, 1997.

Hsu, H. Christine, and H. Jeffrey Wei. "Stock Diversification in the U.S. Equity Market," *Business Quest: A Web Journal of Applied Topics in Business and Economics* (2003), http://www.westga.edu/~bquest/2003/diversify.htm (accessed March 31, 2008).

Hulbert, Mark. "Diversify! Well, Not So Fast," *New York Times*, Money & Business/ Financial section (April 14, 2004).

Investopedia, "Growth at a Reasonable Price—GARP," http://www.investopedia .com/terms/g/garp.asp (accessed May 11, 2009).

Kimmel, Jordan. "Nobody Said the Market Is Supposed to Be Easy, but It Is Worth the Challenge!" *Dick Davis Digest* 555 (2005a): 1–2.

Kimmel, Jordan. "Stock Selection or Indexing?" *Financial Planning Magazine* (July 2005b): 15.

Kimmel, Jordan. "Market on Launch Pad—2006 Will Be Better Than Expected . . . " *Dick Davis Digest* 569 (2006a): 1–2.

Kimmel, Jordan. "Too Much Cash . . . Not Enough Confidence," emailed to contacts, march 14, 2006b.

Kimmel, Jordan. "Expand Your Horizons: The Market Already Did," *Dick Davis Digest* Vol. 596 (2007): 1–2.

Kimmel, Jordan. "All Aboard! This Profit Ship Is Sailing!" *Equities Magazine* (October 2008a): 32.

Kimmel, Jordan. "Focus on the Few True Superlatives—And Just Tune Out the Rest . . . " *Dick Davis Digest* Vol. 626 (2008b): 1–2.

Kimmel, Jordan. "Banking on Growth," *Equities Magazine* (Summer 2008c): 32.

Kimmel, Jordan. "Eat Well and Prosper," Forbes.com, http://www.forbes.com/ personalfinance/2008/06/16/agrium-fertilizer-lindsay-pf-ii-in_jk_0616soapbox_ inl.html (accessed June 16, 2008d).

Kimmel, Jordan. "Picks and Shovels," *Equities Magazine* (May 2008e): 27.

Kimmel, Jordan. "Profitable Investing with Jordan Kimmel," VoiceAmerica Business Network, http://www.modavox.com/VoiceAmericaCMS/Webmodules/ NowPlaying.aspx?BroadcastId=29727&ShowId=50&ScheduleTime=8&Schedul eDate=4/3/08 (accessed April 2008f).

Kimmel, Jordan. "Profiting from Online Business," *Equities Magazine* (September 2008g): 15.

Kimmel, Jordan. "Wall Street Has the Problems—Not Main Street," *Dick Davis Digest* Vol. 619 (2008h): 1–2.

Kitchens, Susan. "Passport to Profits," Forbes.com (May 5, 2008), http://www .forbes.com/business/global/2008/0505/054.html (accessed March 31, 2009).

Krass, Peter. *The Book of Investing Wisdom.* Hoboken, NJ: John Wiley & Sons, 1999.

Loeb, Gerald, and Ken Fisher. *The Battle for Investment Survival.* Hoboken, NJ: John Wiley & Sons, 2007.

Lowenstein, Louis. *The Investor's Dilemma.* Hoboken, NJ: John Wiley & Sons, 2008.

Lynch, Peter. *One Up on Wall Street: How to Use What You Already Know to Make Money in the Market.* Philadelphia: Running Press, 1989.

Markowitz, Harry. "Portfolio Selection," *The Journal of Finance* Vol. 7 (1952): 77–91.

Moody, Michael. "From the Money Managers: Earnings Are Meaningless," Dorsey Wright & Associates (www.Dorseywright.com).

Munger, Charlie, with Peter D. Kaufman. *Poor Charlie's Almanack: The Wit and Wisdom of Charles T. Munger,* Expanded 2nd ed. Belmont, CA: Wadsworth Publishing, 2008.

Munger, Charlie, and Warren Buffett. "Berkshire Hathaway's Warren Buffett & Charlie Munger," *Outstanding Investor Digest* Vol. 21 (2008): 20.

National Organization for Research at the University of Chicago. "2004 Survey of Consumer Finances," Federal Reserve Board, http://www.federalreserve.gov/PUBS/oss/oss2/2004/scf2004.zip (accessed June 20, 2008).

Navellier, Louis. *Emerging Growth Newsletter,* https://iplacereports.com/index.asp?sid=QP1213

Niederman, Derrick. *The Inner Game of Investing.* Hoboken, NJ: John Wiley & Sons, 1999.

O'Neil, William. *24 Essential Lessons for Investment Success, Learn the Most Important Investment Techniques from the Founder of* Investor's Business Daily. New York: McGraw-Hill, 1999.

O'Neil, William. *The Successful Investor: What 80 Million People Need to Know to Invest Profitably and Avoid Big Losses.* New York: McGraw-Hill, 2003.

Poterba, James M. "The Impact of Population Aging on Financial Markets," Working Paper 1085. Cambridge, MA: National Bureau of Economic Research, 2004.

Schwager, Jack. *The New Market Wizards.* New York: HarperCollins, 1994.

Schwartz, Peter J. "Wall Street's Top Earners: Your Pain, Their Gain," Forbes.com, http://www.forbes.com/2008/04/15/paulson-falcone-earners-biz-wall-cz_js_0415wallstreet.html (accessed March 31, 2009).

Schwartz, Peter J. "Wall Street's Top Earners: Your Pain, Their Gain," *Forbes* (April 15, 2008) http://www.forbes.com/2008/04/15/paulson-falcone-earners-biz-wall-cz_js_0415wallstreet.html (accessed March 31, 2009).

Sperandeo, Victor. *Trader Vic: Methods of a Wall Street Master.* Hoboken, NJ: John Wiley & Sons, 1993.

Taleb, Nassim Nicholas. *Fooled by Randomness: The Hidden Role of Chance in Life and in the Markets.* New York: Thomson/Texere, 2004.

Taleb, Nassim Nicholas. *The Black Swan: The Impact of the Highly Improbable.* New York: Random House, 2007.

Tortoriello, Richard. "A Quantitative View of the Stock Market," *Equities Magazine* (October 2008a): 14–15.

Tortoriello, Richard. *Quantitative Strategies for Achieving Alpha.* New York: McGraw-Hill, 2008b.

Sapp, Travis, and Xuemin (Sterling) Yan. "Security Concentration and Active Fund Management: Do Focused Funds Offer Superior Performance?" *The Financial Review* Vol. 43 (2008): 27–49.

U.S. Government Accountability Office. "Baby Boom Generation: Retirement of Baby Boomers Is Unlikely to Precipitate Dramatic Decline in Market Returns, but Broader Risks Threaten Retirement Security," http://www.gao.gov/new .items/d06718.pdf (accessed March 31, 2009).

U.S. Securities and Exchange Commission, Office of Investor Education and Assistance. "Beginners' Guide to Asset Allocation, Diversification, and Rebalancing," http:// www.sec.gov/investor/pubs/assetallocation.htm (accessed March 31, 2009).

The Wall Street Transcript Corporation. "The Wall Street Transcript," http://www .twst.com (accessed July 7, 2008).

Ward, Sandra. "War, Peace and Dividends," *Barron's* (September 11, 2006).

AUTHOR'S NOTE

One of the keys to investing is to identify what to buy—and then when to buy it. Creating watch lists of companies that you are interested in, along with tracking several different sectors or industry groups, helps to keep you organized and aware of market conditions. Using technical indicators can often help you to better time your buys and sells, enabling you to maximize your profits.

Over the course of my career, I have used more than a dozen different programs to view charts and technical indicators for stocks. Throughout this book, I share several of these charts that resulted in some of our most profitable trades in the past—with hopes of showing you exactly what I look for.

My friends at TCNet have been nice enough to offer a complimentary trial of their product in this book. Please see the following for details.

Try TeleChart2007 for 30 days at www.Worden.com. Services include:

- An indexed stock market databank maintained locally on your hard drive with over 250 WatchLists every day;
- Sortable rankings with built-in technical and fundamental criteria (or find data based on custom formulas or an indicator from a chart you are viewing);
- Daily chart lessons including a note window and an archive of charting lessons with illustrations, updated daily by the Wordens, including Don Worden's aftermarket report;
- Industry and exchange-traded fund (ETF) analysis including access to WatchLists and comparison charts to get a feel for stock and industry trends; and
- Access to proprietary indicators.

If you choose to continue your subscription after 30 days, you get the features described here for $29.99 per month (or save more with yearly prepaid specials). Visit www.Worden.com for more information. Please mention code AF153 when you order.

INDEX